Student Resource Handbook

Prepared by

Marcia Swanson
Greater Albany Public Schools
Albany, Oregon

Karen A. Swenson
Department of Mathematics
Oregon State University

Mathematics
for
Elementary Teachers

A CONTEMPORARY APPROACH

Gary L. Musser
William F. Burger
Oregon State University

Macmillan Publishing Company
New York
Collier Macmillan Publishers
London

Macmillan Publishing Company
866 Third Avenue, New York, New York 10022

Collier Macmillan Canada, Inc.

Printing: 4 5 6 7 8   Year: 9 0 1 2 3 4 5 6 7

ISBN: 0-02-385440-5

PREFACE

This handbook has been designed to illustrate and provide practice in the use of effective learning strategies for the mathematics classroom. These strategies are used to provide the pre-service teacher with opportunities to gain understanding of the mathematical concepts and content of the elementary school program within the context of effective mathematics instruction.

Students who use this handbook as a companion to the textbook *Mathematics for Elementary Teachers, A Contemporary Approach* by Gary Musser and William Burger will not only enhance their own learning, but will also begin to place that learning within the framework of the elementary classroom.

You may be using this handbook as part of a course focusing on mathematical content or on the methods of teaching mathematics, or perhaps your course combines the components of content and methods. In whatever situation, this handbook has features to enrich your classroom and study. Each section can be identified by its unique icon. These key components are described in the following paragraphs.

Warm-up

Just as athletes or musicians need a time of warm-up before a competition or performance, a warm-up is also beneficial for students. This section allows students to engage in mathematical thinking and to focus on the task so that the learning time may be more productive. In this section, we provide an opportunity to review and apply the problem-solving strategies presented in the textbook.

Hands-on-activities

This is the developmental phase of the chapter. It is through hands-on activities that mental images of a concept are developed. The purpose of this section is not only to teach "how to" perform the mathematical operations that are required, but also "why to" perform the operations based on an understanding of the concepts that underlie these operations.

These activities provide exposure to a variety of materials and how they can be used in the elementary school classroom. And since research shows that prospective teachers use manipulatives in their teaching in the same manner in which they are taught, this exposure to the use of materials is vital. In all of these activities it is beneficial to approach them as a student just learning the concept. Imagine how an elementary school student would respond.

For each activity we have stated an objective. While there are many forms for writing objectives, it is important as future teachers to be aware of this aspect of any activity used. Not all concepts from the textbook are developed in the section of hands-on activities. For example, there are no activities for solving algebraic equations in Chapter 9. Some of the activities develop the concepts more quickly than would be practical in an elementary school classroom. Yet they do serve as a foundation for an expanded series of appropriate activities.

We have attempted to make this handbook as self-contained as possible. Some hands-on activities refer to materials cards. These are found at the back of the handbook and are numbered according to the activity (Materials Card 13.6 goes with Activity 6 of Chapter 13, for example). Some commercial materials are available and can be used if you have them. The multibase pieces in Chapters 2 and 4 can be replaced with Dienes blocks and the centimeter strips in Chapters 3 and 6 can be replaced with Cuisenaire rods. Other items used include cubes, dice, a metric tape, graph paper, and a protractor.

Mental Math

This section provides a chance to develop flexibility in thinking about mathematics. Students are encouraged to extend their ability to think about mathematics and to reason about the answer to mathematical problems. No paper and pencil allowed!

Exercises

In this section, students move from the concrete objects used in the hands-on section to visual representations of these objects and to numerical problems presented without visual assistance. The focus of this section is on application of the material presented in the textbook and in the hands-on section of the handbook. These exercises are presented in creative formats, and we hope you will find them more interesting than usual pencil and paper exercises.

Self-Test

The self-test provides immediate feedback on student progress so that deficiencies can be recognized and corrected before they become too ingrained and so that progress can be realized and supported through reinforcement of correct responses. Students should use this section to self-prescribe further study as needed. The material included on the self-test is covered in the textbook chapter but may go beyond what is contained in the hands-on activities.

Solutions

This section provides a chance for students to verify results. Solutions and explanations (where appropriate) are included for all sections of the handbook chapter. Students should use this section only after having worked through the handbook activities so that the experience more closely matches the experiences of students in the elementary classroom.

Resource Articles

For students who wish to extend their learning, these articles are taken from professional journals used by classroom teachers. Use of such resources will develop and extend the student's repetoire of teaching ideas.

We hope that you will find this handbook to be both helpful and enjoyable. Approaching mathematics with a spirit of curiosity and enjoyment can do much to enhance learning. We have enjoyed preparing this material with you in mind and sincerely wish you success in making use of it.

In Appreciation . . .

We express our appreciation to the following for their assistance in preparing the Student Resource Handbook:

. . . to Gary Musser and Bill Burger for their faith in us in asking us to participate in this project and their support during its preparation,

. . . to Gary Ostedt and Bob Clark of Macmillan Publishing for their support of our ideas and expertise in producing these materials,

. . . to Marilyn Wallace for her work with the graphic design of these materials on the computer,

. . . to Steve Welsh for his artistic and technical contributions,

. . . to Beverly Wilmert, administrative officer of the Mathematics Department, for expediting matters when needed,

. . . to Charles Peckham and Rhonda Morgan of the Oregon State University Department of Printing for producing film negatives on the Linotronic 300,

. . . to the people of Apple Computer, Adobe Systems, and Aldus Pagemaker for making desktop publishing with the Macintosh available,

. . . to Marcia's husband, Dennis and children, Kelli and Craig, for their encouragement and sacrifice, and finally,

. . . to the elementary education students of Oregon State University for their suggestions and contributions.

Marcia L. Swanson
Karen A. Swenson

CONTENTS

1. Introduction to Problem Solving   1

2. Sets, Whole Numbers, and Numeration   15

3. Whole Numbers – Operations and Properties   25

4. Whole Number Computations – Mental, Written, and Electronic   41

5. Number Theory   55

6. Fractions   69

7. Decimals, Percent, Ratio and Proportion   85

8. Integers   105

9. Rational Numbers and Real Numbers, with an Introduction to Algebra   121

10. Statistics   133

11. Probability   149

12. Geometric Shapes   167

13. Measurement   187

14. Geometry Using Triangle Congruence and Similarity   207

15. Geometry Using Coordinates   221

16. Geometry Using Transformations   235

Materials Cards   255

1

Introduction to Problem Solving

THEME:
1. **Understand the Problem**
2. **Devise a Plan**
3. **Carry Out the Plan**
4. **Look Back**

WARM-UP

**Strategy Review:
Guess and Test.**
The guess and test strategy presented in Chapter 1 will help you solve these problems.

Hazel sold $65 worth of banquet tickets. Adult tickets cost $4 and student tickets cost $3. How many adult tickets did she sell?

Arrange the digits 1, 2, 3, 4, and 5 in the boxes so that the sum is the same in both directions.

Can you find another arrangement? What sums are possible?

HANDS-ON ACTIVITIES

The activities in this chapter are designed to give you practice in using the problem-solving strategies presented in Chapter 1 of the text. See if you can name the strategy or strategies you find useful for solving each problem.

OBJECTIVE: **Use problem-solving strategies**

You Will Need: Materials Card 1.1

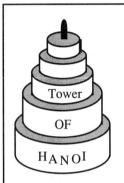

Tower
OF
HANOI

LEGEND:
Monks of
ancient Hanoi
needed to move
a tower of sacred
stones. The
stones were to
be kept on poles
at all times and
were so heavy
they could only
be moved one at
a time. Never
could a larger
stone be placed
on a smaller
one.

1. Place circles 3, 2, and 1 on peg A in that order.
    Your task is to move your stack to either peg B or C following
    these rules:

    Move only one circle at a time.
    Never put a larger circle on top of a smaller one.
    Circles must stay on a peg at all times— (except when being
    moved).
    Each time a circle is moved— count one move.

    What is the minimum number of moves required to transfer the
    stack to peg B or C?

2. Repeat the activity using 4 circles; 5 circles; 6 circles.
    Keep a record of moves required using this chart:

Number of Circles	Number of Moves
3	
4	
5	
6	

3. How many moves would be required to move a stack built from
    10 circles?   100 circles? n circles?

4. What strategy or strategies did you try in solving this problem?

OBJECTIVE: **Use problem-solving strategies**

You Will Need: 3 pennies and 3 nickels

1. Place pennies in the 3 squares on the left and nickels in the 3 squares on the right.
    Leave the center square empty.   Your task is to switch the positions of the coins.
    The coins may move forward either by a direct move or by jumping another coin. No
    backward moves.

    How many moves are required?

2. Try the activity using other numbers of coins. Keep the same number of coins on each side of the center square. In each case, the center square is the only extra square used.

Number of Coins per Side	Number of Moves
1	
2	
3	
4	
n	

3. What problem-solving strategy did you find most useful in solving this problem?

OBJECTIVE: **Use problem-solving strategies**

You Will Need: Materials Card 1.3

Josephine the carpenter has been hired to patch a 2' by 12' hole on the side of a barn. She has only a 3' by 8' piece of plywood with which to make a patch. Since she wants to use as few pieces as possible, she wants to make only one cut. Show how Josephine can cut the plywood with only one cut to fill the 2' by 12' hole. Hint: The cut is not necessarily straight.

What problem-solving strategy was most useful in solving this problem?

OBJECTIVE: **Use problem-solving strategies**

You Will Need: A handful of toothpicks

1. Use 17 toothpicks to make this figure:  Remove 6 toothpicks leaving 2 squares.

2. Use 12 toothpicks to make this figure: Reposition (do not remove) 3 toothpicks leaving 3 squares, all the same size.

3. Use 6 toothpicks to make 4 triangles.

4. Use 3 toothpicks to write 9. (No fair bending them.)

5. What problem-solving strategies did you find useful in solving these problems?

   **OBJECTIVE:**   **Use problem-solving strategies**

You Will Need: Materials Card 1.5

1. Find all the shapes that are rectangles two cubes wide. Write the number for each rectangle.

    _____ , _____ , _____ , _____ , _____ , _____

    What is special about these numbers ?

2. Find all the shapes that are not rectangles two cubes wide. Write the number for each shape.

    _____ , _____ , _____ , _____ , _____ , _____

    What is special about these numbers?

3. Choose two even-numbered shapes. Put them together. Record the shape and the addition equation.

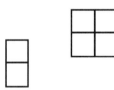

even

2 + 4 = 6   __ + __ = __

    Repeat four times. Record the answers and tell if they are odd or even. What do you notice about adding two even numbers?

4. Choose two odd-numbered shapes. Put them together. Record the shape and the addition equation. Repeat four times. Record the answers and tell if they are odd or even. What do you notice about adding two odd numbers?

5. Choose one even-numbered shape and one odd-numbered shape. Put them together. Record the shape and the addition equation. Repeat 4 times. Record the answers and tell whether they are odd or even. What do you notice about adding one odd number and one even number?

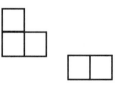

6. Write a statement that summarizes your findings in this activity.

OBJECTIVE: **Use problem-solving strategies**

Remember Josephine the carpenter? She has another hole in the barn to repair.

The hole is 10' by 10'.

Josephine has a 9' by 12' piece of plywood with which to make the patch, but it has an 8' by 1' hole in the middle of it as shown:

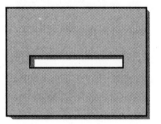

Can it be cut into 2 pieces to fit the 10' by 10' hole?   Draw a picture of your solution.

MENTAL MATH

Can you cut a cake into
8 pieces with exactly 3 cuts?

Can you cut a doughnut into 12 pieces with exactly 3 cuts?

Fill in the missing numbers:

__2__, __5__, __11__, ____, __47__, ____

EXERCISES

INTUITIVELY OBVIOUS?

The first step in problem solving involves understanding the problem. This includes reading carefully and thinking clearly. And, while intuition may give helpful insights, first impressions may need to be double-checked. For instance, consider these...

DIRECTIONS:

For each question on the following page, choose the correct answer and put the letter on the line preceding the question. Then, with a straightedge, follow the specific instructions given to connect those points on the diagram shown.

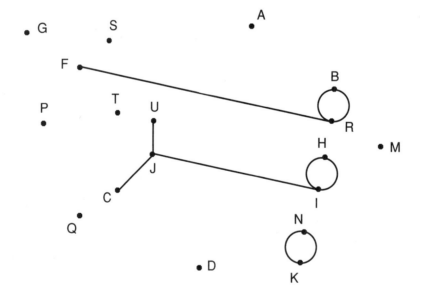

____1. How much dirt is there in a hole 5 meters long, 4 meters wide, and 2 meters deep?

   A. 40 cubic meters   B. no dirt

____2. Is it legal for a man to marry his widow's sister?

   R. yes   S. no

____3. From the bottom of a 24-foot well, a spider can climb up 4 feet each day, but slips back 2 feet each night. In how many days does he escape the well?

   F. 11 days   G. 12 days

____4. Wishing to get a long night's sleep, you go to bed at 8:00 in the evening and set the alarm (on a regular alarm clock) for 9:00 the next morning. How much sleep will you get?

   P. 13 hours   Q. 1 hour

____5. What is the fewest number of ducks if there are two ducks before a duck, two ducks behind a duck, and a duck in the middle?

   J. 5 ducks   K. 3 ducks

____6. Judy had a dozen apples in her office. She ate all but 5. How many were left?

   H. 5 apples   I. 7 apples

____7. Two U.S. coins have a total value of 30 cents. One coin is not a nickel. What are the two coins?

   T. quarter, nickel   U. not possible

____8. How many 3-cent stamps are there in a dozen?

   C. 12 stamps   D. 4 stamps

____9. A train leaves Chicago for Los Angeles, travelling at a rate of 125 kilometers per hour. Another train leaves Los Angeles an hour later, travelling at 75 kilometers per hour. When the two trains meet, which train is nearer to Los Angeles?

   M. faster one   N. neither one

Connect the letter answers to questions 1 through 5 in order. Lift your pencil. Now connect the answers to questions 6 through 9 in order. Can you build the figure you have drawn?

A MAZE OF PATTERNS

Looking for patterns is one of the strategies for problem solving. Many patterns have been known and studied for centuries, but for those who are new to patterns, it takes some practice to develop the skill. Try these...

DIRECTIONS:

Find the number to replace a letter in the pattern. Then, in the maze, shade in the path that connects the diamond containing that letter with the diamond containing the replacement number.

PASCAL'S TRIANGLE:

```
      1   1
    1   2   1
  1   3   3   1
1   4   E   4   1
    .   N   5   1
    .       C   6   1
    .           G   7   1
```

NUMERICAL SEQUENCES:

1, 4, 7, 10, O, G

1, 4, 9, 16, W

FIBONACCI SEQUENCE:

1, 1, 2, 3, 5, 8, K, W

TRIANGULAR NUMBERS:

1   3   6   10   N

START

For a compliment, read your path.

SELF-TEST

A bottle and a cork together cost $1.00. If the bottle costs 90 cents more than the cork, how much does the cork cost? (Items 1 - 3)

1. In understanding the problem, each of the following statements is true *except*

    a. We know the combined cost of the bottle and cork is $1.
    b. We know the cork costs 10 cents.
    c. We know the bottle costs 90 cents more than the cork.
    d. We are asked to find the cost of the cork.

2. You decide to use the strategy of using a variable to solve this problem. Therefore, you let *c* represent the cost of the cork in cents. The cost of the bottle in cents is represented by

    a. $100 + c$ b. 90   c. $c + 90$ d. none of these

3. Proceeding to solve this problem, you find that the cost of the bottle is

    a. 95 cents   b. 90 cents   c. 10 cents   d. 5 cents

How can you bring exactly 2 liters of water from a pond when you have only a 4-liter pail and a 7-liter pail? (Items 4 -7)

4. In understanding the problem, each of the following statements is true *except*

    a. You have only two pails, one that holds 4 liters and the other 7 liters.
    b. You have no other container to hold water.
    c. You want to return with exactly 2 liters in one of the pails.
    d. You are not allowed to pour out any water.

5. What is the fewest number of steps in order to get exactly 3 liters in one pail? Consider each time you fill a pail or pour out a pail as a separate step.

    a. 1 step   b. 2 steps   c. 3 steps   d. more than 3 steps

6. The shortest solution to the problem involves

    a. filling up the 7-liter pail twice.   b. filling up the 4-liter pail five times.
    c. filling up the 4-liter pail four times. d. none of these steps.

7. If, instead, you had a 6-liter pail and a 10-liter pail, which of the following exact amounts could you bring back?

    a. 3 liters   b. 5 liters   c. 8 liters   d. 9 liters

Given an n-gon (a polygon with n sides), draw all possible diagonals. How many diagonals are there? (Items 8 - 10)

8. In understanding the problem, each of the following statements is true *except*

   a. You are looking for the maximum number of diagonals.
   b. All possible segments are drawn connecting nonadjacent vertices.
   c. Each vertex of the n-gon will be an endpoint of only 2 diagonals.
   d. There are n vertices of the polygon.

9. Which of the following strategies could be used?
   (i) Solve a simpler problem - consider polygons with 3 sides, 4 sides, etc.
   (ii) Use a variable - let s be the number of vertices, then find the number of diagonals from each vertex, and the total number of diagonals.
   (iii) Make a list (table) - record number of diagonals for 3-gon, 4-gon, etc.

   a. i and ii only   b. i and iii only   c. ii and iii only   d. all of i, ii, and iii

10. You set up the following chart and look for a pattern.

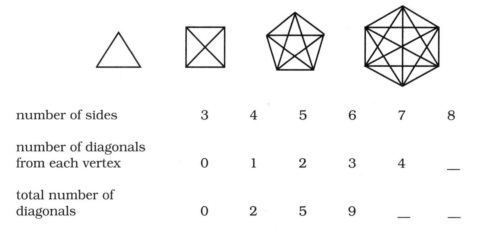

number of sides	3	4	5	6	7	8
number of diagonals from each vertex	0	1	2	3	4	__
total number of diagonals	0	2	5	9	__	__

Which of the following is *not* a valid conclusion to draw?

   a. The number of diagonals from each vertex of an n-gon is $n - 3$.
   b. The number of diagonals possible in an octagon (8 sides) is 20.
   c. The number of diagonals in an n-gon is an increase of $(n - 2)$ over the number of diagonals in an $(n - 1)$-gon.
   d. The number of diagonals in an n-gon is the number of vertices, n, times the number of diagonals from each vertex, $n - 3$.

SOLUTIONS

Warm-up
One possible solution is that she sold 14 adult tickets. Can you find another solution?

One possible solution is: 5   Yes, possible sums are 8, 9, and 10.
                  4 1 3
                    2

Hands-on Activities

Activity 1
1. 7 moves

2.

Number of circles	Number of moves
3	7
4	15
5	31
6	63

3. 1023, $2^{100} - 1$, $2^n - 1$

4. Look for a pattern and solve a simpler problem.

Activity 2
1. 15 moves

2.

Number of coins	Number of moves	
1	3	n-p-n
2	8	n-pp-nn-pp-n
3	15	n-pp-nnn-ppp-nnn-pp-n
4	24	n-pp-nnn-pppp-nnnn-pppp-nnn-pp-n
n	$n(n+2)$	

3. Again, you might look for a pattern.

Activity 3
See the drawing.
To solve this problem, you are drawing a picture.

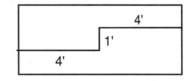

Activity 4

1. The squares are not necessarily the same size.

2.

3. This figure will be three-dimensional.
4. Your numeral will look like this: IX
5. Guess and test, solve a simpler problem

Activity 5

1. 2, 4, 6, 8, 10, 12   They are all even numbers.
2. 1, 3, 5, 7, 9, 11   They are all odd numbers.
3. The sum is always an even number.
4. The sum is always an even number.
5. The sum is always an odd number.
6. The sum of two even numbers is even; the sum of two odd numbers is even; and the sum of an odd and an even number is odd.

Activity 6

See the drawing:

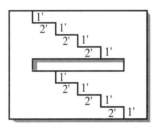

Mental Math

The first cut through your cake could be horizontal as illustrated:

Cut the doughnut as shown:

Missing numbers: 23, 95

Exercises

INTUITIVELY OBVIOUS?
    1. B **2.** S **3.** F **4.** Q **5.** K **6.** H **7.** T **8.** C **9.** N

A MAZE OF PATTERNS
    Pascal's Triangle: E-6, N-10, C-15, G-21
    Numerical Sequences: O-13, G-16, W-25
    Fibonacci Sequence: K-13, W-21
    Triangular numbers: N-15
    Pathway: NICE WORK!

Self-Test

1. b   **2.** c   **3.** a   **4.** d   5. b   **6.** a   **7.** c   **8.** c   **9.** d   **10.** d

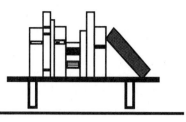

RESOURCE ARTICLES

Bush, William S., and Ann Fiala. "Problem Stories: A New Twist on Problem Posing." *Arithmetic Teacher* 34 (December 1986): 6-9. *Suggestions for writing problem-solving stories.*

Campbell, Patricia F. "Using a Problem-solving Approach in the Primary Grades." *Arithmetic Teacher* 32 (December 1984): 11-14. *Use of problem solving to promote understanding of addition and subtraction.*

Charles, Randall I. "The Role of Problem Solving." *Arithmetic Teacher* 32 (February 1985): 48-50. *Characteristics of problem solving that promote mathematical thinking.*

Day, Roger P. "A Problem-Solving Component for Junior High School Mathematics." *Arithmetic Teacher* 34 (October 1986): 14-17. *Suggestions for emphasizing the process of solving problems.*

Easterday, Kenneth E., and Clara A. Clothiaux. "Problem-solving Opportunities." *Arithmetic Teacher* 32 (January 1985): 18-20. *Use student questions to design activities.*

Gilbert-Macmillan, Kathleen, and Steven J. Leitz. "Cooperative Small Groups: A Method for Teaching Problem Solving." *Arithmetic Teacher* 33 (March 1986): 9-11. *Instructional setting for improving students' problem-solving skills.*

Havel, Phyllis. "Students Categorize, Then Solve Problems." *Arithmetic Teacher* 33 (November 1985): 19-23. *Using previously acquired knowledge, skills, and understanding.*

Johnson, James E. "Do You Think You Might Be Wrong? Comfirmation Bias in Problem Solving." *Arithmetic Teacher* 34 (May 1987): 13-16. *Activities involved in creating and relinquishing hypotheses.*

Jones, Billie M. "Put Your Students in the Picture for Better Problem Solving." *Arithmetic Teacher* 30 (April 1983): 30-33. *Presentation of problem solving using record-setting events and a personalized approach.*

Knifong, J. Dan, and Grace M. Burton. "Understanding Word Problems." *Arithmetic Teacher* 32 (January 1985): 13-17. *General strategies for solving word problems.*

Krulik, Stephen, and Jesse A. Rudnick. "Developing Problem-Solving Skills." *Mathematics Teacher* 78 (December 1985): 685-692, 697-698. *Activities using "make an organized list" and "search for a pattern."*

Krulik, Stephen, and Jesse A. Rudnick. "Strategy Gaming and Problem Solving--an Instructional Pair Whose Time Has Come!" *Arithmetic Teacher* 31 (December 1983): 26-29. *Uses and adaptations of strategy games to develop problem-solving abilities.*

Leutzinger, Larry P. "Ideas." *Arithmetic Teacher* 34 (January 1987): 19-24. *Activities for interpreting story problems, drawing their own conclusions, and making guesses.*

Newman, Claire M., and Susan B. Turkel. "The Class Survey: A Problem-solving Activity." *Arithmetic Teacher* 32 (May 1985): 10-12. *Collecting, organizing, and drawing conclusions from data.*

O'Daffer, Phares G. "Problem Solving: Tips for Teachers." *Arithmetic Teacher* 32 (September 1984 through May 1985). *Spotlight on a different problem-solving strategy each month.*

Suydam, Marilyn N. "Research Report: Problem Solving." *Arithmetic Teacher* 31 (May 1984): 36. *Brief summary of research findings.*

Van de Walle, John A., and Helen Holbrook. "Patterns, Thinking, and Problem Solving." *Arithmetic Teacher* 34 (April 1987): 6-12. *Pictorial and numeric patterns used to develop problem-solving thinking strategies.*

Van de Walle, John A., and Charles S. Thompson. "Let's Do It: Promoting Mathematical Thinking." *Arithmetic Teacher* 32 (February 1985): 7-13. *Activities to promote development of general problem-solving skills.*

Wheatley, Charlotte L., and Grayson H. Wheatley. "Problem Solving in the Primary Grades." *Arithmetic Teacher* 31 (April 1984): 22-25. *Activities to achieve problem-solving readiness in early childhood.*

Willcutt, Bob. "Stamp Collector's Nightmare, Phase Two." *Arithmetic Teacher* 31 (September 1983): 43-46. *Extensions of a problem to a variety of levels of difficulty.*

Wright, Jone Perryman, and Nancy Kight Stevens. "Improving Verbal Problem-solving Performance." *Arithmetic Teacher* 31 (October 1983): 40-42. *Suggestions for using language-experience approach to involve students in problem solving.*

2 Sets, Whole Numbers, and Numeration

THEME: Grouping and Place Value

WARM-UP

Strategy Review:
Use a Variable.
For these problems, you might find that using a variable will be helpful. See Chapter 1 if you need to review.

A total of 20 children and dogs are playing in the park. If you counted their legs, you would get 56 in all. How many children and how many dogs are there?

Sue has 2 brothers. She is 3 times as old as Michael, her youngest brother. The age of her other brother, Jon, is the difference between Sue's and Michael's ages. The sum of all their ages is 36. How old is Jon?

HANDS-ON ACTIVITIES

The activities in this chapter are designed to give you experience in working with the concepts of place value and regrouping. To make the experience more like that of your future students, you will be working in bases other than base ten with which you are already familiar.

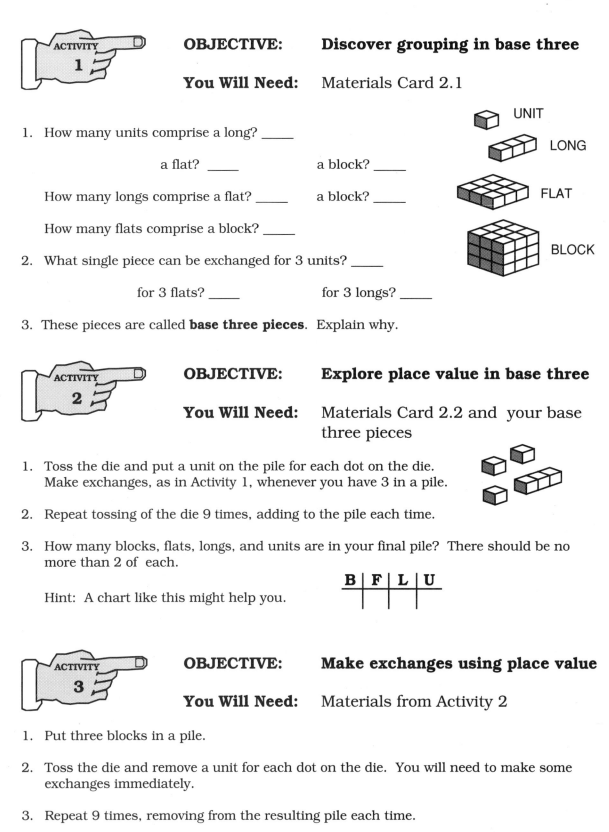

ACTIVITY 1

OBJECTIVE: **Discover grouping in base three**

You Will Need: Materials Card 2.1

UNIT

LONG

FLAT

BLOCK

1. How many units comprise a long? _____

           a flat? _____   a block? _____

   How many longs comprise a flat? _____   a block? _____

   How many flats comprise a block? _____

2. What single piece can be exchanged for 3 units? _____

              for 3 flats? _____   for 3 longs? _____

3. These pieces are called **base three pieces**. Explain why.

ACTIVITY 2

OBJECTIVE: **Explore place value in base three**

You Will Need: Materials Card 2.2 and your base three pieces

1. Toss the die and put a unit on the pile for each dot on the die. Make exchanges, as in Activity 1, whenever you have 3 in a pile.

2. Repeat tossing of the die 9 times, adding to the pile each time.

3. How many blocks, flats, longs, and units are in your final pile? There should be no more than 2 of each.

   Hint: A chart like this might help you.

B	F	L	U

ACTIVITY 3

OBJECTIVE: **Make exchanges using place value**

You Will Need: Materials from Activity 2

1. Put three blocks in a pile.

2. Toss the die and remove a unit for each dot on the die. You will need to make some exchanges immediately.

3. Repeat 9 times, removing from the resulting pile each time.

4. Record on a chart the blocks, flats, longs, and units left in the pile.

OBJECTIVE: **Represent a number in base three**

You Will Need: Your base three pieces and a handful of paper clips

1. Place a pile of paper clips (or other small objects) in front of you.

2. Represent the number of clips in the pile, as illustrated, using as few base three pieces as possible. Record the number in a chart. *Try to think in base three.*

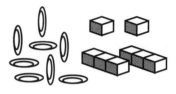

3. Repeat parts 1 and 2 several times, recording the number of pieces on your chart each time.

OBJECTIVE: **Write numerals to represent base three pieces**

You Will Need: Your base three pieces

1. The numeral that describes these pieces is written 1022_3 (one block, no flats, two longs, two units). The subscript indicates a grouping by threes.

   What numeral describes these pieces?

2. Use your base three pieces to represent these numerals, and draw a picture of each.
   a. 112_3 b. 1012_3 c. 1102_3 d. 1120_3

3. Using your drawings, arrange the numbers in part 3 from least to greatest. How can you arrange them by just looking at the numerals?
   Explain why.

Now think about base ten.

4. How many units would make up the longs, flats, and blocks in base ten?

5. A child writes 201 for 21 and 400,203 for 423. Show on these charts how 21 and 423 can be represented with base ten pieces.

   How would you help a student see there is a difference between 201 and 21?

6. How could you show these base ten arithmetic problems to second graders using base ten pieces? Make a sketch to show your answer.

   a.   365
       + 486
       _____

   b.   432
       - 276
       _____

ACTIVITY 6   **OBJECTIVE: Use Venn diagrams to represent sets**

1. Place these numbers in the correct portion of the Venn Diagram:

   2, 3, 4, 6, 8, 9, 10,
   12, 14, 15, 16, 18, 20, 21, 22

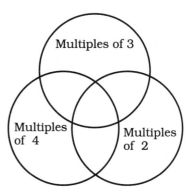

   Why would this be a better diagram? Explain.

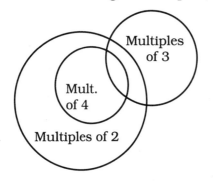

2. Write a description for the intersecting sets described by this diagram:

    5   7   3   18
    11   9   6
         13   15   12

3. Draw a Venn diagram that will fit the following:

    Multiples of 6 less than 100
    Multiples of 15 less than 100
    Multiples of 3 less than 100

    Place the numbers 1 to 100 in your diagram.

MENTAL MATH

Write the base 5 numeral that correctly represents the solution to each equation.

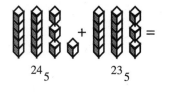

24_5 23_5

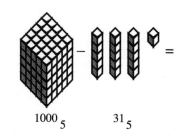

1000_5 31_5

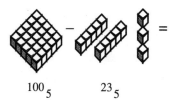

100_5 23_5

EXERCISES

HIDDEN MESSAGE

To find the hidden message, follow these directions:

- Choose any numeral in the left-hand column.

- Find its corresponding base ten expression in the right-hand column.

- Put the letter in the blank with the corresponding problem number in the message below.

- Keep making matches until you have discovered the message!

NUMERALS

1. 112_{12}
2. 320_4
3. 100010_2
4. 11111_2
5. 111_5
6. 111000_2
7. 200_7
8. 211_5
9. 70_8
10. 343_5
11. 124_8
12. $2T_{12}$
13. 2120_3
14. 51_6

BASE TEN

U	73
T	84
S	31
R	158
P	65
N	196
M	13
L	69
I	27
H	43
F	106
E	98
C	49
B	34
A	56

$\overline{\rule{1em}{0pt}}$ $\overline{\rule{1em}{0pt}}$ $\overline{\rule{1em}{0pt}}$ $\overline{\rule{1em}{0pt}}$ $\overline{\rule{1em}{0pt}}$ $\quad$ $\overline{\rule{1em}{0pt}}$ $\overline{\rule{1em}{0pt}}$ $\overline{\rule{1em}{0pt}}$ $\quad$ $\overline{\rule{1em}{0pt}}$ $\quad$ $\overline{\rule{1em}{0pt}}$ $\overline{\rule{1em}{0pt}}$ $\overline{\rule{1em}{0pt}}$ $\overline{\rule{1em}{0pt}}$ $\overline{\rule{1em}{0pt}}$!
12 8   4   10 5   9   1   7   2   3 13 6 14 11

MAZE CRAZE !

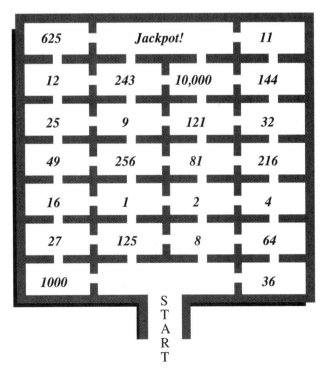

Each room in this maze contains a number. Twelve of these numbers are correct answers to the problems below.

In each problem, a particular digit in the numeral is underlined. Identify the base ten value of that place. Circle your answer in the maze.

(For $\underline{4}32_5$ you would circle 25.)

Keep doing problems until you can draw a path that goes *only* through rooms containing correct answers. (It might not go through all of the correct answers.)

$36\underline{1}_9$ $3\underline{2}410_5$ $\underline{2}120_3$ $78T\underline{3}_{12}$
$1\underline{0}10111_2$ $56\underline{1}13_7$ $53\underline{1}402_6$
$100\underline{1}1_2$ $9\underline{T}1E_{12}$ $11\underline{2}2012_3$
$322\underline{1}30_4$ $2\underline{3}6797_{10}$

SELF-TEST

1. The possible number of different 1-1 correspondences between two three-member sets is

   a. 1   b. 2   c. 3   d. 6

2. Which of the following sets are equivalent, but not equal?

   a. {a, b, c}, {a, c, b}   b. {a, b}, {1, 2}   c. {a, b, c}, {a, c}   d. {a, b, d, e}, {1, 2, 3, 4, 5}

3. If M = {a, b, c}, N = {b, c, d}, and P = {a, b, c, d}, which of the following is *false*?

   a. M $\subseteq$ P   b. N $\subset$ P   c. N $\subseteq$ M   d. None of a, b, or c.

4. If A and B are sets, A is a proper subset of B, and A is equivalent to B, then which must be true?

   a. B $\subseteq$ A   b. A = B   c. B is an infinite set   d. None of a, b, or c.

5. If A, B, and C are three sets, which of the following are equal sets?
   (Hint: Use a Venn Diagram.)
   (i) (A - B) $\cup$ (B - C)   (ii) (A $\cup$ B) - C   (iii) (A $\cup$ B) - (B $\cap$ C)

   a. i and ii   b. i and iii   c. ii and iii   d. None of a, b, or c.

6. Which of the following sets would a child use to answer the question, "How many elements are in {a, b, c, d, e}?"

   a. {0, 1, 2, 3, 4}   b. {1, 2, 3, 4, 5}   c. {2, 4, 6, 8, 10}   d. None of a, b, or c.

7. The number for this set suggested
   by the grouping (in base 3) has

   a. A 1 in the third place from the right.
   b. A 1 in the second place from the right.
   c. No 1 in its numeral.
   d. None of a, b, or c.

8. How many longs are needed to represent 422 using as few base 6 pieces as possible?

   a. 5   b. 4   c. 2   d. None of a, b, or c.

9. How many zeros are required to be able to write $4 \cdot 8^7 + 6 \cdot 8^2 + 2$ in its standard base 8 representation?

   a. 6   b. 5   c. 4   d. None of a, b, or c.

10. When 983_{12} is changed into its *base 10* numeral, the hundreds digit is:

    a. 1   b. 2   c. 7   d. None of a, b, or c.

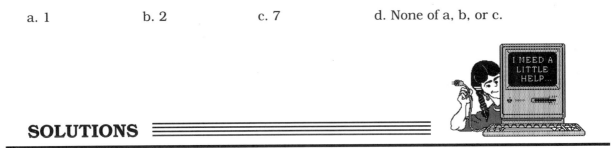

SOLUTIONS

Warm-up

12 children and 8 dogs. Let x = number of children, then $20 - x$ = number of dogs. Then the number of legs = $2x + 4(20 - x) = 56$.

12 years old. Let x = Michael's age. Sue's age = $3x$ and Jon's age = $3x - x$ or $2x$. The sum of their ages is 36, so $3x + 2x + x = 36$.

Hands-on Activities

Activity 1
1. 3 units, 9 units, 27 units; 3 longs, 9 longs; 3 flats
2. A long, a block, a flat
3. Since 3 of one piece can be exchanged for the next larger piece.

Activity 2
Answers will vary. Note: you must not have 3 pieces of any one size. Any 3 must be exchanged as in Activity 1.

Activity 3
Answers will vary.

Activity 4
Answers will vary. Check to be sure you are making exchanges when needed.

Activity 5
1. 102_3

2.

	B	F	L	U
a.		1	1	2
b.	1	0	1	2
c.	1	1	0	2
d.	1	1	2	0

3. 112_3, 1012_3, 1102_3, 1120_3
The numbers can be arranged from least to greatest by comparing the value of each place from left to right. Look at (b) and (d) for example: The first digit on the left is the same, but by checking the second digit from the left, we know that $1120_3 > 1012_3$.

4. 10 units would comprise a long, 100 units a flat, and 1000 units a block.

5. 2 longs and 1 unit; 4 flats, 2 longs and 3 units
Have the student work with the pieces to see that in 201 the 2 represents the number of flats and in 21 the 2 represents the number of longs, etc.

6. a.   Have the students represent each number, add the pieces together, and make exchanges.
b.   Have the students represent 432 and then ask them to take away 276, making exchanges when necessary.

Activity 6

1. All multiples of 4 are also multiples of 2, so the second diagram is better.

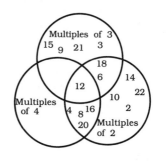

2. Odds and multiples of 3

3. All multiples of 6 and 15 are also multiples of 3.

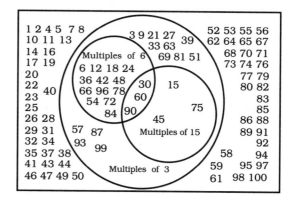

Mental Math

102_5 414_5 22_5

Exercises

HIDDEN MESSAGE		
1. 158	**6.** 56	**11.** 84
2. 56	**7.** 98	**12.** 34
3. 34	**8.** 56	**13.** 69
4. 31	**9.** 56	**14.** 31
5. 31	**10.** 98	
Bases Are A Blast!		

MAZE CRAZE !
Circle these answers: 9   125   27
1   32   49   216   2   144   81
64   10,000
The path through the maze is:
125, 1, 2, 81, 216, 32, 144, 10000, JACKPOT!
Remember: Use this pattern to determine the place value in any base (n for example)...n^5 n^4 n^3 n^2 n 1

Self-Test

1. d   **2.** b   **3.** c   **4.** c   **5.** b   **6.** b   **7.** b   **8.** b   **9.** b   **10.** d

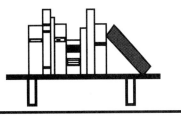

RESOURCE ARTICLES

Beattie, Ian D. "The Number Namer: An Aid to Understanding Place Value." *Arithmetic Teacher* 33 (January 1986): 24-28. *Builds bridge between iconic representation of a number and its symbolic representation.*

Burton, Grace M. "Teaching the Most Basic Basic." *Arithmetic Teacher* 32 (September 1984): 20-25. *Explores the teaching of place value.*

Clements, Douglas H., and Leroy G. Callahan. "Number or Prenumber Foundational Experiences for Young Children: Must We Choose?" *Arithmetic Teacher* 31 (November 1983): 34-37. *Suggests a variety of activities with counting, simple addition, and subtraction.*

Harrison, Marilyn, and Bruce Harrison. "Developing Numeration Concepts and Skills." *Arithmetic Teacher* 33 (February 1986): 18-21, 60. *Activities for place value, multiples, and rounding.*

Liedtke, Werner. "Young Children— Small Numbers: Making Numbers Come Alive." *Arithmetic Teacher* 31 (September 1983): 34-36. *Includes activities for first graders concerning numbers 5 and 6.*

Nelson, Marvin N., H. Clifford Clark, and Marvin N. Tolman. "The Human Computer (Nudging Along Together)." *Arithmetic Teacher* 32 (March 1985): 24-25. *Understanding place value through number bases.*

Payne, Joseph N. "Ideas." *Arithmetic Teacher* 34 (September 1986): 26-32. *Activities with Egyptian numerals.*

Shaw, Jean M. "Let's Do It: A-Plus for Counters." *Arithmetic Teacher* 31 (September 1983): 10-14. *Using counters to develop number concepts and operations.*

Shaw, Jean M. "Let's Do It: Punchy Mathematics." *Arithmetic Teacher* 31 (October 1983): 10-14. *Using a paper punch to develop mathematical ideas including numbers.*

Suydam, Marilyn N. "Research Report: The Process of Counting." *Arithmetic Teacher* 33 (January 1986): 29. *Research findings on development of counting skills.*

Van de Walle, John and Charles S. Thompson. "Let's Do It: Partitioning Sets for Number Concepts, Place Value, and Long Division." *Arithmetic Teacher* 32 (January 1985): 6-11. *Using manipulatives to develop number concepts, counting skills, and place value concepts.*

3

Whole Numbers – Operations and Properties

THEME:

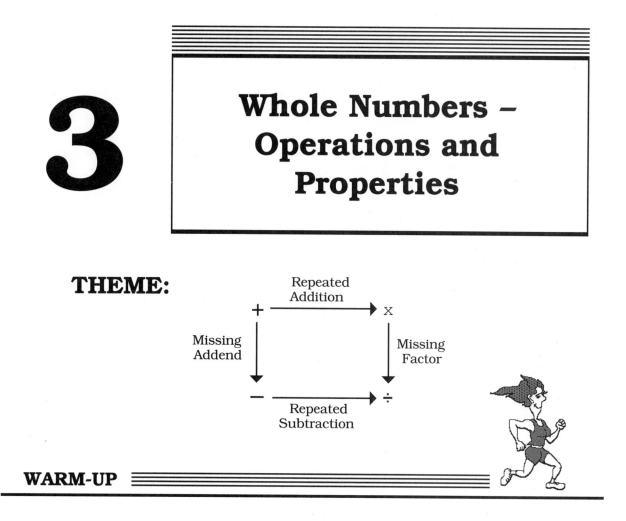

Repeated Addition

Missing Addend

Missing Factor

Repeated Subtraction

WARM-UP

Strategy Review:
Look for a Pattern.
In Chapter 1, the strategy of looking for a pattern was discussed. Try that strategy to solve these problems.

Fill in the blanks: 1, 1, 2, 3, 5, ___ , ___

Five people met at a business meeting. Each person shook hands with every other person exactly once. How many handshakes were exchanged altogether?

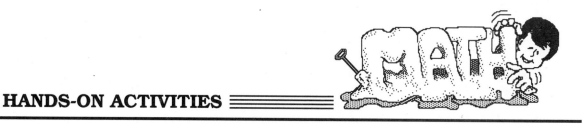

HANDS-ON ACTIVITIES

The first activities in this chapter are designed to help you understand the concept of addition and discover properties of addition.

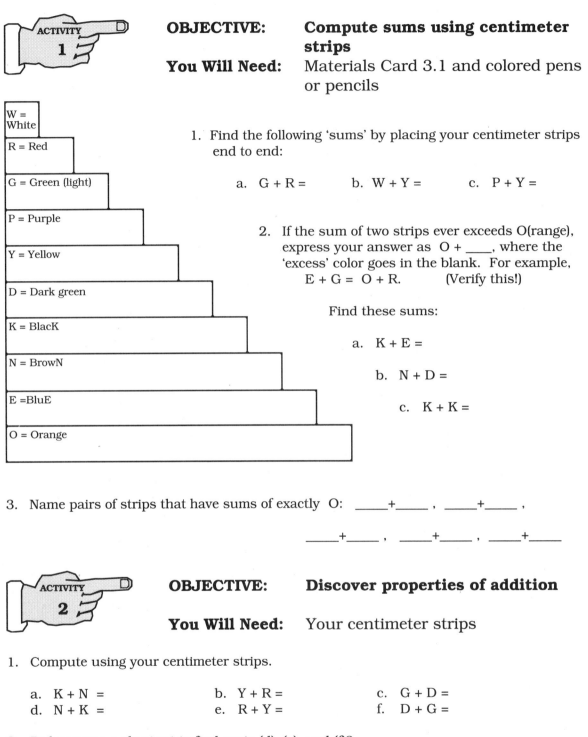

ACTIVITY 1

OBJECTIVE: **Compute sums using centimeter strips**

You Will Need: Materials Card 3.1 and colored pens or pencils

W = White
R = Red
G = Green (light)
P = Purple
Y = Yellow
D = Dark green
K = BlacK
N = BrowN
E = BluE
O = Orange

1. Find the following 'sums' by placing your centimeter strips end to end:

     a.   G + R =   b.   W + Y =   c.   P + Y =

2. If the sum of two strips ever exceeds O(range), express your answer as O + ____, where the 'excess' color goes in the blank. For example, E + G = O + R.   (Verify this!)

     Find these sums:

     a.   K + E =

     b.   N + D =

     c.   K + K =

3. Name pairs of strips that have sums of exactly O: ____+____ , ____+____ ,

     ____+____ , ____+____ , ____+____

ACTIVITY 2

OBJECTIVE: **Discover properties of addition**

You Will Need: Your centimeter strips

1. Compute using your centimeter strips.

     a.   K + N =   b.   Y + R =   c.   G + D =
     d.   N + K =   e.   R + Y =   f.   D + G =

2. Did you use a shortcut to find parts (d), (e), and (f)?
     Explain.

If you did not use a shortcut, look for one now. Hint: compare (a) and (d).

3. Fill in the portion of this table above the dotted line.

+	W	R	G	P	Y
W	R	G			D
R					
G					
P					
Y					

4. Use your discovery of a short-cut in part 2 to complete the rest of the table.

Write a statement that explains the property of addition that helps to simplify your task here.

OBJECTIVE: **Discover properties of addition**

You Will Need: Your centimeter strips and the table in Activity 2

1. Compute these sums:

   a. W + R =
   c. R + Y =

   b. (W + R) + Y =
   d. W + (R + Y) =

2. Compare your results in (b) and (d) above. What do you notice?

Write a general statement that summarizes your findings.

The next activities in this chapter deal with the concept of subtraction.

OBJECTIVE: **Represent subtraction using a missing addend**

You Will Need: Your centimeter strips

1. Solve the following:
    a. Y + _____ = O   b.   O - Y = _____
    c. K + _____ = O + R   d.   (O + R) - K = _____
    e   D + _____ = O + P   f.   (O + P) - D = _____

2. How are (a) and (b) above related?
    What is the relationship between (e) and (f)?

3. Make another pair of sums that are related in the same way.

OBJECTIVE: **Compute differences using an addition table**

You Will Need: Your centimeter strips

1. This table is the one you should have obtained in Activity 2. Without using your centimeter strips, but using the table to the right, find the following differences.

+	W	R	G	P	Y
W	R	G	P	Y	D
R	G	P	Y	D	K
G	P	Y	D	K	N
P	Y	D	K	N	E
Y	D	K	N	E	O

   a. N - Y = _____   b. O - Y = _____

   c. K - P = _____   d. P - R = _____

Use your centimeter strips to check your results.

The concepts of '**greater than**' and '**less than**' are explored in the next activity.

OBJECTIVE: **Describe 'greater than' and 'less than' using addition**

You Will Need: Your centimeter strips

1. Order the following strips from smallest to greatest.

    Y   O   N   P   D

2. Complete the following:

    a. Y + _____ = N   Y is _____ (shorter, longer) than N.
    b. Y + _____ = O   O is _____ (shorter, longer) than Y.
    c. N + _____ = O   R is _____ (shorter, longer) than O.

3. Since Y + G equals N, what do we know is true of the relationship between Y and N? between G and N?

Explain how addition can be used to order two strips; that is, how addition can be used to show that one strip is longer than another.

---

4. Insert the correct symbol (>, <, or =) in each of the following:

    a. Y + N_____P + D   b. P + O_____N + D   c. P + Y_____D + N

The next set of activities in this chapter will be helpful in understanding the concept of multiplication and for discovering properties of multiplication. The results may seem simple to you, but try thinking as a student just introduced to the idea.

OBJECTIVE: **Use a set model for multiplication**

You Will Need: Materials Card 3.7

1. Make 3 groups of 4 cubes.

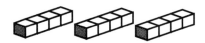

   How many cubes are there altogether?____
   This shows that $3 \times 4 = 12$.

2. Use cubes to represent these products. Record.

   a. $6 \times 3 =$ ____   b. $3 \times 9 =$ ____
   c. $8 \times 5 =$ ____   d. $2 \times 8 =$ ____
   e. $4 \times 7 =$ ____   f. $7 \times 8 =$ ____

3. Take 24 cubes. Find and record four multiplication facts that can be shown about 24.

   a. ____ $\times$ ____ $= 24$ b. ____ $\times$ ____ $= 24$

   c. ____ $\times$ ____ $= 24$ d. ____ $\times$ ____ $= 24$

OBJECTIVE: **Use an array model for multiplication**

You Will Need: Materials from Activity 7

1. Make a 5 by 7 array of cubes.
   How many cubes are in the array?____
   Record: $5 \times 7 =$ ____

2. Make arrays of cubes to represent these products.
   Record:
   a. $7 \times 6 =$ ____   b. $7 \times 7 =$ ____
   c. $4 \times 9 =$ ____   d. $9 \times 8 =$ ____

OBJECTIVE: **Discover properties of multiplication**

You Will Need: Materials from Activity 7

1. Make a 3 by 5 array and a 5 by 3 array of cubes.
   Record: $3 \times 5 =$ ____ $5 \times 3 =$ ____

What do you observe about these two equations?

2. Use cubes and your shortcut from part 1 to solve these multiplication equations:

    a. $9 \times 3 =$ ____   b. $8 \times 7 =$ ____   c. $12 \times 6 =$ ____
    d. $3 \times 9 =$ ____   e. $7 \times 8 =$ ____   f. $6 \times 12 =$ ___

3. Make 4 arrays, each 2 by 3. How many cubes are there altogether?____
    Record: $4 \times (2 \times 3) =$ _____

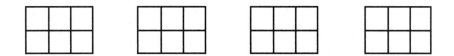

    Make 3 arrays, each 4 by 2. How many cubes are there altogether?____
    Record: $(4 \times 2) \times 3 =$ _____

    What do you notice about your results?

4. Write two multiplication equations using the numbers 2, 5, and 6.

    ___ $\times$ (___ $\times$ ___) = ____   ___ $\times$ (___ $\times$ ___) = ____

    What do you notice about the solution to each equation?

Write a general statement to explain your results.

---

5. Make 2 groups of 5 cubes. Add to that, 2 groups of 3 cubes. How many cubes are there altogether?____ Record $(2 \times 5) + (2 \times 3) =$ _____

    Now make 2 groups of 8 cubes. How many cubes are there altogether?____
    Record: $2 \times (5 + 3) =$ _____

    What do you notice about your results in each case?

Write a general statement to explain your results.

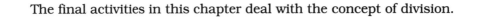

The final activities in this chapter deal with the concept of division.

ACTIVITY 10

OBJECTIVE: **Use a set model for division**

You Will Need: Materials from Activity 7

1. Take 24 cubes. Divide the cubes into groups of 6. How many groups of 6 are there?_____ This shows 24 ÷ 6 using a set of objects.

2. Take 40 cubes. Compute 40 ÷ 8 by dividing the 40 cubes into groups of 8. How many groups are there?_____ Record: 40 ÷ 8 = _____

3. Use cubes to solve these division problems. Record:

    a. 48 ÷ 3 = _____   b. 52 ÷ 4 = _____   c. 68 ÷ 4 = _____   d. 72 ÷ 12 = _____

ACTIVITY 11

OBJECTIVE: **Use an array model for division**

You Will Need: Materials from Activity 7

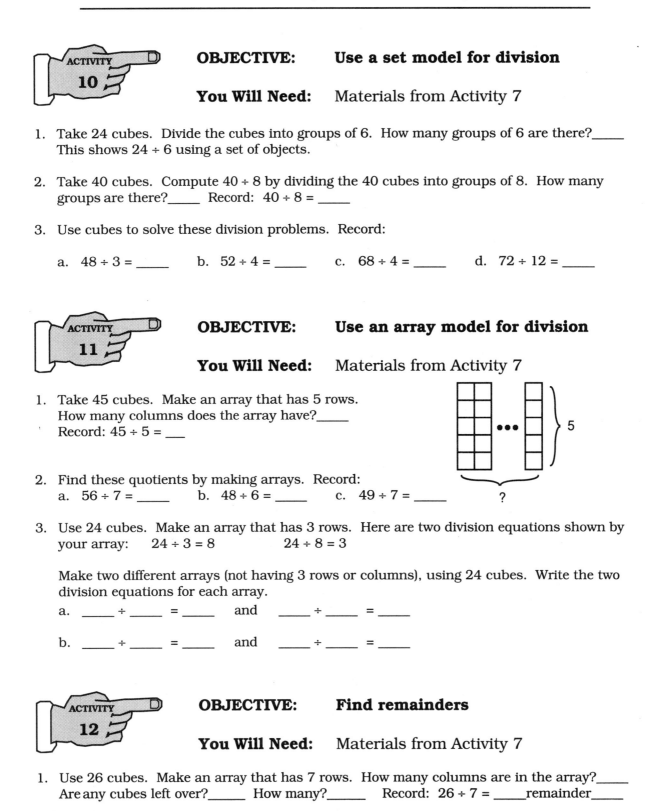

1. Take 45 cubes. Make an array that has 5 rows. How many columns does the array have?_____ Record: 45 ÷ 5 = ___

2. Find these quotients by making arrays. Record:
    a. 56 ÷ 7 = _____   b. 48 ÷ 6 = _____   c. 49 ÷ 7 = _____

3. Use 24 cubes. Make an array that has 3 rows. Here are two division equations shown by your array: 24 ÷ 3 = 8   24 ÷ 8 = 3

    Make two different arrays (not having 3 rows or columns), using 24 cubes. Write the two division equations for each array.

    a. _____ ÷ _____ = _____   and   _____ ÷ _____ = _____

    b. _____ ÷ _____ = _____   and   _____ ÷ _____ = _____

ACTIVITY 12

OBJECTIVE: **Find remainders**

You Will Need: Materials from Activity 7

1. Use 26 cubes. Make an array that has 7 rows. How many columns are in the array?_____ Are any cubes left over?_____ How many?_____ Record: 26 ÷ 7 = _____ remainder _____

2. Use 20 cubes. Make arrays to solve these problems:

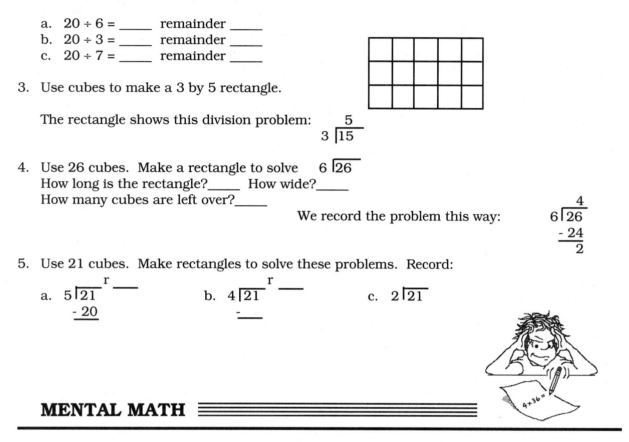

   a. 20 ÷ 6 = _____ remainder _____
   b. 20 ÷ 3 = _____ remainder _____
   c. 20 ÷ 7 = _____ remainder _____

3. Use cubes to make a 3 by 5 rectangle.

   The rectangle shows this division problem:
   $$3\overline{)15}\ ^5$$

4. Use 26 cubes. Make a rectangle to solve $6\overline{)26}$
   How long is the rectangle?_____ How wide?_____
   How many cubes are left over?_____

   We record the problem this way:
   $$6\overline{)26}\ ^4$$
   $$-24$$
   $$\overline{2}$$

5. Use 21 cubes. Make rectangles to solve these problems. Record:

   a. $5\overline{)21}\ ^{r\,\_\_}$
       -20

   b. $4\overline{)21}\ ^{r\,\_\_}$
       $-$ ___

   c. $2\overline{)21}$

MENTAL MATH

Add as you trace the correct path through each maze.
You may pass through each square only once.
You must obtain the result in the triangle.

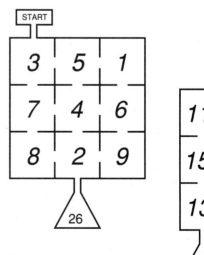

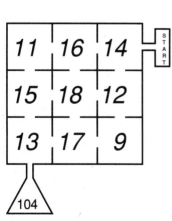

Multiply as you trace the correct path through this maze. You may pass through each square once.

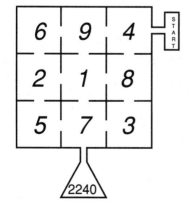

EXERCISES

Proper-T-Practice

Each of the following computations could be simplified by applying one of the properties listed at the right below. For each computation, identify the property or properties used and place the code letter on the line in front of the computation.

Properties of Whole Numbers

___1. $(96 + 56) + 44 = 196$ (C)   commutativity for addition

___2. $(56 \times 29) + (56 \times 71) = 5600$ (M)   associativity for addition

___3.   (E)   identity for addition
    $\Big\}$ $132 + (51 + 68) = 251$
___4.   (H)   commutativity for multiplication

___5. $4 \times (250 \times 29) = 29000$ (A)   associativity for multiplication

___6. $21 + (39 + 0) = 60$ (I)   identity for multiplication

___7. $(121 \times 49) - (21 \times 49) = 4900$ (T)   distributivity for multiplication over addition

___8.
    $\Big\}$ $8 \times (57 \times 125) = 57000$
___9.   (S)   distributivity for multiplication over subtraction

___10. $(56 \times 1) \times 4 = 224$

___11. $(46 \times 27) + (54 \times 27) = 2700$

Now unscramble these 11 code letters to identify a subject that is an art and a tool, as well as a science.

— — — — — — — — — — —

Want Ads

Needed: Doctors who know how to operate.

Skills required: +, -, ×, ÷, and ( )
Tools Available: 3, 5, 6, 7, 9

First of all, you are to choose three different tools to complete the following operations successfully. Remember that multiplication and division are done before addition and subtraction, unless grouping symbols indicate otherwise. There may be several correct answers.

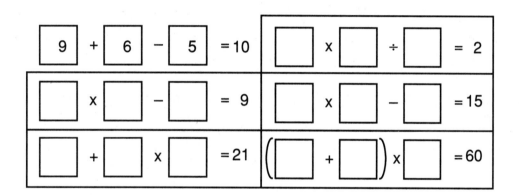

Now that you are getting proficient, you choose any of the operations as well as four different tools (don't forget parentheses can be used).

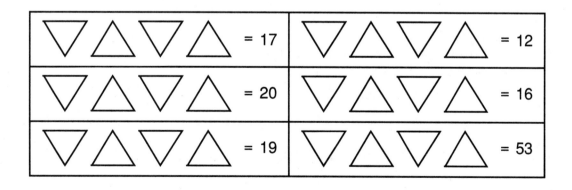

SELF-TEST

1. Using the set union definition of the addition of whole numbers, which of the following pairs of sets could be used to show that 2 + 4 is 6?

   a. {a, b} and {b, c, d, e}
   b. {2} and {4}
   c. {x, y} and {x, y, z, w}
   d. {1, 3} and {2, 4, 6, 8}

2. Which of the following is *not* an example of the commutative property?

   a. (3 + 4) + 5 = 5 + (3 + 4)
   b. 9 + 8 = 8 + 9
   c. (2 + 4) + (5 + 6) = (5 + 6) + (2 + 4)
   d. (6 + 3) + 2 = 6 + (3 + 2)

3. Which of the following properties is *not* used in the computation below?

   a. Distributivity
   b. Associativity
   c. Commutativity
   d. None of a, b, or c.

   $$5(37 + 43) = 5((30 + 7) + 43)$$
   $$= 5(30 + (7 + 43))$$
   $$= 5(30 + 50)$$
   $$= 5 \cdot 30 + 5 \cdot 50$$

4. Which statement is *false*? W is the set of whole numbers.

   a. $a - 0 = a$ for all $a \in W$
   b. $a - b = b - a$ for some $a, b \in W$
   c. $(a - b) - c = a - (b - c)$ for all $a, b, c \in W$
   d. $a - b \in W$ for some $a, b \in W$

5. Using this addition table find (A - B) - C.

   a. A   b. B   c. C   d. D

+	A	B	C	D
A	A	B	C	D
B	B	C	D	A
C	C	D	A	B
D	D	A	B	C

6. Which two of the following models represent the same multiplication problem?

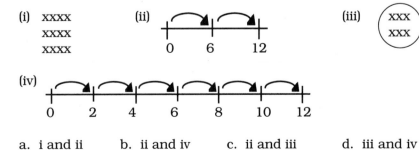

   (i) xxxx
        xxxx
        xxxx

   a. i and ii   b. ii and iv   c. ii and iii   d. iii and iv

7. Which of the following does *not* model division?

    a. There are n objects. You can place them in m equivalent piles. How many will be in each pile?

    b. There are n objects. You can place the objects in a rectangular array with m rows. How many columns are there?

    c. There are n objects. You can make m piles. How many objects will each pile contain?

    d. There are n objects. You can make piles of m objects each. How many piles will you obtain?

8. If a divided by b gives a quotient of c and a remainder d, then

    a. $ac + d = b$ b. $bc = a + d$

    c. $bc = a - d$ d. $ac - d = b$

9. The quotients $6 \div 3$ and $3 \div 6$ can be used to show that

    (i) Division of whole numbers is *not* associative.
    (ii) Division of whole numbers is *not* commutative.
    (iii) The whole numbers are *not* closed under division.

    a. i only   b. iii only   c. i and iii only   d. ii and iii only

10. Which of these is *false*?

    a. $3^4 \cdot 3^5 = 3^3 \cdot 3^6$ b. $4^2 = 2^4$

    c. $5^4 \div 5^2 = 5^{4+2}$ d. $4^3 \cdot 6^3 = 2(2^3 \cdot 3^3)$

SOLUTIONS

Warm-up
8, 13   10 handshakes

Hands-on Activities

Activity 1
1. a. Y   b. D   c. E
2. a. O + D   b. O + P   c. O + P
3. E + W, N + R, K + G, D + P, Y + Y

Activity 2
1. a. O + Y   b. K   c. E   d. O + Y   e. K   f. E
2. Use commutativity and results from (a), (b), and (c).

3. Row 1: P, Y; Row 2: P, Y, D, K; Row 3: D, K, N; Row 4: N, E; Row 5: O
4. The first column has the same entries as the first row, etc.
  $a + b = b + a$ This is called the commutative property of addition.

Activity 3
1. a. G   b. N   c. K   d. N
2. They are the same.
  $(a + b) + c = a + (b + c)$ This is called the associative property of addition.

Activity 4
1. a. Y   b. Y   c. Y   d. Y   e. N   f. N
2. Subtraction is the inverse of addition.
3. K + R = E if and only if E - R = K or E - K = R. There are many other answers.

Activity 5
1. a. G   b. Y   c. G   d. R

Activity 6
1. P < Y < D < N < O
2. a. G, shorter   b. Y, longer   c. R, shorter
3. Y < N, G < N
  If two strips form a third strip, then each of the two is less than the third.
4. a. >   b. =   c. <

Activity 7
1. 12
2. a. 18   b. 27   c. 40   d. 16   e. 28   f. 56
3. a. 4, 6   b. 3, 8   c. 2, 12   d. 1, 24
  (Your answers may be in a different order.)

Activity 8
1. 35
2. a. 42   b. 49   c. 36   d. 72

Activity 9
1. 15, 15 Same answer. This is the commutative property of multiplication.
2. a. 27   b. 56   c. 72   d. 27   e. 56   f. 72
3. 24, 24, 24, 24 Equal
4. $2 \times (5 \times 6) = 60$ $(2 \times 5) \times 6 = 60$ Equal $a \times (b \times c) = (a \times b) \times c$ This is the associative property of multiplication.
5. 16,   10 + 6 = 16,   16,   2 × 8 = 16 Equal $a \times (b + c) = a \times b + a \times c$ This is called the distributive property of multiplication over addition.

Activity 10
1. 4
2. 5, 5
3. a. 16   b. 13   c. 17   d. 6

Activity 11

1. 9, 9
2. a. 8   b. 8   c. 7
3. a. $24 \div 4 = 6$ and $24 \div 6 = 4$
   b. $24 \div 2 = 12$ and $24 \div 12 = 2$ (Your answers may be in a different order.)

Activity 12

1. 3, Yes, 5, 3, 5
2. a. 3, 2   b. 6, 2   c. 2, 6
4. 6, 4, 2
5. a. 4, 1   b. 5, 1   c. 10, 1

Mental Math

3, 5, 1, 6, 9, 2;   14, 16, 11, 15, 18, 17, 13;   4, 8, 1, 2, 5, 7

Exercises

Proper-T-Practice
   1. M   **2.** T   **3-4.** M, C   **5.** A   **6.** E   **7.** S   **8-9.** A, H
   10. I   **11.** T   **MATHEMATICS**

Want Ads (There may be more than one correct answer.)

$$3 \times 6 \div 9 = 2$$

$3 \times 5 - 6 = 9$ $3 \times 7 - 6 = 15$
$6 + 3 \times 5 = 21$ $(3 + 7) \times 6 = 60$
$5 + 6 + 9 - 3 = 17$ $3 \times 5 + 6 - 9 = 12$
$5 \times 6 - 3 - 7 = 20$ $(3 + 5) \times (9 - 7) = 16$
$5 \times 6 \div 3 + 9 = 19$ $3 \times 6 + 5 \times 7 = 53$

Self-Test

1. d 2. d 3. c 4. c 5. b 6. c 7. c 8. c 9. d 10. d

RESOURCE ARTICLES

Baroody, Arthur J. "Children's Difficulties in Subtraction: Some Causes and Cures." *Arithmetic Teacher* 32 (November 1984): 14-19. *Analyzes children's informal subtraction strategies.*

Falco, Thomas. "Multiplication Clue: A Game Activity for the Classroom." *Arithmetic Teacher* 31 (October 1983): 36-37. *Learning game reinforcing multiplication facts.*

Flexer, Roberta J. "The Power of Five: The Step before the Power of Ten." *Arithmetic Teacher* 34 (November 1986): 5-9. *Method of teaching addition and subtraction without counting or rote memorization.*

Greene, Gary. "Math-Facts Memory Made Easy." *Arithmetic Teacher* 33 (December 1985): 21-25. *Instructional strategies to help students learn addition and subtraction facts.*

Hendrickson, A. Dean. "Verbal Multiplication and Division Problems: Some Difficulties and Some Solutions." *Arithmetic Teacher* 33 (April 1986): 26-33. *Examples of situations requiring multiplication and/or division.*

Madell, Rob. "Children's Natural Processes." *Arithmetic Teacher* 32 (March 1985): 20-22. *How children in grades K-3 add and subtract.*

Quintero, Ana Helvia. "Children's Conceptual Understanding of Situations Involving Multiplication." *Arithmetic Teacher* 33 (January 1986): 34-37. *Activities to help students understand concept of multiplication.*

Quintero, Ana Helvia. "Conceptual Understanding of Multiplication: Problems Involving Combinations." *Arithmetic Teacher* 33 (November 1985): 36-39. *Analyzes multiplication word problems.*

Rightsel, Pamela S., and Carol A. Thornton. "72 Addition Facts Can Be Mastered by Mid-Grade 1." *Arithmetic Teacher* 33 (November 1985): 8-10. *Sequence of activities presented.*

Swart, William L. "Some Findings on Conceptual Development of Computational Skills." *Arithmetic Teacher* 32 (January 1985): 36-38. *A case for conceptual rather than mechanized approach.*

Thompson, Charles S., and A. Dean Hendrickson. "Verbal Addition and Subtraction Problems: Some Difficulties and Some Solutions." *Arithmetic Teacher* 33 (March 1986): 21-25. *Presents different context for verbal addition and subtraction problems.*

Thompson, Charles S. and John Van de Walle. "Let's Do It: Modeling Subtraction Situations." *Arithmetic Teacher* 32 (October 1984): 8-12. *Manipulative to abstract variations of take-away and comparison subtraction problems.*

Thompson, Charles S. and John Van de Walle. "Let's Do It: The Power of 10." *Arithmetic Teacher* 32 (November 1984): 6-11. *Using a 10-frame to teach addition and place value.*

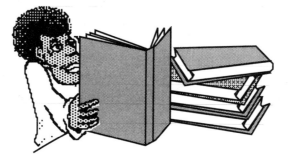

4

Whole Number Computations —Mental, Written, and Electronic

THEME: Understanding Algorithms

WARM-UP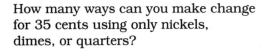

Strategy Review: Make a List.
The strategy of making a list was presented in Chapter 1. It will be useful in solving these problems.

How many ways can you make change for 35 cents using only nickels, dimes, or quarters?

What possible scores can you get by hitting the target with 3 darts?

HANDS-ON ACTIVITIES

What is an algorithm? In mathematics, **algorithms** are the mechanical 'how-to-do-it' part of the curriculum. For example, the step-by-step procedures you follow as you add a column of numbers or do a long division problem are algorithms. In Chapter 3, we looked at the 'concepts' of addition, subtraction, multiplication, and division— that is, the basic ideas of what is happening when we perform these operations. The activities in this chapter will help you gain further insight into 'how-to-do' these operations.

41

OBJECTIVE: **Use the chip abacus to add and subtract in base 3**

You Will Need: Materials Card 4.1

For many of these activities you will be using a **chip abacus.** The chip abacus consists of a sheet of paper with lines drawn as shown.

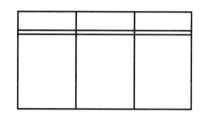

The columns represent the various place values– depending on the base. Numbers are represented by putting chips in the appropriate columns.

Example:

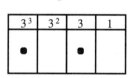

327 is represented as on a base ten abacus.

As you use the chip abacus to explore the operations of addition and subtraction, see if you can explain how the algorithms *you* use to add and subtract are illustrated.

1. Write the base three numerals that are represented by these diagrams:

a.

3^3	3^2	3	1

b.

3^3	3^2	3	1

c.

3^3	3^2	3	1

_____   _____   _____

2. Represent these numerals on your chip abacus.

a. 221_3 b. 120_3 c. 12_3 d. 1002_3

3. Your chip abacus can be used to find a sum such as $112_3 + 212_3$ as follows:

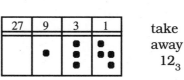

The chip abacus can be used to find a difference such as $211_3 - 12_3$ as follows:

211_3

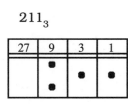

Exchange until each column has at least the number to be taken away.

take away 12_3

Compute these on your chip abacus.

a. $212_3 + 22_3$

b. $121_3 + 21_3 + 12_3$

c. $1212_3 - 221_3$

d. $1111_3 - 212_3$

How could you do these problems without your abacus? Did you use an algorithm? Explain.

4. Compute the following *without* using your abacus:

a. $\begin{array}{r} 1221_3 \\ + 2122_3 \\ \hline \end{array}$

b. $\begin{array}{r} 2211_3 \\ - 1212_3 \\ \hline \end{array}$

Check your answers using your abacus.

We can also look more closely at the operation of multiplication by using the chip abacus. As you do the next activity, think about the algorithm *you* use to do multiplication.

 **OBJECTIVE:** **Use the chip abacus to multiply in base 3**

You Will Need: Materials from Activity 1

1. Show 121_3 on your abacus.

2. Put two *more* 121_3's on your abacus and simplify (no column should have more than two chips after simplification).

3. Compare your results with 121_3. How are they alike? How are they different?

4. The result obtained in part 2 was three times 121_3, or $10_3 \times 121_3$. Can you suggest a shortcut for multiplying any number (in base 3) by 10_3? by 100_3?

5. Find the product $2_3 \times 102_3$, by putting 102_3 on your abacus twice and then simplifying (making exchanges).

$$2_3 \times 102_3 = \rule{2cm}{0.4pt}$$

6. Now see if you can combine what you have learned in this activity to do the following computation. Hint: Associativity and commutativity will help you to do this problem.

$$20_3 \times 102_3 = \rule{2cm}{0.4pt}$$

7. Now use distributivity to do this problem:

$$21_3 \times 102_3 = (20_3 + 1_3) \times 102_3 = (20_3 \times 102_3) + (1_3 \times 102_3)$$

Check this problem using your abacus if you need to.

8. Combine what you have learned in this activity to find these products:

   a. $12_3 \times 111_3 = \rule{2cm}{0.4pt}$ b. $21_3 \times 21_3 = \rule{2cm}{0.4pt}$

   c. $21_3 \times 201_3 = \rule{2cm}{0.4pt}$ d. $12_3 \times 120_3 = \rule{2cm}{0.4pt}$

The chip abacus provides a manipulative for addition and multiplication. As an alternative to the standard algorithm, it may be easier to do, but it requires more time or space to perform the computation. In the next activities, we will look at other methods for addition and multiplication, using a **lattice**.

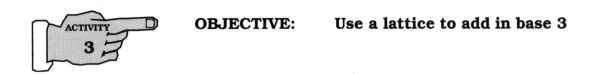

OBJECTIVE: **Use a lattice to add in base 3**

1. Examine this addition procedure:

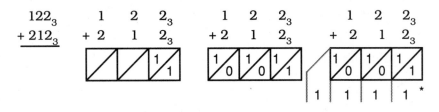

*This sum was obtained by adding down the "diagonals".

2. Is this a correct procedure?   Try it on these. Remember that no subscript indicates base ten.

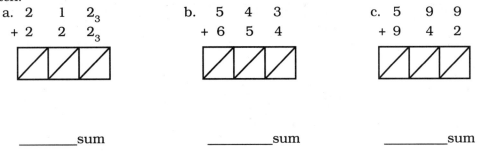

a. $2 \quad 1 \quad 2_3$
$+ 2 \quad 2 \quad 2_3$

_____sum

b. $5 \quad 4 \quad 3$
$+ 6 \quad 5 \quad 4$

_____sum

c. $5 \quad 9 \quad 9$
$+ 9 \quad 4 \quad 2$

_____sum

Is this a correct procedure in all three cases?

Show how this relates to the standard addition algorithm you usually use.

   OBJECTIVE: **Use the lattice method for multiplication**

1. Examine this multiplication method:

    34 × 56

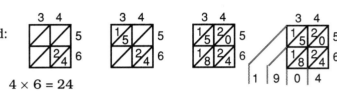

    4 × 6 = 24

    By adding down the diagonals and carrying, we see that 34 × 56 = 1904.

2. Try this method again.

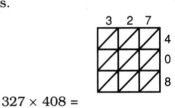

    19 × 35 =   72 × 38 =

3. Try this method with 3-digit numbers.

    165 × 219 =   327 × 408 =

    ┌───┐
    │   Use the notion of place value to explain why this method works. │
    │   │
    │   │
    │   │
    └───┘

    ───
    We have looked at models for algorithms in addition, subtraction, and
    multiplication. In the next activity we will use base 10 pieces to look
    at a concrete model for the division algorithm.
    ───

   OBJECTIVE: **Find quotients using base 10 pieces**

    You Will Need: Materials Card 4.5

1. Represent 23 in base 10 pieces. You should have 2 longs and 3 units. Now divide
    those pieces into two equal piles. Each pile has _____longs and _____units.
    Are there any units left over?_____ How many?_____ Leftover units are called the
    remainder.

    23 ÷ 2 = _____longs_____units, remainder_____ or 23 ÷ 2 = 11, remainder 1

2. Divide the pieces representing 23 into 3 equal piles. Why is this problem more difficult than 23 ÷ 2?

    23 ÷ 3 = _____longs_____units, remainder_____

3. Represent 376 in base 10 pieces. Now divide the pieces into 3 piles.
    Hint: Always begin with the largest pieces and work down to the units.

    Record: 376 ÷ 3 =___flats___longs___units, remainder___

4. Perform these computations using your base 10 pieces.

    a. 1042 ÷ 5 = _f _l _u, r_   b. 572 ÷ 3 = _f _l _u, r_

    c. 76 ÷ 12 = _l _u, r_   d. 95 ÷ 6 = _l _u, r_

    | Explain how this method is like the standard division algorithm. |

MENTAL MATH

Find the correct path to the calculator.

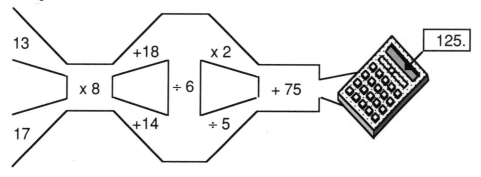

EXERCISES

Worm Work

In going through my great-grandmother's attic recently, I found the following homework page. However, over the years, hungry worms have done their share of damage. Repair the damage by finding the missing digits.

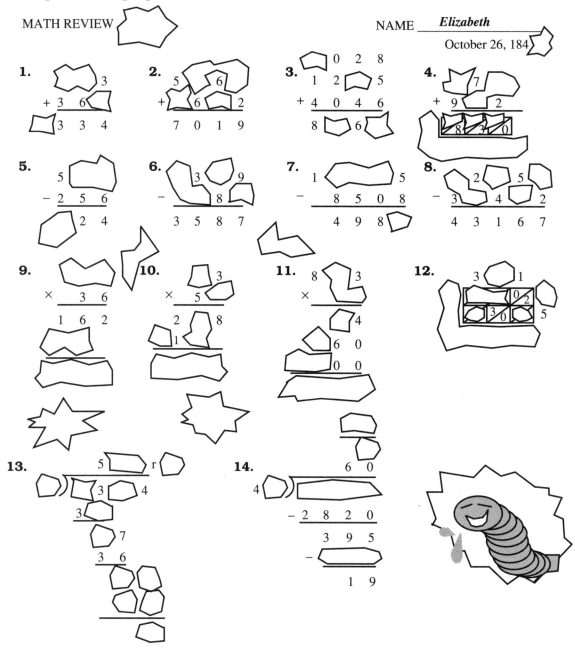

P.S. The year this paper was written was a perfect square. What year was it?

CALCULATOR CAPERS

What did the old woman who lived in a shoe admire most about her husband? Put your head and calculator together to discover the answer. Complete the problems below and discover the patterns. Find the answers that replace the boxes on the calculator keys below. Find the same number in the calculator display given and shade that portion.

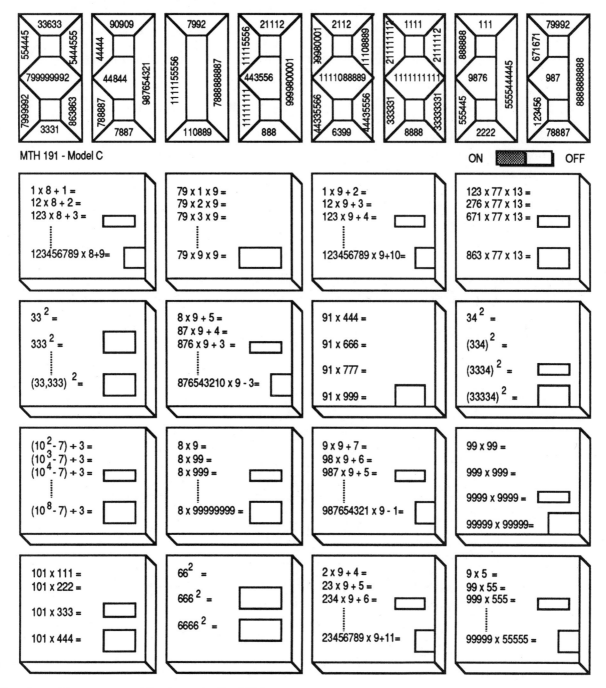

Now turn the page upside down to find the answer.

SELF-TEST

1. Which of the following computations can be simplified using distributivity?

   a. 34(17 + 83)   b. 20(5 × 163)   c. 17 + (13 + 42)   d. 27 × 7 + 27 × 3

2. Which of the following illustrates the left-to-right addition method for finding 35 + 41?

   a. 30 + 40 + 5 + 1   b. 30 + 5 + 40 + 1
   c. 5 + 1 + 30 + 40   d. None of a, b, or c.

3. Fill in the correct values for this intermediate
   addition algorithm. Then find the sum of the
   numbers in the three boxes.

   a. 6   b. 5
   c. 7   d. None of a, b, or c.

   ```
        4  8  9  2
      + 7  6  5  9
               1  1
            1 □  0
         □  4  0  0
      1  1 □  0  0
   ```

4. In performing this subtraction problem, we eventually express 50,000 as

   a. 4000 + 900 + 90 + 9   b. 40000 + 900 + 90 + 10
   c. 40000 + 9000 + 900 + 90 + 9   d. None of a, b, or c.

   ```
      5 0 0 0 0
    -   2 3 9 2
   ```

5. The subtraction problem at the right was done
   by the *subtract-from-base* algorithm. The 3
   in the answer was obtained by calculating

   ```
          2
          3̸ 2
        -   9
          2 3
   ```

   a. (10 - 9) + 2   b. 12 - 9
   c. □ , where 9 + □ = 12   d. None of a, b, or c.

6. Find the indicated product by
   completing the lattice to the right.

   a. 15,125   b. 14,125
   c. 15,200   d. 15,225

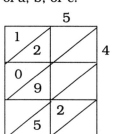

7. Fill in the correct values for this intermediate multiplication algorithm.
   Then find the sum of the numbers in the four boxes.

   a. 13   b. 15
   c. 17   d. None of a, b, or c.

   ```
         274
       ×  38
         32
        560
      □□00
       □20
      2100
     □000
   ```

8. The y in the division problem to the right equals

    a. 2   b. 5
    c. 7   d. None of a, b, or c.

$$
\begin{array}{r}
47\,\boxed{}\boxed{}\boxed{}\boxed{}\,y \\
\underline{-\ \text{x x x x}\ \ 30} \\
\text{x x x} \\
\underline{-\ \text{x x x}\ \ 10} \\
\text{x x x} \\
\underline{-\ \text{x x x}\ \ 6} \\
1\ 3
\end{array}
$$

9. Find the remainder for 6,289,214 divided by 92,365.

    a. 68   b. 8,394   c. 571,555   d. None of a, b, or c.

10. Which of the following are equal?

    (i) $37_8 + 124_8$ (ii) $354_8 - 152_8$ (iii) $32_8 \times 5_8$

    a. i and ii   b. i and iii   c. ii and iii   d. None of a, b, or c.

SOLUTIONS

Warm-up
6 ways   3, 7, 11, 12, 15, 16, 20, 21, 25, 30

Hands-on Activities

Activity 1
1. a. 212_3 b. 1010_3 c. 1201_3
2. a. 0, 2, 2, 1 chips   b. 0, 1, 2, 0 chips   c. 0, 0, 1, 2 chips   d. 1, 0, 0, 2 chips
3. a. 1011_3 b. 1001_3 c. 221_3 d. 122_3
   Use the usual addition or subtraction algorithm, regrouping by 3's
4. a. 11120_3 b. 222_3

Activity 2
2. 1210_3
3. Multiplying by 3 has shifted 121_3 one place to the left.
4. Shift the numeral one place to the left. For 100_3, shift two places left.
5. 211_3
6. 2110_3
7. 2212_3
8. a. 2102_3 b. 1211_3 c. 11221_3 d. 2210_3

Activity 3

2. Yes   a. 1211_3 b. 1197   c. 1541   Yes, it avoids some carrying.
Places are added, then regrouped diagonally instead of vertically.

Activity 4

2. 19×35—   Row 1: 0, 3, 2, 7   Row 2: 0, 5, 4, 5   Product: 665
     72×38—   Row 1: 2, 1, 0, 6   Row 2: 5, 6, 1, 6   Product: 2736
3. 165×219—   Row 1: 0, 2, 1, 2, 1, 0   Row 2: 0, 1, 0, 6, 0, 5
          Row 3: 0, 9, 5, 4, 4, 5   Product: 36135

     327×405—   Row 1: 1, 2, 0, 8, 2, 8   Row 2: 0, 0, 0, 0, 0, 0
          Row 3: 2, 4, 1, 6, 5, 6   Product: 133416

Places are multiplied, then regrouped diagonally. For example, in the product 327×408 the intersection of the "3" column and the "4" row represents $300 \times 400 = 120000$.

Activity 5

1. 1, 1   Yes, 1, 1, 1, 1
2. You need to exchange longs for units.   0 longs 7 units, remainder 2
3. 1, 2, 5 r 1
4. a. 2, 0, 8 r 2   b. 1, 9, 0 r 2   c. 0, 6 r 4   d. 1, 5 r 5
We start from the left dividing up the bigger pieces first and proceed to the right.

Mental Math

17, 8, 14, 6, 2, 75

Exercises

Worm Work

1. 973 + 361 = 1334

2. 5367 + 1652 = 7019

3. 3028 + 1295 + 4046 = 8369

4. 978 + 962 = [diagram] = 1940

5. 580 - 256 = 324

6. 4369 - 782 = 3587

7. 13495 - 8508 = 4987

8. 82659 - 39492 = 43167

9.
```
    27
  ×36
   162
    81
   972
```

10.
```
    43
  × 56
   258
   215
  2408
```

11.
```
   873        or        823
  ×  8                 ×  8
    24                   24
   560                  160
  6400                 6400
  6984                 6584
```

12.

13.
```
      562r2
  6)3374
    30
    37
    36
    14
    12
     2
```

14.
```
           68
            8
           60
  47)3215
   - 2820
      395
    - 376
       19
```

Calculator Capers

Top Row:	987, 987654321, 6399, 1111, 1111111111, 671671, 863863
Second Row:	110889, 1111088889, 7887, 7888888887, 90909, 11115556, 1111155556
Third Row:	3331, 33333331, 7992, 799999992, 8888, 8888888888, 99980001, 9999800001
Bottom Row:	33633, 44844, 443556, 44435556, 2112, 211111112, 554445, 5555444445

hIS ShOES

Self-Test

1. d **2.** a **3.** b **4.** d **5.** a **6.** d **7.** d **8.** b **9.** b **10.** c

RESOURCE ARTICLES

Abel, Jean, Glenn D. Allinger, and Lyle Andersen. "Popsicle Sticks, Computers, and Calculators: Important Considerations." *Arithmetic Teacher* 34 (May 1987): 8-12. *Use of teaching aids to help students learn the concept and algorithm for division.*

Bates, Tom, and Leo Rousseau. "Will the Real Division Algorithm Please Stand Up?" *Arithmetic Teacher* 33 (March 1986): 42-46. *Approaches and applications of the division algorithm.*

Beattie, Ian D. "Modeling Operations and Algorithms." *Arithmetic Teacher* 33 (February 1986): 23-28. *Rationale for using manipulatives.*

Broadbent, Frank W. "Lattice Multiplication and Division." *Arithmetic Teacher* 34 (January 1987): 28-31. *Extends lattice method to division.*

Cheek, Helen Neely, and Olson Melfried. "A Den of Thieves Investigates Division." *Arithmetic Teacher* 33 (May 1986): 34-35. *Activity using distributive connotation of division.*

Ewbank, William A., and John L. Ginther. "Subtraction Drill with a Difference." *Arithmetic Teacher* 31(January 1984): 49-51. *Collection of number games and puzzles to supplement textbook.*

Grossman, Anne S. "A Subtraction Algorithm for the Upper Grades." *Arithmetic Teacher* 32 (January 1985): 44-45. *Subtraction by the equal addition method.*

Haigh, William E. "The Only Way To Do It Is To Undo It." *Arithmetic Teacher* 31 (November 1983): 24-25. *Illustrates relationship between inverse operations.*

Hall, William D. "Division with Base-Ten Blocks." *Arithmetic Teacher* 31 (November 1983): 21-23. *Provides transition from manipulatives to written division algorithm.*

Lessen, Elliott I., and Carla L. Cumblad. "Alternatives for Teaching Multiplication Facts." *Arithmetic Teacher* 31 (January 1984): 46-48. *Suggests alternative sequence to teaching multiplication facts.*

Meyer, Ruth A., and James E. Riley. "Multiplication Games." *Arithmetic Teacher* 33 (April 1986): 22-25. *Variety of games for drill and practice of multiplication.*

Pearson, Eleanor S. "Summing It All Up: Pre-1900 Algorithms." *Arithmetic Teacher* 33 (March 1986): 38-41. *Algorithms for operations.*

Pereira-Mendoza, Lionel. "Using English Sentences and Pictures for Practice in Mathematics." *Arithmetic Teacher* 32 (September 1984): 34-38. *Game for self-checking practice with addition and subtraction.*

Reys, Robert E. "Testing Mental-Computation Skills." *Arithmetic Teacher* 33 (November 1985): 14-16. *Suggestions for testing mental-computation skills in the classroom.*

Richbart, Lynn A. "Fun and Arithmetic Practice with Days and Dates." *Arithmetic Teacher* 32 (January 1985): 48. *Practice in dividing, multiplying, adding, subtracting, and using simple algebraic expressions.*

Young, Jerry L. "Uncovering the Algorithms." *Arithmetic Teacher* 32 (November 1984): 20. *Method for diagnosing students' problems with applying algorithms.*

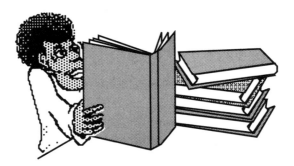

5 Number Theory

THEME: Composing and Decomposing with Primes

Strategy Review:
Solve a Simpler Problem.
To solve these problems, begin by solving a simpler version first. See Chapter 1 for a review of this strategy.

A restaurant has 23 square tables that seat 1 person on each side. How many people can be seated at a banquet if one long, rectangular table is made by pushing the 23 tables together?

Craig and 6 of his friends have telephones. Each friend talks with every other friend exactly once each day. How many phone calls are made each day?

HANDS-ON ACTIVITIES

What is a factor? The numbers 2 and 3 are **factors** of 6 because $2 \times 3 = 6$. The list of all the factors of 6 is 1, 2, 3, and 6. In order to deal with the concepts in this chapter, you need to have a clear understanding of factors. Activity 1 will help you understand factors.

ACTIVITY 1

OBJECTIVE: **Investigate factors**

You Will Need: Materials Card 5.1

1. Use 12 cubes. Make a 3 by 4 rectangle. 3 and 4 are called factors of 12.

3 [rectangle]

4

   Use the 12 cubes again. Make a 2 by 6 rectangle. 2 and 6 are also factors of 12.

   Use the 12 cubes again. Make a 1 by 12 rectangle. 1 and 12 are also factors of 12. Record all the factors of 12:

   _____ , _____ , _____ , _____ , _____ , _____

2. Use 15 cubes. Find all of the factors of 15 by making rectangles. Record the factors of 15:

   _____ , _____ , _____ , _____

3. Find all of the factors of each number by making rectangles. Record.

   a. 4 _____ b. 9 _____

   c. 18 _____ d. 20 _____

   e. 25 _____ f. 36 _____

4. Which numbers in part 3 have an odd number of factors?

   _____ , _____ , _____ , _____

   What is the special name for these numbers?

When two numbers have the same factor or factors, they are said to have **common factors**. Both 4 and 6 have 2 as a factor. Therefore, 2 is a common factor of 4 and 6. Activity 2 will give you more information about common factors.

OBJECTIVE: **Find the greatest common factor**

You Will Need: Materials from Activity 1

1. Make 3 different rectangles, using 16 cubes for each rectangle.
    Record:

    _____ by _____ , _____ by _____ , _____ by _____

    Record the factors of 16: _____ , _____ , _____ , _____ , _____

2. Make 4 different rectangles, using 24 cubes for each rectangle.
    Record:

    _____ by _____ , _____ by _____ , _____ by _____ , _____ by _____

    Factors of 24:   _____ , _____ , _____ , _____ , _____ , _____ , _____ , _____

3. List the factors that 16 and 24 have in common:

    _____ , _____ , _____ , _____

    These factors are called the **common factors** of 16 and 24.
    Which of these factors is the largest? _____
    This is called the **greatest common factor (GCF)**.

4. Find the common factors of 15 and 20. Record: _____ , _____

    What is the greatest common factor of 15 and 20? _____

5. Find the greatest common factor of each pair of numbers:

    a. 12 and 18 _____   b. 8 and 12 _____

    c. 9 and 12 _____   d. 12 and 24 _____

    CHALLENGE: Find the greatest common factor of 12, 16, and 20.

The **multiples** of a number are found by multiplying that number by
the counting numbers. For example, the multiples of 3 are 3, 6, 9, 12 . . .
Activity 3 will give you additional practice in finding multiples.

OBJECTIVE: **Investigate multiples**

You Will Need: Materials from Activity 1

1. Make a 4 by 1 rectangle. How many cubes are in the rectangle?_____
    4 is called a multiple of 4.

    Now make a 4 by 2 rectangle. How many cubes are in the rectangle?_____
    8 is also a multiple of 4.

    Now make a 4 by 3 rectangle. How many cubes are in the rectangle?_____
    12 is also a multiple of 4.

2. Make 6 more rectangles with 4 cubes on one side. Use the rectangles to find six more multiples of 4.

    Record: _____ , _____ , _____ , _____ , _____ , _____

3. Make rectangles to find six multiples of each number.

    a. 3 _____   b. 7 _____

    c. 5 _____   d. 6 _____

When two numbers have the same number as a multiple, they are said
to have a **common multiple**. You can always find a common multiple
by multiplying the two numbers together, but it is important to know how
to find the **least common multiple (LCM)**. Activity 4 will help you
understand common multiples.

OBJECTIVE: **Find least common multiples**

1. For each multiple of 2, shade in the triangle in the upper left corner of the box in the grid given on the next page (2 and 4 have been done for you). For each multiple of 3, use vertical lines to shade in the triangle in the upper right corner of the box (3 and 6 have been done for you).

    List the common multiples (those with both a solid and striped triangle) of 2 and 3 less than 100:

    Which number is the least common multiple of 2 and 3?_____

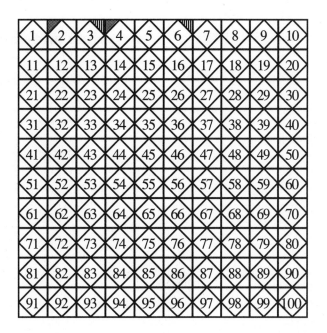

2. For all of the multiples of 4 use horizontal lines to shade in the triangle in the lower left corner of the box.

    Use dots to shade in the lower right corner of the box for each multiple of 6.

    List the common multiples of 4 and 6 less than 100:

    What is the least common multiple of 4 and 6?_____

3. Find the least common multiple for each pair of numbers.
    Hint: Instead of shaded triangles, use bits of paper to cover the multiples of 3, then 5.

    a. 3 and 5 _____   b. 4 and 7 _____   c. 9 and 6 _____   d. 2 and 8 _____

    What can you say about the bits of paper and the common multiples?

    the least common multiples?

4. Find the least common multiple for each group of numbers.

    a. 2, 3, and 5 _____   b. 3, 6, and 8 _____   c. 3, 4, and 7 _____   d. 2, 5, and 9 _____

Some numbers have exactly 2 factors; these numbers are called **prime** numbers. Numbers that have more than two factors are called **composite** numbers. This activity will demonstrate a method for finding prime and composite numbers.

OBJECTIVE: **Find prime and composite numbers**

You Will Need: Materials from Activity 1

1. Make a rectangle using 3 cubes. Draw your rectangle here:

    Can you make a different rectangle with 3 cubes?_____
    The dimensions of the rectangle are the factors of 3. Record the factors of 3: _____ , _____

2. Make two different rectangles using 4 cubes in each rectangle. (Remember: A square is also a rectangle.) Draw your rectangles here:

    Record the factors of 4: _____ , _____ , _____

3. Make all of the different rectangles that can be made for each number. Record all of the factors for each number here:

    a. 18_____   b. 27_____

    c. 23_____   d. 29_____

    Circle each number for which you could make only one rectangle.

    > The numbers you have circled are **primes** because they have exactly two factors, themselves and 1. (The number 1 is not prime because it has only one as a factor.)

4. On the next grid, cross out 1 and circle 2. Then cross out all the multiples of 2. Now circle 3 and cross out all the multiples of 3. What is the next number that has not been crossed out? _____ Circle it and cross out all of its multiples.

    Continue in this manner until all of the numbers on the grid are circled or crossed out.

1	2	3	4	5	6	7	8	9	10
11	12	13	14	15	16	17	18	19	20
21	22	23	24	25	26	27	28	29	30
31	32	33	34	35	36	37	38	39	40
41	42	43	44	45	46	47	48	49	50
51	52	53	54	55	56	57	58	59	60
61	62	63	64	65	66	67	68	69	70
71	72	73	74	75	76	77	78	79	80
81	82	83	84	85	86	87	88	89	90
91	92	93	94	95	96	97	98	99	100

> The circled numbers are the primes less than 100. List them here:

5. The numbers on the grid, except 1, that are crossed out are called composite numbers because they have more than two factors. Take 6 for example. Build as many different rectangles as you can using 6 cubes. Draw your rectangles here:

Did you find two different rectangles?_____

Record the factors of 6: _____ , _____ , _____ , _____

6 is a composite number because it has more than two factors. Which of these factors are prime numbers? _____ , _____

6 can be written as the product of primes: $2 \times 3 = 6$

6. Build as many different rectangles as you can using 10 cubes. Draw your rectangles here:

Is 10 a composite number?_____

Record the factors of 10: _____ , _____ , _____ , _____

Write 10 as the product of primes: _____ × _____ = 10

7. Build as many different rectangles as you can using 30 cubes. Record your rectangles:

Is 30 a composite number?_____

What are the factors of 30?

_____ , _____ , _____ , _____ , _____ , _____ , _____ , _____

Write 30 as the product of primes: _____ × _____ × _____ = 30

8. Write these composite numbers as products of primes.

a. 14 = _____ × _____   b. 15 = _____ × _____

c. 12 = _____ × _____ × _____   d. 16 = _____ × _____ × _____ × _____

e. 50 = _____ × _____ × _____   f. 24 = _____ × _____ × _____ × _____

Can every composite number be written as the product of primes?_____
If two people each correctly factor the same number into prime factors, how will their factorizations be alike?

How might they differ?

MENTAL MATH

OBSERVE THIS PATTERN:

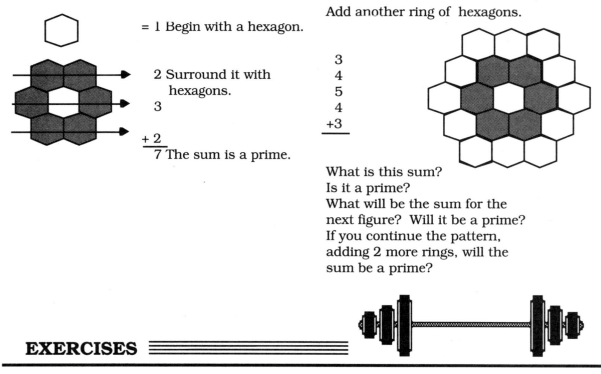

= 1 Begin with a hexagon.

2 Surround it with
   hexagons.
3

+ 2
——
7 The sum is a prime.

Add another ring of hexagons.

3
4
5
4
+3
——

What is this sum?
Is it a prime?
What will be the sum for the
next figure? Will it be a prime?
If you continue the pattern,
adding 2 more rings, will the
sum be a prime?

EXERCISES

STAINED GLASS DISCOVERY

This exercise is divided into four frames. In each frame, shade each region that contains
a number divisible by the given number. You should find 7 of these regions in each frame.

Divisible by 3

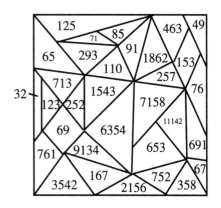

Divisible by 9

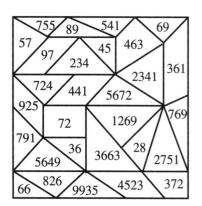

Divisible by 8

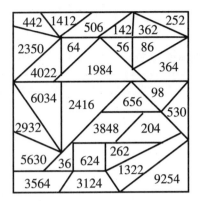

Divisible by 6

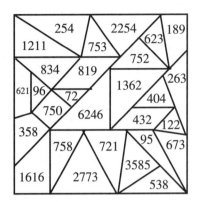

Which one is the swan?____ the cat?____ the profile of a man's head?____
the whale?____

A TIMELY TAIL

DIRECTIONS: A special message is written in code at the bottom of the page. To decode it, determine what number should replace each letter in the factor trees below. Each time this number appears in the code, write the letter above it.

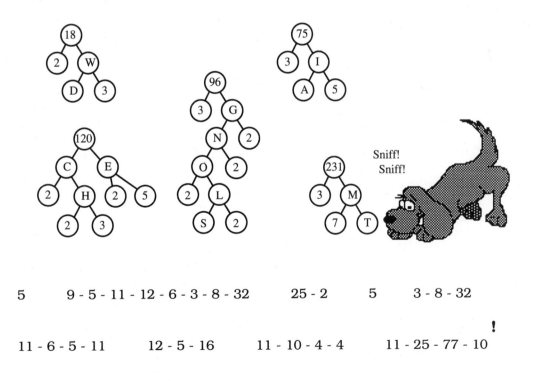

Sniff!
Sniff!

5   9 - 5 - 11 - 12 - 6 - 3 - 8 - 32   25 - 2   5   3 - 8 - 32

                                                                        !

11 - 6 - 5 - 11   12 - 5 - 16   11 - 10 - 4 - 4   11 - 25 - 77 - 10

What do Alexander the Great and Smokey the Bear have in common?

DIRECTIONS: Find the greatest common factor or least common multiple for the numbers given on the left. Draw a straight line connecting each problem with its answer. Each line will cross a number and a letter, as the first problem indicates. Wherever the number appears in the code below, fill in the letter.

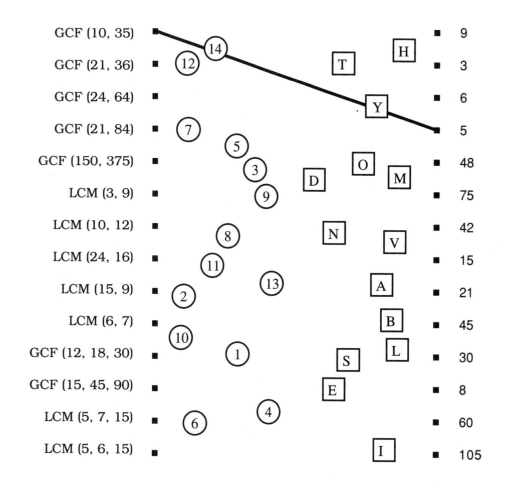

GCF (10, 35)   — 9
GCF (21, 36)   — 3
GCF (24, 64)   — 6
GCF (21, 84)   — 5
GCF (150, 375) — 48
LCM (3, 9)   — 75
LCM (10, 12)   — 42
LCM (24, 16)   — 15
LCM (15, 9)   — 21
LCM (6, 7)   — 45
GCF (12, 18, 30) — 30
GCF (15, 45, 90) — 8
LCM (5, 7, 15)   — 60
LCM (5, 6, 15)   — 105

Y
12 - 5 - 4 - 14   2 - 10 - 12 - 5   5 - 1 - 13 - 4

12 - 5 - 4   11 - 1 - 8 - 4

8 - 6 - 3 - 3 - 7 - 4   9 - 1 - 8 - 4

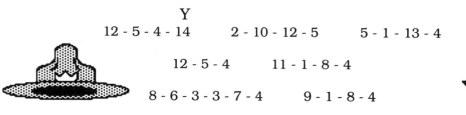

SELF-TEST

1. Which of a, b, or c is *false?*

    a. 68 is a multiple of 17   b. 111 is a prime
    c. 19 is a divisor of 76   d. None of a, b, or c is false.

2. Which of the following does *not* divide 1357924860?

    a. 9   b. 4   c. 6   d. 8

3. Given the following prime factor tree, the sum of the unknown prime factors is:

    a. 22   b. 18   c. 15   d. 4

4. If $a = 2^7 \cdot 3^3 \cdot 5^2$, which of the following is *false?*

    a. 15 divides a b. 12 divides a c. 21 divides a d. 75 divides a

5. By the fundamental theorem of arithmetic, if $2^4 \cdot 6^3 \cdot 3^5 = 2^7 \cdot 3^x$, then x must be

    a. 5   b. 8   c. 12   d. None of a, b, or c.

6. 144 is the LCM for which pair of numbers below?

    a. 36, 16   b. 27, 24   c. 12, 18   d. None of a, b, or c.

7. Find the *sum* of the GCF and the LCM of 8, 22, and 46.

    a. 1518   b. 2530   c. 1024144   d. 2026

8. The LCM is $2^2 \cdot 3^3 \cdot 5^2 \cdot 13$ and the GCF is $2^2 \cdot 3^2 \cdot 13$. One number is 1404, what is the *sum* of the digits of the other number?

    a. 9   b. 8   c. 7   d. None of a, b, or c.

9. If p and q are primes (but neither is 2), then

    a. $2p$ is prime   b. $p + q$ is prime
    c. $p + q$ is composite   d. $p + q$ is an odd number

10. The number of divisors of 425 is

    a. 6   b. 8   c. 4   d. 3

SOLUTIONS

Warm-up

48 people. 1 table = 4 seats, 2 tables = 6 seats, 3 tables = 8 seats, etc.
21 calls (to count them, label the callers A, B, C, D, E, F, G)

AB AC AD AE AF AG
BC BD BE BF BG
CD CE CF CG
DE DF DG
EF EG
FG

Hands-on Activities

Activity 1
1. 1, 2, 3, 4, 6, 12
2. 1, 3, 5, 15
3. a. 1, 2, 4   b. 1, 3, 9   c. 1, 2, 3, 6, 9, 18   d. 1, 2, 4, 5, 10, 20
       e. 1, 5, 25   f. 1, 2, 3, 4, 6, 9, 12, 18, 36
4. 4, 9, 25, 36, Square numbers

Activity 2
1. 1 by 16, 2 by 8, 4 by 4,   1, 2, 4, 8, 16
2. 1 by 24, 2 by 12, 3 by 8, 4 by 6,   1, 2, 3, 4, 6, 8, 12, 24
3. 1, 2, 4, 8   GCF = 8
4. 1, 5   GCF = 5
5. a. 6   b. 4   c. 3   d. 12   CHALLENGE = 4

Activity 3
1. 4, 8, 12
2. Answers may vary— possibly 16, 20, 24, 28, 32, 36
3. Answers may vary— possibly 3, 6, 9, 12, 15, 18;   7, 14, 21, 28, 35, 42;
       5, 10, 15, 20, 25, 30;   6, 12, 18, 24, 30, 36

Activity 4
1. 6, 12, 18, 24, 30, 36, 42, 48, 54, 60, 66, 72, 78, 84, 90, 96   LCM = 6
2. 12, 24, 36, 48, 60, 72, 84, 96   LCM = 12
3. a. 15   b. 28   c. 18   d. 8
       Two bits of paper on a square indicates common multiple. First one to occur is LCM.
4. a. 30   b. 24   c. 84   d. 90

Activity 5

1. 1 by 3, No other rectangle can be made. 1, 3
2. 1 by 4 and 2 by 2; 1, 2, 4
3. a. 1, 2, 3, 6, 9, 18   b. 1, 3, 9, 27   c. 1, 23   d. 1, 29
    23 and 29 should be circled.
4. 5;
    2, 3, 5, 7, 11, 13, 17, 19, 23, 29, 31, 37, 41, 43, 47, 53, 59, 61, 67, 71, 73, 79, 83, 89, 97
5. 1 by 6 and 2 by 3;   Yes;   1, 2, 3, 6;   2 and 3
6. 1 by 10 and 2 by 5;   Yes;   1, 2, 5, 10; $2 \times 5 = 10$
7. 1 by 30, 2 by 15, 3 by 10, and 5 by 6; Yes;
    1, 2, 3, 5, 6, 10, 15, 30; $2 \times 3 \times 5 = 30$
8. a. 2×7 b. 3×5 c. $2 \times 2 \times 3$ d. $2 \times 2 \times 2 \times 2$ e. $2 \times 5 \times 5$ f. $2 \times 2 \times 2 \times 3$
    Yes;   They will contain the same prime factors. The factors may be listed in a different order.

Mental Math

The sum is 19, a prime. The next sums are 37, a prime, 61, a prime, and 91, not a prime.

Exercises

STAINED GLASS DISCOVERY

Divisible by 3: 123, 252, 69, 6354, 7158, 11142, 153; the cat.
Divisible by 9: 234, 441, 72, 36, 3663, 1269, 45; the swan.
Divisible by 8: 64, 56, 1984, 2416, 656, 3848, 624; the profile of a man's head.
Divisible by 6: 834, 96, 750, 72, 6246, 1362, 432; the whale.

A TIMELY TAIL

18: W = 9, D = 3   75: I = 25, A = 5   96: G = 32, N = 16, O = 8, L = 4, S = 2
120: C = 12, H = 6, E = 10   231: M = 77, T = 11
A watchdog is a dog that can tell time!

What do Alexander the Great and Smokey the Bear have in common?
GCF (21, 36) = 3   LCM (15, 9) = 45
GCF (24, 64) = 8   LCM (6, 7) = 42
GCF (21, 84) = 21   GCF (12, 18, 30) = 6
GCF (150, 375) = 75   GCF (15, 45, 90) = 15
LCM (3, 9) = 9   LCM (5, 7, 15) = 105
LCM (10, 12) = 60   LCM (5, 6, 15) = 30
LCM (24, 16) = 48
They both have the same middle name.

Self-Test

1. b   **2.** d   **3.** b   **4.** c   **5.** b   **6.** a   **7.** d   **8.** a   **9.** c   **10.** a

RESOURCE ARTICLES

Beattie, Ian D. "Building Understanding with Blocks." *Arithmetic Teacher* 34 (October 1986): 5-11. *Activities illustrating concrete forms of factors and multiples.*

Bezuszka, Stanley J. "A Test for Divisibility by Primes." *Arithmetic Teacher* 33 (October 1985): 36-38. *General divisibility algorithm for prime numbers.*

Brown, G. W. "Searching for Patterns of Divisors." *Arithmetic Teacher* 32 (December 1984): 32-34. *Practice in examining divisors.*

Dearing, Shirley Ann, and Boyd Holtan. "Factors and Primes with a T square." *Arithmetic Teacher* 34 (April 1987): 34. *Technique for finding all factors of a number.*

Dockweiler, Clarence J. "Palindromes and the 'Law of 11'." *Arithmetic Teacher* 32 (January 1985): 46-47. *Classifying numbers through palindromes.*

Edwards, Flo McEnery. "Geometric Figures Make the LCM Obvious." *Arithmetic Teacher* 34 (March 1987): 17-18. *An approach using geometric figures to find LCM and GCF.*

Hopkins, Martha H. "Number Facts - or Fantasy." *Arithmetic Teacher* 34 (March 1987): 38-42. *Shares past and present beliefs about specific numbers.*

Lamb, Charles E., and Lyndal R. Hutcherson. "Greatest Common Factor and Least Common Multiple." *Arithmetic Teacher* 31 (April 1984): 43-44. *Strategies for avoiding misconceptions about GCF and LCM and computational algorithms.*

Litwiller, Bonnie H., and David R. Duncan. "Pentagonal Patterns in the Addition Table." *Arithmetic Teacher* 32 (April 1985): 36-38. *Activities and patterns involving the addition table.*

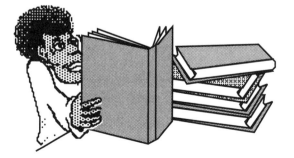

6

Fractions

THEME: Understanding Fractions and their Operations

WARM-UP

Strategy Review: Draw a Picture.
You may find these problems easier to solve if you draw a picture to help you visualize the problem. This strategy was introduced in Chapter 1.

A sleepy snail wants to climb to the top of a sunflower 10 feet tall so that he can check out the snails in the neighbor's yard. Each day he climbs up 3 feet, but at night he slides back down 2 feet as he sleeps. How many days will it take him to reach the top of the sunflower?

The South High football team wears consecutive numbers starting with 1. If they form a circle in numerical order, number 1 is directly across from number 17. How many players are on the team?

HANDS-ON ACTIVITIES

The following activities show two distinct ways to represent fractions. We will use a measurement model and an area model. For the first activity, let's look at a representation using lengths.

OBJECTIVE: **Represent fractions using a measurement model**

You Will Need: Materials Card 6.1

1. For this part, let an ORANGE represent the whole number 1. Place an ORANGE strip in front of you. Now find the strip that represents 1/2 by putting together 2 identical strips of another color that measure the same length as an ORANGE. For example:

ORANGE	
YELLOW	YELLOW

Since ORANGE is equal to 1, YELLOW is equal to _____. Now use your centimeter strips to find the value of:

a. RED = _____   b. WHITE = _____

2. Now let BROWN be equal to the whole number 1. What color represents each of these fractions:

a. 1/2 = _____   b. 1/8 = _____

c. 1/4 = _____   d. 1 1/4 = _____
How did you solve (d) above? Hint: Use a BROWN and your answer to (c).

Now find the strips that are equal to these values, (BROWN = 1):

e. 1 1/8 = _____   f. 3/4 = _____   g. 3/8 = _____

3. Use BLUE as the unit. Find the value of these strips:

a. WHITE = _____   b. LIGHT GREEN = _____

4. Complete the following.

a. WHITE = 1/2 of _____   b. RED = 1/2 of _____

c. _____ = 1/2 of BROWN   d. _____ = 1/2 of DARK GREEN

In Activity 1 we used the linear measurement model to represent fractions.
Next, we will use an area model.

OBJECTIVE: **Use an area model to represent fractions**

You Will Need: Materials Card 6.2

1. Lay the circle in front of you. Find the two pieces that will exactly cover the circle. Each of these pieces is equal to _____ of the circle. Label each of these pieces 1/2.

2. Find the three pieces that exactly cover the circle. Each of these pieces is equal to _____ of the circle. Label them.

    Continue in this manner until all of the pieces are labelled.

3. Now find the following fractions of the circle: (Draw a picture to record your findings.)

    a. 2/3   b. 3/8   c. 5/6

    d. 3/4   e. 7/8   f. 1 1/2

    +--+
    | Explain how fractions can be represented using an area model. |
    | |
    | |
    | |
    +--+

OBJECTIVE: **Solve a problem using the area model for fractions**

You Will Need: Materials Card 6.3

1. Determine what fractional part of the large square is represented by each of these pieces:

    a. large triangle = _____   b. medium triangle = _____
    c. small triangle = _____   d. small square = _____
    e. parallelogram = _____   f. large square = _____

2. Which 3 different pieces have the same area (represent the same fractional part of the large square)?

        _____   _____   _____

We have looked at several ways to represent fractions. The following activity will address the concept of **equivalent fractions**– fractions that represent the same relative amount.

 **OBJECTIVE: Find equivalent fractions**

You Will Need: Materials from Activity 2

1. Lay the circle in front of you.
    Find the piece that is 1/3 of the circle.
    Now find two pieces that exactly cover the piece labelled 1/3.
    What is each of these pieces labelled?_____
    We can say that 1/3 is equivalent to two _____pieces − or that 1/3 = 2/6.

2. Find the piece that is 1/2 of the circle. Use your pieces to find three other fractions
    that are equivalent to 1/2.

    _____ = 1/2   _____ = 1/2   _____ = 1/2

    Can you then say that 2/4 = 3/6 = 4/8 = 1/2? _____
    Explain:

3. Now use this procedure to find fractions equivalent to the following:

    a. 2/3   b. 1/4   c. 3/3   d. 3/4   e. 4/8   f. 5/6

    Why is the last problem difficult with these pieces?

    Write some fractions that are equivalent to 5/6 without using the pieces.

Now that you can represent fractions and find equivalent fractions, you are
ready to perform the operations of addition, subtraction, multiplication, and
division with fractions. Again, we will use the measurement and area models
of fractions.

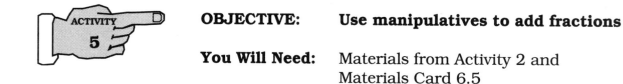 **OBJECTIVE: Use manipulatives to add fractions**

You Will Need: Materials from Activity 2 and
                       Materials Card 6.5

1. Using the circle and the circle pieces from Activity 2, place the piece marked 1/2 and the
    piece marked 1/3 on the circle as illustrated:

Using only one size of pieces, find pieces that will exactly cover the 1/2 and 1/3. Which fractional piece did you use?_____ How many 1/6-pieces will cover 1/2 plus 1/3?_____ We can say 1/2 + 1/3 = ___/6.

2. Now use your method in part 1 to solve these problems:

a.
$\frac{1}{4}$ = _____
$\frac{1}{8}$

c. 3/8 + 1/8 = _____

d. 3/6 + 1/3 = _____

b. 1/2 + 1/4 = _____

e. 5/8 + 1/2 = _____

3. Now test yourself. Construct the die on Materials Card 6.5. Roll the die three times. Pick up the pieces indicated by each roll. Use the method in part 1 to compute the sum on each turn. Repeat 4 times. Record the rolls and sum on each turn.

a. ____ + ____ + ____ = ____

b. ____ + ____ + ____ = ____

c. ____ + ____ + ____ = ____

d. ____ + ____ + ____ = ____

Were you able to use the method in part 1 for all of your sums?____ Why might you encounter difficulties with this method? Hint: Look at a problem like 1/3 + 1/4 + 1/8.

ACTIVITY 6

OBJECTIVE: **Use the measurement model to add fractions**

You Will Need: Your centimeter strips from Activity 1

1. Let ORANGE be equal to 1. Find the fractional value of these combinations:

a. RED + WHITE = _____

b. LIGHT GREEN + PURPLE = _____

c. BROWN + YELLOW = _____

d. BLUE + WHITE = _____

Why might it be helpful to change these lengths to combinations of REDs, YELLOWs, and WHITEs before finding the fractional value?

2. Let BROWN equal 1. Find the fractional value of these combinations:

a. DARK GREEN + WHITE = _____

b. BLUE + BLUE = _____

c. YELLOW + RED = _____

d. ORANGE + DARK GREEN = _____

3. Let DARK GREEN be the unit. Find the least number of centimeter strips that will give the following sums:

a. $1/2 = $ _____ + _____   b. $1/3 = $ _____ + _____

c. $2/3 = $ _____ + _____ or _____ + _____   d. $1\ 1/3 = $ _____ + _____

Could you find more than one solution for (d)? Show other solutions (there are 4 altogether):

Now let's look at some models for understanding the operation of subtraction with fractions. In the next activities we will use a "take-away" model and the "missing-addend" method.

OBJECTIVE: **Use the take-away model for subtraction**

You Will Need: Circle pieces from Activity 2

1. Place the circle in front of you. For the problem $7/8 - 1/4$, place 7 of the 1/8-pieces on the circle as illustrated:

1/8 sections   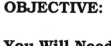 

Now take away enough pieces to cover the 1/4-piece (see above). How many 1/8-pieces remain on the circle?_____ We can say seven 1/8-pieces take away one 1/4-piece equals _____1/8-pieces or $7/8 - 1/4 = $ _____.

2. Use your pieces to solve these problems:

a. $5/6 - 1/3 = $ _____   b. $5/8 - 1/2 = $ _____   c. $3/8 - 1/8 = $ _____   d. $5/6 - 1/4 = $ _____

Why is (d) a difficult problem to do using the method?

OBJECTIVE: **Use the missing-addend method of subtraction**

You Will Need: Your centimeter strips from Activity 1

1. In order to find what ORANGE - DARK GREEN equals using the missing-addend approach, you need to fill in the following blank: DARK GREEN + _____ = ORANGE. In other words, ORANGE - DARK GREEN is whatever you add to DARK GREEN to equal ORANGE.

ORANGE	
DARK GREEN	**?**

What is the result?

2. Let BROWN = 1. Use your centimeter strips to find BROWN - RED = _____ or RED + _____ = BROWN. Draw a picture to show your results.

   In this case, RED = 1/4. What fraction represents the solution to the above problem? _____ Therefore, we can say 1 - 1/4 = _____ since 1/4 + _____ = 1.

3. Use your centimeter strips to solve these problems. Let DARK GREEN = 1.

   a. DARK GREEN - LIGHT GREEN = _____
       since LIGHT GREEN + _____ = DARK GREEN.
       Thus, 1 - ____ = ____ since ____ + ____ = 1
   b. 1 - 1/3 = ____ since 1/3 + ____ = 1
       DARK GREEN - _____ = _____
       since _____ + _____ = DARK GREEN.

4. Let BROWN = 1.   Solve these problems using your strips and the missing-addend model.

   a. 1 - 1/2 = ____   b. 3/4 - 1/4 = ____

   c. 1/2 + ____ = 3/4   d. 3/4 + ____ = 1 1/2

5. Now see if you can compute these differences using the missing-addend method:

   a. 5/6 - 1/3 = ____ or 1/3 + ____ = 5/6   (Use DARK GREEN = 1)

   b. 2 1/4 - 3/8 = ____ or 3/8 + ____ = 2 1/4 (Use BROWN = 1)

   c. 1 3/4 - 1/3 = ____ or 1/3 + ____ = 1 3/4 (Use ORANGE + RED = 1)

6. Why is the choice for 1 so important?

   How can you choose the appropriate color?

7. Show two ways to represent this statement:
       "Two and one-sixth minus two-thirds equals ____."

We have worked with the operations of addition and subtraction. In this next activity we will be looking at an area model for multiplication of fractions.

ACTIVITY 9

OBJECTIVE: **Use manipulatives to multiply fractions**

You Will Need: Materials Card 6.9

1. We can solve problems of the type $2 \times 1/3$ using the fractional pieces of the square. (Note: Label the fractional pieces from Materials Card 6.9 as you cut them out.) For example:

    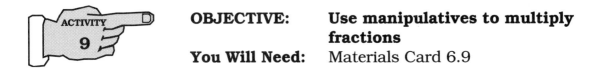

    Use this method to solve these problems:

    a. $3 \times 1/4 = $ _____   b. $5 \times 1/6 = $ _____

    c. $4 \times 1/8 = $ _____   d. $3 \times 1/3 = $ _____

2. Can you use this method to solve problems of the following type: $1/3 \times 1/4 = $ _____ ?

    While the area model is useful in solving this type of problem, a new aspect of the area model must be developed.

3. Cut out the squares on Materials Card 6.9. Using one square, we will do the following problem:

    $$1/3 \times 1/4 = \underline{\quad}$$

    First fold the square lengthwise into quarters as illustrated:

    Fold in half   Fold in half again   You have now divided the square into fourths.

    Now, without unfolding the quarters, fold into thirds in the opposite direction, as illustrated:

    Fold up one third   Fold again   Now color or shade the top only.

    Unfold the paper. It should look like this:

    What fractional portion of the square is shaded? _____

    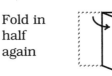

We can see that 1/3 of 1/4 = 1/12 because the paper is divided into 12 equal sections and one of those is shaded. So, 1/3 × 1/4 means 1/3 of 1/4.

4. Try the paper folding method to solve these problems:

   a. 1/2 × 1/4 = _____   b. 1/3 × 1/3 = _____

5. Will the paper folding method also work to solve these problems?_____

   a. 1/2 × 2/3 = _____   b. 2/3 × 3/4 = _____

What adjustments must you make to do these problems?
Hint: Unfold before refolding or coloring.

What is 3/4 × 3/4 ?_____ Draw a picture to show the folded square for this problem.

The final activity deals with division of fractions. We will use the centimeter strips to look at a model for representing division of fractions by both whole numbers and fractions, as well as division of whole numbers by fractions.

OBJECTIVE: **Use manipulatives to divide fractions**

You Will Need: Centimeter strips from Activity 1

1. First we will look at problems of this type: 1/2 ÷ 1/4 .

   Using BROWN = 1, find the strip that equals 1/2. What color is that strip?_____

   What color is the strip that equals 1/4?_____

   How many 1/4-strips equal a 1/2-strip?_____

   We can say that PURPLE ÷ RED = 2 since 2 answers the question, "How many 1/4-strips are in a 1/2-strip?" By this method, we see that 1/2 ÷ 1/4 = 2.

   Use your centimeter strips to solve these problems.   Hint: Think "How many 1/8's are in 3/4?" Find 3/4 of 1, then see how many 1/8's will equal the length 3/4.

   a. 3/4 ÷ 1/8 = _____   b. 7/8 ÷ 1/8 = _____

2. Now let's look at a method for solving problems like $2/3 \div 3$.
    Let BLUE equal 1. What piece = 1/3?_____ Put 2 of these pieces together.
    What 3 pieces of the same length will equal this representation of 2/3?_____
    What fractional part of BLUE does RED equal?_____
    Hint: You may need to break both the BLUE and RED into WHITEs to answer that
    question.
    By this method, we see that $2/3 \div 3 = 2/9$ since 3 of the 2/9-strips are the same length as
    the 2/3-strip.

    Try these: Let BROWN = 1.
    Hint: Think "What fractional piece used 3 times equals 3/8?"

    a. $3/8 \div 3 =$ _____   b. $3/4 \div 2 =$ _____   c. $1/2 \div 4 =$ _____   d. $3/4 \div 6 =$ _____

3. Finally, let's look at problems of the type: $3 \div 1/4$.
    Let PURPLE = 1. What color strip = 1/4?_____
    Build a representation of 3 using PURPLE as illustrated:

PURPLE	PURPLE	PURPLE

    Now, using the strip that equals 1/4 of PURPLE, build a representation equal to 3
    PURPLE strips. How many of these smaller pieces did you use?_____

    We can show that $3 \div 1/4 = 12$ because it takes 12 of the 1/4's to equal 3.
    Try these:

    a. $5 \div 1/2 =$ _____   b. $6 \div 1/4 =$ _____   c. $2 \div 1/2 =$ _____   d. $1 \ 1/2 \div 3/4 =$ _____

    CHALLENGE:
    a. Use the cm strips to show $2/3 \div 1/4$. Use ORANGE + RED = 1.
    b. Use the cm strips to find $3/7 \div 1/2$.
        (First choose a convenient length for 1.)

MENTAL MATH ═══════════════════════

THE RANGE GAME

Use the digits 1 through 9 to see how many fractions you
can find within the given range. Example:
$3/8 < 1/2 < 9/16$. Write your fractions here:

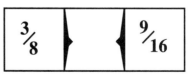

Now, play the game with a partner. Score 1 point for each correct fraction, lose 1 point for
each error. Play until one person gets 10.

EXERCISES

THE MOUSE RACE

These hungry mice have spied a chunk of cheese. To reach the cheese, they must find a path from their current location that travels through equivalent fractions. Which two mice will go hungry?

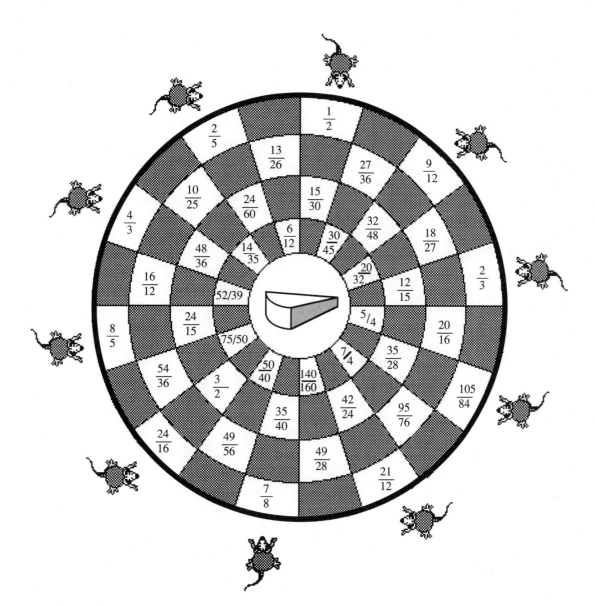

YOU CAN'T FIT A SQUARE PEG INTO A ROUND HOLE!

DIRECTIONS: Use the fractions given on the left to fill in the missing holes on the right. The results should give true equations across and down.

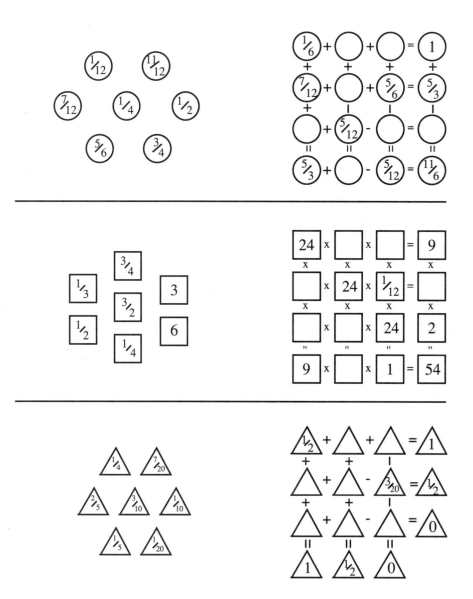

SELF-TEST

1. Which of the following diagrams does *not* represent the same number as the other two?

   a. A
   b. B
   c. C
   d. None of a, b, or c.

   A. 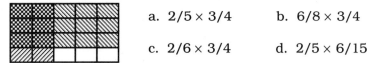   B.   C.

2. Which of the following is *not* in simplest form?
   (i) 45/64   (ii) 108/135   (iii) 369/492

   a. i and ii   b. ii and iii   c. ii only   d. None of a, b, or c.

3. If 12/40 = 15/*a*, then the sum of the digits in *a* is

   a. 5   b. 6   c. 8   d. None of a, b, or c.

4. What is the reciprocal of 2 3/8?

   a. 8/19   b. 19/8   c. 2 8/3   d. 22/4

5. Compute, write in simplest form, and then add your numerator and denominator.

   $$1/10 + 13/18$$

   a. 328   b. 82   c. 164   d. None of a, b, or c.

6. This model is used to represent:

   a. 2/5 × 3/4   b. 6/8 × 3/4

   c. 2/6 × 3/4   d. 2/5 × 6/15

7. 1 1/3 ÷ 5/6 =

   a. 8/5   b. 1 2/5   c. 1/15   d. None of a, b, or c.

8. Which of the following is *not* helpful in simplifying this computation?

   $$(5/7 \cdot 13/19) \cdot 7/5$$

   a. Commutativity for multiplication   b. Associativity for multiplication
   c. Inverse for multiplication   d. Distributivity

9. If the following numbers are arranged from least to greatest, which one will be in the middle?

    3/7, 2/9, 5/13, 7/11, 5/12

    a. 3/7   b. 5/12   c. 5/13   d. 7/11

10. Which of these fractions is between 7/15 and 8/13 ?

    a. 3/5   b. 2/5   c. 2/3   d. None of a, b, or c.

SOLUTIONS

Warm-up

He will climb out on day number 8.   There are 32 players on the team.

Hands-on Activities

Activity 1
1. 1/2   a. 1/5   b. 1/10
2. a. PURPLE b. WHITE c. RED   d. ORANGE e. BLUE f. DARK GREEN   g. LIGHT GREEN
3. a. 1/9   b. 1/3   **4.** a. RED   b. PURPLE   c. PURPLE   d. LIGHT GREEN

Activity 2
1. 1/2   **2.** 1/3   **3.** a.   b.   c.   d.   e.   f.
    By dividing the area into equal-sized sections, the fractional model is illustrated.

Activity 3
1. a. 1/4   b. 1/8   c. 1/16   d. 1/8   e. 1/8   f. 1
2. Medium triangle, small square, and parallelogram

Activity 4
1. 1/6, 1/6   **2.** 2/4, 3/6, 4/8 ; Yes, they cover the same portion of the circle.
3. a. 4/6   b. 2/8   c. 4/4   d. 6/8   e. 1/2   f. 10/12
    There are no divisions of the circle that exactly cover 5/6.   5/6 = 10/12 = 15/18 = 20/24

Activity 5
1. 1/6, 5, 5   **2.** a. 3/8   b. 3/4   c. 1/2   d. 5/6   e. 9/8 or 1 1/8
3. Answers may vary. You don't have a common denominator available.

Activity 6
1. a. 3/10 b. 7/10 c. 1 3/10 d. 1   **2.** a. 7/8 b. 2 1/4 c. 7/8 d. 2
3. a. RED + WHITE   b. WHITE + WHITE   c. LIGHT GREEN + WHITE or RED + RED
    d. PURPLE + PURPLE, RED + DARK GREEN, YELLOW + LIGHT GREEN, BLACK + WHITE

Activity 7
1. 5, 5, 5/8   **2.** a. 3/6 or 1/2   b. 1/8   c. 2/8 or 1/4   d. 7/12 There are no 1/12 pieces.

Activity 8
1. PURPLE   **2.** DARK GREEN, DARK GREEN, 3/4, 3/4, 3/4
3. a. LIGHT GREEN, LIGHT GREEN, 1/2, 1/2, 1/2 + 1/2
   b. 2/3, 2/3, RED, PURPLE, RED + PURPLE
4. a. 1/2   b. 1/2   c. 1/4   d. 3/4   **5.** a. 3/6 or 1/2   b. 1 7/8   c. 1 5/12
6. You need to be able to represent both fractions relative to that length. Choose the length
   that represents the least common multiple.
7. 2 1/6 - 2/3 = _____ , 2/3 + _____ = 2 1/6

Activity 9
1. a. 3/4   b. 5/6   c. 4/8   d. 3/3   **2.** See part 3
3. 1/12   **4.** a. 1/8 b. 1/9   **5.** Yes   a. 2/6
   b. 6/12   Partially unfold the square before folding in
   the opposite direction. 9/16

Activity 10
1. PURPLE, RED, 2   a. 6   b. 7   **2.** LIGHT GREEN, 3 RED, 2/9   a. 1/8   b. 3/8
   c. 1/8 d. 1/8   **3.** WHITE, 12   a. 10   b. 24   c. 4   d. 12/6 or 2

CHALLENGE
   a. 2/3 ÷ 1/4 = 8/3 = 2 2/3. It takes 2 2/3
      of the 1/4-strip to equal 2/3.

   b. 3/7 ÷ 1/2 = 6/7. It takes 6/7 of the
      1/2-strip to equal 3/7.

Mental Math
Answers will vary.

Exercises
THE MOUSE RACE
1/2 = 13/26 = 15/30 = 6/12   2/5 = 10/25 = 24/60 = 14/35
4/3 = 16/12 = 48/36 = 52/39   24/16 = 54/36 = 3/2 = 75/50
7/8 = 49/56 = 35/40 = 140/160   21/12 = 49/28 = 42/24 = 7/4
105/84 = 95/76 = 35/28 = 5/4   2/3 = 18/27 = 32/48 = 30/45
Hungry Mice are 8/5 and 9/12.

YOU CAN'T FIT A SQUARE PEG INTO A ROUND HOLE!
Round Holes:	Square Holes:	Triangular Holes:
First row: 3/4, 1/12	First row: 3/4, 1/2	First row: 1/10, 2/5
Second row: 1/4	Second row: 3/2, 3	Second row: 3/10, 7/20
Third row: 11/12, 1/2, 5/6	Third row: 1/4, 1/3	Third row: 1/5, 1/20, 1/4
Fourth row: 7/12	Fourth row: 6	

Self-Test
1. b   **2.** b   **3.** a   **4.** a   **5.** b   **6.** a   **7.** a   **8.** d   **9.** b   **10.** a

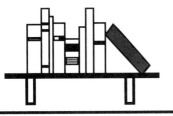

RESOURCE ARTICLES

Beede, Rudy B. "Dot Method for Renaming Fractions." *Arithmetic Teacher* 33 (October 1985): 44-45. *Ideas at manipulative level leading to abstract.*

Brown, G.W. "Searching for Patterns of Divisors." *Arithmetic Teacher* 32 (December 1984): 32-34. *Practice in examining divisors prior to fraction work.*

Chiosi, Lou. "Fractions Revisited." *Arithmetic Teacher* 31 (April 1984): 46-47. *Instructional strategies that lend meaning to notion of a fraction.*

Edge, Douglas. "Fractions and Panes." *Arithmetic Teacher* 34 (April 1987): 13-17. *Activities using window panes to extend knowledge of fractions.*

Ettline, J. Fred. "A Uniform Approach to Fractions." *Arithmetic Teacher* 32 (March 1985): 42-43. *A look at two common student-difficulties in computing with fractions.*

Kalman, Dan. "Up Fractions! Up n/m!" *Arithmetic Teacher* 32 (April 1985): 42-43. *Addition of fractions by graphing ordered pairs.*

Steiner, Evelyn E. "Division of Fractions: Developing Conceptual Sense with Dollars and Cents." *Arithmetic Teacher* 34 (May 1987): 36-42. *An eight-level monetary model for division of fractions.*

Sweetland, Robert D. "Understanding Multiplication of Fractions." *Arithmetic Teacher* 32 (September 1984): 48-52. *Using Cuisenaire rods.*

Tierney, Cornelia C. "Patterns in the Multiplication Table." *Arithmetic Teacher* 32 (March 1985): 36-40. *Activities that provide foundation for work with fractions.*

Van de Walle, John, and Charles S. Thompson. "Let's Do It: Fractions with Fraction Strips." *Arithmetic Teacher* 32 (December 1984): 4-9. *Fraction concept tasks.*

Wiebe, James H. "Discovering Fractions on a 'Fraction Table'." *Arithmetic Teacher* 33 (December 1985): 49-51. *Materials for discovering concepts about operations on fractions.*

Zawojewski, Judith S. "Ideas." *Arithmetic Teacher* 34 (December 1986): 18-25. *Activities using region model for fractions.*

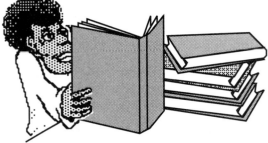

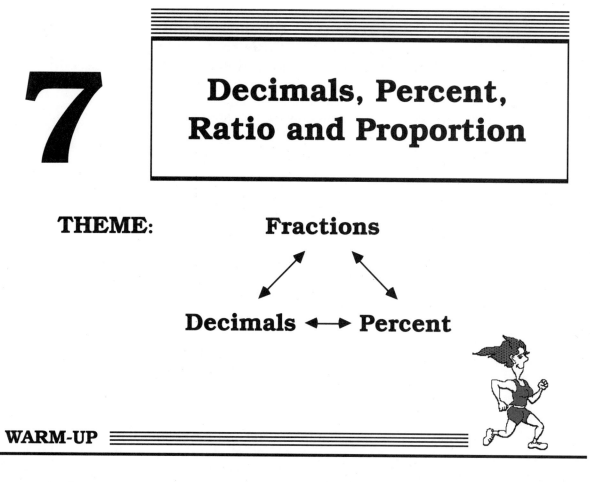

7

Decimals, Percent, Ratio and Proportion

THEME: Fractions

Decimals ←→ Percent

WARM-UP

Strategy Review:
Use Indirect Reasoning.
In Chapter 4, the strategy of using indirect reasoning was explained. Use that strategy to help you in solving these problems.

Three baseball players, Chuck, Mark, and Paul, play for Chicago, Montreal, and Philadelphia. No player's city starts with the same letter as his name. Paul has never been to Chicago. Who plays for Philadelphia?

Ann, Amy, Alice, and Angie like apples, apricots, asparagus, and anchovies. Ann hates vegetables. One of Alice's friends loves all kinds of fish. Amy can't eat crunchy food because she wears braces. Angie loves green food. Amy has never met Alice. Who likes anchovies?

HANDS-ON ACTIVITIES

Decimals give us a convenient way to represent fractions. The first activities in this chapter will introduce you to decimals as well as their numerals, names, and operations.

 **OBJECTIVE:**   **Extend understanding of place value to decimals**

You Will Need: Materials Card 7.1

1. Remember that our place value system evolved from grouping by tens. As we move from right to left on our chip abacus, how are the values of the adjacent columns related?

100	10	1

2. How are the values of the adjacent columns related as we move from left to right?

3. If moving from any column to the column on its left is described as "grouping by tens", how would you describe moving from any column to the column on its right?

4. Use your observations above to extend this chip abacus to the right. Label the missing place values:

100	10	1	___	___	___

5. We can distinguish where the whole numbers end and the fractional parts begin by using a marker which we will call the **decimal point marker**. Place the decimal point marker on the chip abacus above. This marker will separate the 1 and 1/10 columns. Fill in the place values in the drawings below:

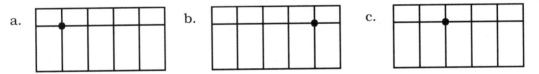

6. Using the chip abacus in Materials Card 7.1, represent the following:

   a. 321.04   b. 3.2104   c. 32.104

   Can you do all of them by simply placing the 3, 2, 1, and 4 chips and then moving just the decimal point marker?

7. Write the expanded fractional form for the numbers above. For example,

   321.04 = 3(100) + 2(10) + 1+ 0(1/10) + 4(1/100)

   3.2104 =

   32.104 =

OBJECTIVE: **Write numerals and word names**
for number representations

You Will Need: Your chip abacus

1. Use chips to represent these numbers on your abacus. Record your results on the abacus by writing numerals. In reading decimals, notice that the decimal is read as "and".

    Example: Two and twelve hundredths = 2.12

Exchanging

   a. Thirty two and thirteen hundredths = _____

   b. Five and twenty one thousandths = _____

   Write the word names for these numerals:

   c. 10 10/1000 =

   d. 34 11/100 =

   e. 5 15/1000 =

2. Write the numerals and the word names for the numbers illustrated below:

   a.   b.   c.

3. Move your decimal point markers in part 2 one column to the right and write the new numerals and word names.

OBJECTIVE: **Multiply and divide decimals by 10**

You Will Need: Your chip abacus

1. Represent 3.57 on this abacus:

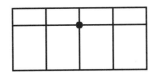

Multiply 3.57 by 10 and represent the product on this abacus:

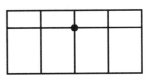

Could you obtain the second abacus simply by moving the decimal point marker on the first abacus?

Repeat the steps above by representing 1.72 on the first abacus and 1.72 times 10 on the second abacus. How do your results compare?

Represent 6.13 on the first abacus. Predict your results on the second abacus if you multiply 6.13 by 10.

Describe a shortcut you can use when multiplying by 10, by 100, by 1000.

2. Represent 3.57 on this abacus:

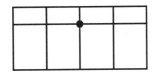

Divide 3.57 by 10 and represent the quotient on this abacus:

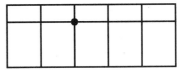

Could you obtain the second abacus simply by moving the decimal point marker on the first abacus?

Now represent 1.72 on the first abacus and 1.72 divided by 10 on the second abacus. How do your results compare with the first set of numbers?

Represent 6.13 on the first abacus and then compute 6.13 divided by 10 mentally without using your abacus.

Describe a shortcut to use when dividing by 10, by 100, by 1000.

---

3. Think about what you have done in this activity. What is the effect on a number represented on an abacus when the decimal point marker is moved one column to the right?

   What about moving it two columns to the right?

   One column to the left?

   Two columns to the left?

4. Describe the decimal point marker moves that are equivalent to the following procedures:

   a. multiplying by 10   b. dividing by 1000

   c. dividing by 10   d. multiplying by 10,000

Write a statement that tells how the number and direction of moves of the decimal point marker are related to the number of zeros and the operation being used.

OBJECTIVE: **Compare addition and subtraction of whole numbers and decimals**

You Will Need: Your chip abacus

1. Compute these using your chip abacus:

   a. 31.12 + 4.6 = _____

   b. 5.213 + 0.4 = _____

   c. 3.12 - 1.5 = _____

   d. 13.213 - 7.508 = _____

2. Compute these using your chip abacus:

   a. 3112 + 460 = _____

   b. 5213 + 400 = _____

   c. 312 - 150 = _____

   d. 13,213 - 7,508 = _____

3. Relate the problems in part 1 with their counterparts in part 2 and explain how addition or subtraction of decimals is related to addition or subtraction of whole numbers.

In the text you have read about the relationship between fractions, decimals, and percent. We have done activities to help you understand the meanings of fractions and decimals. The next activity will help you understand the meaning of percent.

OBJECTIVE: **Use the chip abacus to understand percent**

You Will Need: Your chip abacus

1. The notation $n\%$ means $n \cdot (1/100)$, or $n/100$. For example, $20\% = 20 \cdot (1/100) = 20/100 = 0.20$. Both the original whole number part of the percent and the decimal can be represented on the chip abacus.

EXAMPLE:

20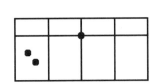

20% or 0.2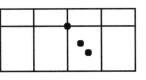

For each percent given, represent the whole number part of the percent on your chip abacus. Then represent these percents as decimals on your chip abacus. Record your results in the drawings below:

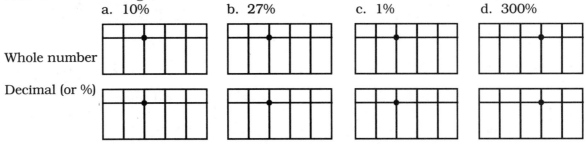

a. 10%   b. 27%   c. 1%   d. 300%

Whole number

Decimal (or %)

2. Look at the results above. If you are given the decimal, could you find the equivalent percent by simply moving your decimal point marker?_____
Explain:

If you were given the percent, could you find the equivalent decimal by moving your decimal point marker?_____
Explain:

> What is the relationship between the decimal and its equivalent percent?

3. Represent the following numbers on your abacus. Then change each percent to its equivalent decimal and vice versa by moving only your decimal point marker.

a. 42%   b. 0.03   c. 7.5   d. 0.1%

The remainder of this chapter is devoted to the ideas of ratio and
proportion. When you are able to use ratios and know how to
set up proportions you will be able to solve percent problems
more easily. First, let's look at the meaning of ratio.

OBJECTIVE: **Discover the meaning of ratios**

You Will Need: Materials Card 7.6

1. Place the following pieces in a group in front of you:

    2 striped squares   3 dotted squares   4 solid squares

    A **ratio** is an ordered pair of numbers indicating relative amounts. For example, the ratio 2:9 represents the ratio of striped squares to all squares. Another way to show this ratio is in fraction notation:

    2/9 = striped squares/all squares

2. Write the ratios that represent these relationships:

    a. striped squares/dotted squares = _____

    b. solid squares/all squares = _____

    c. dotted squares : all squares = _____:_____

    d. solid : not solid = _____:_____

3. A ratio can show the relationship of a *part to a part* or of a *part to the whole*.   For example, striped squares : all squares shows the relationship of a part to the whole.

    Look at the examples in part 2. Which examples represent the relationship of a part to the whole?_____   Which examples represent the relationship of a part to a part?_____

4. Repeat part 2 using the following pieces:

    4 striped squares   1 dotted square   2 solid squares

    a._____   b._____   c._____   d._____

5. Now place the following pieces in front of you:

    3 striped squares   4 dotted squares   4 solid squares

    Write 4 ratios that relate a part to a part and one ratio that relates a part to the whole:

It is often useful to compare ratios to see if they are equivalent. If you wish to enlarge or reduce a recipe for example, the ratio of each ingredient to the whole amount must stay the same if the results are to be satisfactory. The next activity will give you practice in determining when ratios are equivalent.

OBJECTIVE: **Find equivalent ratios**

You Will Need: Materials Card 7.7

1. Cover a rhombus with triangles. How many triangles exactly cover the rhombus?_____

   We can say there are _____ triangles per rhombus or that the ratio of triangles : rhombuses is _____ : _____ .

   Cover a trapezoid with triangles. How many triangles exactly cover the trapezoid?_____

   We can say there are _____ triangles per trapezoid or that the ratio of triangles : trapezoids is _____ : _____ .

   Cover a hexagon with triangles. How many triangles exactly cover the hexagon?_____

   What is the ratio of triangles : hexagons? _____ : _____

2. Using only the rhombuses, trapezoids, and hexagons, find pieces that have a ratio equivalent to triangles : rhombuses. What are these pieces called?

   _____ and _____

   So we can say that the ratio of _____ : _____ is 2:1.

   Can you find pieces that have the same ratio as triangles : trapezoids? What are these

   pieces called? _____ and _____ .

   So we can say the ratio of _____ : _____ is 3:1.

   Can you find pieces that have the same ratio as triangles : hexagons?_____ Why or why not?

3. Can you design a shape that has a ratio of 4:1 with the rhombus and of 6:1 with the trapezoid?_____ Draw your shape within the outlines below:

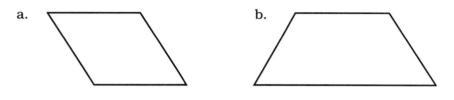

a.   b.

Hint: Use the triangle to find the new shape. What is your new shape called?_____
Draw it here:

4. How many rhombuses does it take to cover a trapezoid?_____ It may be easier to look at this problem in a different way. First form a hexagon from 2 trapezoids. Now cover the trapezoids with rhombuses. There are _____rhombuses and 2 trapezoids, so the ratio of rhombuses to trapezoids is _____: 2. Now let's answer the first question in a different way:

    rhombuses : trapezoids = _____: 1

You have written two ratios that are equivalent to each other. Write two more ratios that are also equivalent to these. Hint: Build 2 hexagons from trapezoids then cover with rhombuses, etc.

When you know how to set up ratios you can solve a variety of problems.
A **proportion** is a statement that two ratios are equal. Proportions are
especially useful in solving percent problems or problems involving
other ratios. For example, suppose that 2 out of 5 students in
elementary education are male. Then, if we know the total
number of students in elementary education, we can
determine the number of male students in
elementary education.

OBJECTIVE: **Use proportions to solve problems**

You Will Need: Materials Card 7.8 and a clock
or watch with a second hand

1. Compute your number of heart beats in one minute as follows: Find your pulse. Count the number of heart beats in 6 seconds. Write that number in the blank numerator below:

$$\frac{\rule{2cm}{0.4pt}}{6 \text{ sec.}} = \frac{n}{60 \text{ sec.}}$$

Now use cross multiplication to find the number of heart beats (n) in one minute. For example, if a heart beats 10 times in 6 seconds the proportion is:

$$\frac{10}{6} = \frac{n}{60} \quad \text{or} \quad 10 \times 60 = 6n \quad \text{or} \quad n = \frac{10 \times 60}{6}$$

In this case the heart beats 100 times in 1 minute.

How many times did *your* heart beat in 1 minute? $n = \rule{2cm}{0.4pt}$

2. Use the information about your own heart rate to determine the following:
How many times does your heart beat in one hour?

Hint: $\dfrac{\text{heart beats}}{\text{minute}} = \dfrac{x}{60 \text{ minutes}}$

At this rate, how many times will your heart beat in one day?_____

one week?_____ one year?_____ 80 years?_____

3. Repeat parts one and two, but first do 25 jumping jacks and then quickly take your pulse. Try resting, running in place, or some other physical activity and then repeat parts one and two.

4. Construct the metric tape on Materials Card 7.8. Measure your height in centimeters. _____

Measure the height of your head in centimeters. _____

To be a professional model, one asset is to have a ratio of height to head height of 8 to 1. Most people have a height : head height ratio of 7:1.

Use a proportion to determine your ratio, e.g.

$$\frac{\text{height}}{\text{head height}} = \frac{n}{1}$$

What is your height : head height ratio? _____ : 1

If a girl is 182 cm tall, what head height should she have in order to be of average height?

$$\frac{182}{n} = \frac{7}{1} \qquad n = \text{_____}$$

What head height should she have in order to qualify as a model?

$$\frac{}{n} = \frac{}{} \qquad n = \text{_____}$$

MENTAL MATH

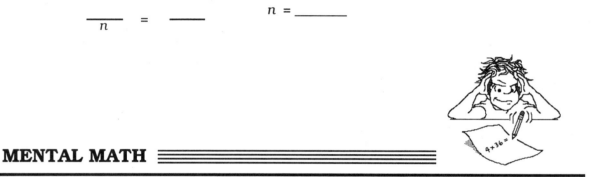

Use proportions to solve these mental math problems. Which item is the better buy?

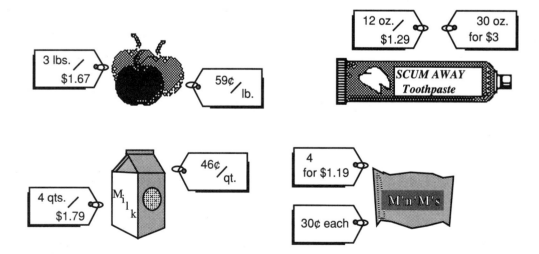

EXERCISES

What did the decimal point say to the dollar sign?

The numbers in the columns below are to be used to complete the problems involving that operation. For example, the numbers in the addition column are to be used to complete the addition problems. An extra number is contained in each column. Determine the number that would replace each numbered circle. Take the letter of the replacement number and place it in the blank that has the same number as the circle. Do as much mentally as you can.

ADDITION		SUBTRACTION		MULTIPLICATION		DIVISION	
N	74.59	W	10.9	S	3.2	E	3.92
A	72.9	N	8.39	H	2.7	I	1.9
H	7.8	O	5.93	E	8.06	I	0.7
E	15.4	A	12.7	M	12.42	T	5
K	17.87	T	6.4	N	10.58	C	6.21
Y	87.9	H	13.13	S	6.08	E	9.69
A	98.6	M	9.28	O	5	B	14.6

smaller
① + ② = 106.4   ⑨ + 57.5 = ⑩   17.3 - ⑰ = smaller ⑱

③ - ④ = 7.2   ⑪ ÷ 5.6 = ⑫   4.6 × ⑲ = ⑳

smaller
⑤ × ⑥ = 40.3   ⑬ - 0.89 = ⑭   56.72 + ㉑ = ㉒

⑦ ÷ ⑧ = 5.1   ⑮ × 1.9 = ⑯   31.05 ÷ ㉓ = smaller ㉔

$23.56

___ ___ ,   ___   ___ ___   ___ ___ ___   ___ ___ ___
 1   12   8   2   13   18   3   9   4   14   7

___ ___ ___   ___ ___ ___ ___ ___   ___ ___ ___ ___ ___!
17   19   5   20   10   21   6   15   23   11   22   24   16

A DREAM COME TRUE !

You have just received a check as a winner in the USA lottery. The check you receive is for $70,000. After paying 21% of that amount in taxes, you go on a shopping spree. Will you be able to buy all the items listed below?

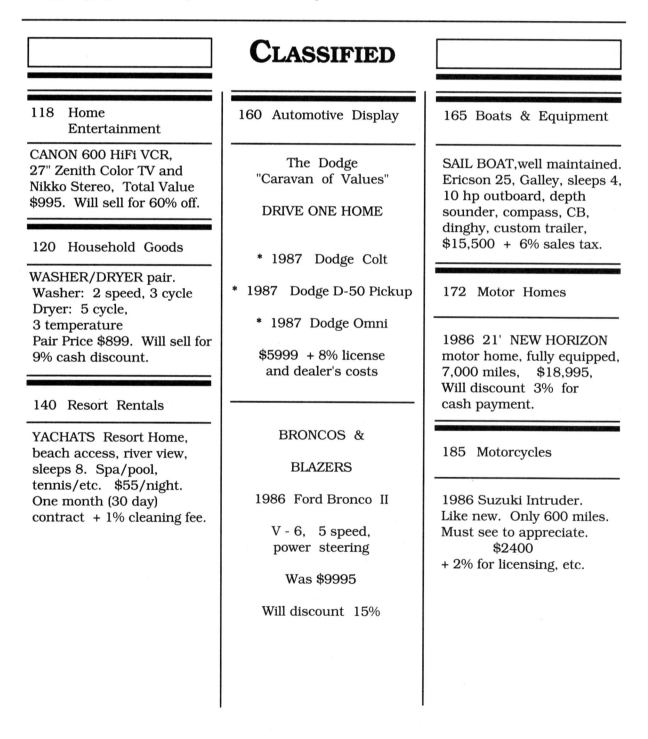

CLASSIFIED

118   Home Entertainment

CANON 600 HiFi VCR, 27" Zenith Color TV and Nikko Stereo, Total Value $995. Will sell for 60% off.

120   Household Goods

WASHER/DRYER pair. Washer: 2 speed, 3 cycle Dryer: 5 cycle, 3 temperature Pair Price $899. Will sell for 9% cash discount.

140   Resort Rentals

YACHATS Resort Home, beach access, river view, sleeps 8. Spa/pool, tennis/etc. $55/night. One month (30 day) contract + 1% cleaning fee.

160   Automotive Display

The Dodge "Caravan of Values"

DRIVE ONE HOME

* 1987   Dodge Colt

* 1987   Dodge D-50 Pickup

* 1987   Dodge Omni

$5999 + 8% license and dealer's costs

BRONCOS &

BLAZERS

1986 Ford Bronco II

V - 6,   5 speed, power steering

Was $9995

Will discount 15%

165   Boats & Equipment

SAIL BOAT, well maintained. Ericson 25, Galley, sleeps 4, 10 hp outboard, depth sounder, compass, CB, dinghy, custom trailer, $15,500 + 6% sales tax.

172   Motor Homes

1986 21' NEW HORIZON motor home, fully equipped, 7,000 miles, $18,995, Will discount 3% for cash payment.

185   Motorcycles

1986 Suzuki Intruder. Like new. Only 600 miles. Must see to appreciate. $2400 + 2% for licensing, etc.

☆ ☆ ☆ **MAGIC STAR** ☆ ☆ ☆

Solve the proportions and ratio problems below. Each problem is designated by a letter and that letter appears in one of the circles in the star. When you find the answer to each problem, put it in the corresponding circle.

A. $10/6 = n/12$

B. $35/n = 21/9$

C. $13/n = 65/95$

D. $4/9 = 16/n$

E. A photo that is 3.5 cm by 6 cm is enlarged. Its new dimensions are n cm by 24 cm. What is n?

F. The scale on a map is given as 6 inches = 75 miles. If you take a 475 mile trip, what would it be on the map (in inches)?

G. The ratio of the weight of an object on Jupiter to its weight on Earth is 8 to 3. How much would an 11.25-pound rock on Earth weigh on Jupiter?

H. If 3.7 grams of salt will dissolve in 10 grams of water, how many grams of salt will dissolve in 100 grams of water?

I. The ratio of boys to girls in a class is 1 : 2. If there are 51 students in the class, how many boys are there?

J. If you can buy 24 pencils for 88 cents, how much will you pay for 15 pencils?

K. If 192 meters of pipe weighs 48 kg, how much pipe would weigh 2 kg?

L. Your car has traveled 93.5 km on 8.5 liters of gas. How many km/liter did your car average?

WHAT IS THE MAGIC OF THE STAR?

SELF-TEST

1. If the expanded form of a number is $3(10^2) + 7 + 4(1/10) + 5(1/10^3)$, then the numeral representing that number has how many digits?

    a. 4   b. 5   c. 6   d. None of a, b, or c.

2. Which of the following numbers is the greatest?

    a. 0.51   b. 0.5101   c. 0.5   d. 0.5097

3. Express $0.\overline{36}$ as a fraction in simplest form. The sum of the numerator and denominator of this fraction is

    a. 136   b. 15   c. 34   d. 135

4. If 0.000004205 is divided by 0.0006001 , the answer is approximately

    a. 0.7   b. 0.07   c. 0.007   d. 0.0007

5. Which of these are equal?   (i) 0.52   (ii) 5.2%   (iii) 13/25

    a. i and ii   b. i and iii   c. ii and iii   d. None of a, b, or c.

6. If a $15.00 shirt is reduced 35% and a $24.00 pair of pants is reduced 15%, what is the total sale price of the two items?

    a. $8.85   b. $19.50   c. $30.15   d. None of a, b, or c.

7. An item was marked up 25% and then this price was marked down 20%. The *net effect* of these two markings is a

    a. 0% markup   b. 2.5% markup
    c. 5% markup   d. Not enough information to work the problem.

8. Which is the best buy?

    a. 13 oz. for 70 cents   b. 27 oz. for $1.68
    c. 24 oz. for $1.36   d. 32 oz. for $2.00

9. Which of the following proportions have the same solution?

    (i) $12/22 = 30/n$ (ii) $15/9 = n/33$ (iii) $n/66 = 135/162$

    a. i and ii only   b. i and iii only
    c. ii and iii only   d. i, ii, and iii

10. Miss Kelley and Mr. Peabody have 25 and 36 children in their classrooms, respectively. The ratio of boys to girls in Miss Kelley's classroom is 3 : 2 and the ratio of girls to all the children in Mr. Peabody's classroom is 1 : 3. If the two classes are combined, the ratio of girls to boys is

    a. 3 : 5   b. 2 : 7   c. 22 : 39   d. 19 : 42

SOLUTIONS

Warm-up

Use a chart to help you organize your information:

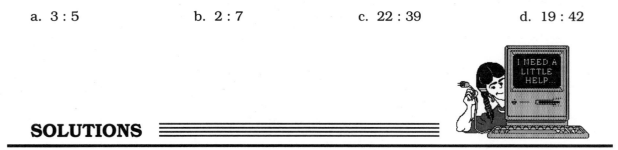

Hands-on Activities

Activity 1
1. 10 times larger
2. 1/10 as large
3. Dividing by 10
4. 1/10, 1/100, 1/1000
5. a. 1, 1/10, 1/100, 1/1000, 1/10000   b. 1000, 100, 10, 1, 1/10
    c. 10, 1, 1/10, 1/100, 1/1000
6. Yes   a. Decimal point after 1
    b. Decimal point after 3
    c. Decimal point after 2
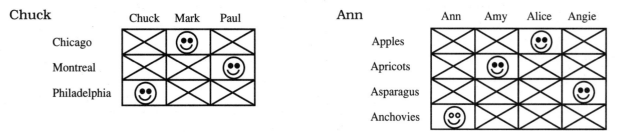
7. 3 + 2(1/10) + 1(1/100) + 4(1/10000);   3(10) + 2 + 1(1/10) + 4(1/1000)

Activity 2
1. a. 32.13   b. 5.021   c. Ten and ten thousandths
    d. Thirty four and eleven hundredths   e. Five and fifteen thousandths
2. a. 13.12   thirteen and twelve hundredths
    b. 3.1032 three and one thousand thirty two ten thousandths
    c. 20.501 twenty and five hundred one thousandths
3. a. 131.2   one hundred thirty one and two tenths
    b. 31.032 thirty one and thirty two thousandths
    c. 205.01 two hundred five and one hundredth

Activity 3

1. 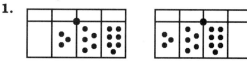 Yes, one place to the right.
The results for 1.72 and 17.2 will be like 3.57 and 35.7. The decimal point in 6.13 will move one place to the right.

Move the decimal one place to the right when multiplying by 10, two places to the right when multiplying by 100, three places to the right when multiplying by 1000.

2. 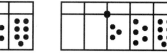 Yes, one place to the left.
The results for 1.72 and .172 will be similar. The decimal point in 6.13 will move one place to the left.

Move the decimal one place to the left when dividing by 10, two places when dividing by 100, and three places when dividing by 1000.

3. It is multiplied by 10. It is multiplied by 100. It is divided by 10. It is divided by 100.

4. a. Move 1 place to the right   b. Move 3 places to the left
c. Move 1 place to the left   d. Move 4 places to the right

Move the decimal point marker to the right or left as many spaces as the power of 10 used, e.g. 10^3 yields 3 spaces right when multiplying and left when dividing.

Activity 4

1. a. 35.72   b. 5.613   c. 1.62   d. 5.705
2. a. 3572   b. 5613   c. 162   d. 5705
3. Each of the addends in part 1 is multiplied by a power of ten to give the problems in part 2. The sum is also multiplied by the same power of 10. The same is true for the subtraction problems.

Activity 5

2. Yes. The percent name is found by multiplying the decimal equivalent by 100.
Yes. Remove the percent sign and move the decimal 2 places to the left.
The % sign simply means "hundredths." These are two ways to name the same number.

3. a. 42% = 0.42   b. 0.03 = 3%   c. 7.5 = 750%   d. 0.1% = 0.001

Activity 6

2. a. 2/3   b. 4/9   c. 3 : 9   d. 4 : 5
3. b & c; a & d
4. a. 4/1   b. 2/7   c. 1 : 7   d. 2 : 5
5. Answers may vary: 3/4 = striped/dotted; 4/4 = dotted/solid; 4/3 = solid/striped; 4/7 = dotted/not dotted;   3 : 11 = striped : all

Activity 7

1. 2, 2, 2 : 1;   3, 3, 3 : 1;   6, 6 : 1
2. Trapezoids & hexagons; trapezoids : hexagons
Yes, rhombuses & hexagons; rhombuses : hexagons
No. You would need a shape smaller than the triangle.
3. Yes, a triangle equivalent to half the given triangle.
4. 1 1/2, 3, 3, 1 1/2 , 6:4, 9:6

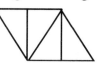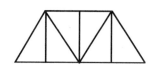

Activity 8
1. Answers will vary.
2. 60 n; 1440 n; 10,080 n; 525,600 n; 42,048,000 n
3. Answers will vary.
4. Answers will vary.

   n = 26 cm head height $182/n$ = $8/1$ n = 22.75 cm

Mental Math
3 lbs. for $1.67   30 oz. for $3.00   4 qts. for $1.79   4 for $1.19

Exercises

What Did the Decimal Point Say to the Dollar Sign?

1 - 7.8	9 - 15.4	17 - 10.9
2 - 98.6	10 - 72.9	18 - 6.4
3 - 13.13	11 - 3.92	19 - 2.7
4 - 5.93	12 - 0.7	20 - 12.42
5 - 5	13 - 9.28	21 - 17.87
6 - 8.06	14 - 8.39	22 - 74.59
7 - 9.69	15 - 3.2	23 - 6.21
8 - 1.9	16 - 6.08	24 - 5

Hi! I am the one who makes cents!

A DREAM COME TRUE!

Yes. You pay $14,700 in taxes, leaving you with $55,300.

Home Entertainment:	$398.00	Sailboat:	$16,430.00
Washer/Dryer:	$818.09	Motor home:	$18,425.15
Resort home:	$1,666.50	Suzuki:	$2,448.00
Dodge:	$6,478.92		
Bronco:	$8,495.75	Total:	$55,160.41

MAGIC STAR

A. 20   **B.** 15   **C.** 19   **D.** 36   **E.** 14   **F.** 38   **G.** 30   **H.** 37

I. 17   **J.** 55   **K.** 8   **L.** 11   Each straight line of four circles totals 100.

Self-Test
1. c   **2.** b   **3.** b   **4.** c   **5.** b   **6.** c   **7.** a   **8.** a   **9.** d   **10.** c

RESOURCE ARTICLES

Boling, Bruce A. "A Different Method for Solving Percentage Problems." *Mathematics Teacher* 78 (October 1985): 523-524. *A unique method presented.*

Coburn, Terrence G. "Percentage and the Hand Calculator." *Mathematics Teacher* 79 (May 1986): 361-367. *Activities using and estimating percentages.*

Dewar, Jacqueline M. "Another Look at the Teaching of Percent." *Arithmetic Teacher* 31 (March 1984): 48-49. *Concrete version of a proportional approach to percent problems.*

Glatzer, David J. "Teaching Percentage: Ideas and Suggestions." *Arithmetic Teacher* 31 (February 1984): 24-26. *Teaching the concept of percentage and ways of finding it.*

Grossman, Anne S. "Decimal Notation: An Important Research Finding." *Arithmetic Teacher* 30 (May 1983): 32-33. *Understanding of decimal notation.*

Hampel, Paul J. "Computer Corner." *Arithmetic Teacher* 32 (September 1984): 46. *Program changing fractions into decimals.*

Hiebert, James. "Research Report: Decimal Fractions." *Arithmetic Teacher* 34 (March 1987): 22-23. *Summarizes research findings and suggests instructional strategies.*

Payne, Joseph N., and Ann E. Towsley. "Ideas." *Arithmetic Teacher* 34 (March 1987): 26-32. *Activities with decimals.*

Quintero, Ana Helvia. "Helping Children Understand Ratios." *Arithmetic Teacher* 34 (May 1987): 17-21. *Describes different levels of difficulties and activities with ratios.*

Wiebe, James H. "Manipulating Percentages." *Mathematics Teacher* 79 (January 1986): 23-26, 21. *Discusses two concrete models.*

8

Integers

THEME: Understanding Integers and their Operations

**Strategy Review:
Draw a Diagram.**
You can refer to
this strategy in
Chapter 2 of the text.

A survey was taken in a school cafeteria. Of the 125 students surveyed, 47 liked hamburgers, 30 liked pizza, and 12 liked both pizza and hamburgers. How many students did not like pizza or hamburgers? Hint: Use a Venn Diagram.

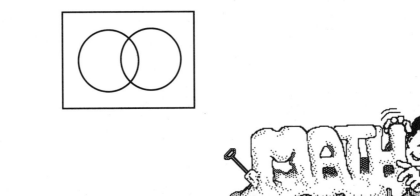

HANDS-ON ACTIVITIES

The first three activities in this chapter are designed to give you practice in representing positive and negative integers using black and red cubes to build models of the integers.

OBJECTIVE: **Build models of integers**

You Will Need: Materials Card 8.1

1. These sets are models of 5 and -6.

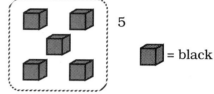 5

= black

-6 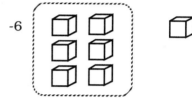 = red

2. Using the cubes from Materials Card 8.1, make models of these integers. Record how each was made:

8   -7   4   -3   -5

OBJECTIVE: **Use opposites to represent 0**

You Will Need: Materials from Activity 1

1. These black and red cubes can be matched in a 1-to-1 correspondence.

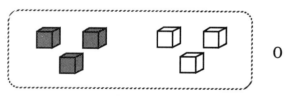 0

We say that the red cubes "cancel" the black cubes (and vice versa) and that the entire set represents the number 0.

Because of this, -3 is called the **opposite** of 3. Also, 3 is called the opposite of -3.

2. Using the black and red cubes, show four different ways to represent 0. Record. Name the pairs of opposites as illustrated:

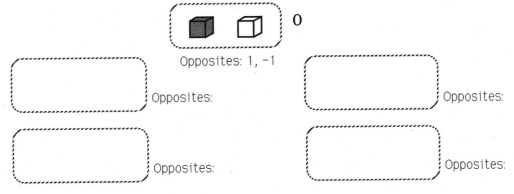

Opposites: 1, −1

Opposites: _____

Opposites: _____

Opposites: _____

Opposites: _____

OBJECTIVE: **Represent integers in alternate ways**

You Will Need: Materials from Activity 1

1. Cubes can be used to represent -6 in many different ways. Two ways are shown below:

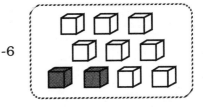

-6

-6

Circle pairs of cubes that cancel each other.

2. Use cubes to show two ways to represent -3. Record. Circle pairs of cubes that cancel each other.

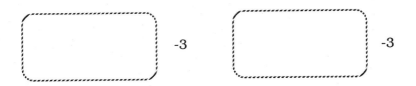

-3

-3

3. Find four ways to represent 5. Record. Circle pairs of cubes that cancel each other.

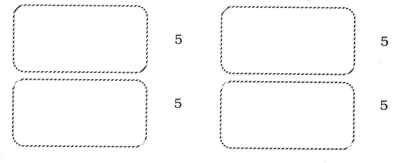

5   5

5   5

Now that you know how to represent integers using the black and red cubes, you are ready to look at models for addition and subtraction of integers.

OBJECTIVE: **Represent addition of integers using black and red cubes**

You Will Need: Materials from Activity 1

1. This model shows how to add 3 and 4 using black cubes:

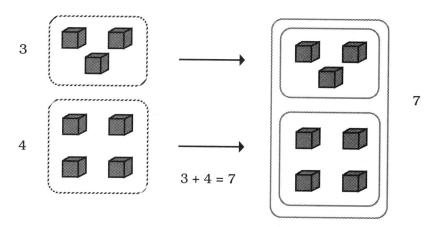

2. Use red cubes and black cubes to find the sum of -5 and 2. Record by picture. Circle the cubes that cancel each other. Record the sum.

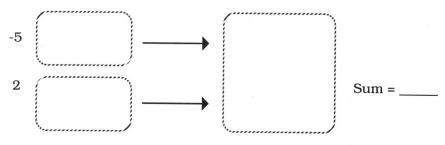

-5

2   Sum = _____

3. Use your cubes to compute and record the following sums:

    a. 7 + (-3) =   b. -4 + (-3) =   c. -8 + 2 =

    ┌───┐
    │   State a rule for adding integers.   │
    │   │
    │   │
    │   │
    │   │
    │   │
    └───┘

4. Use your rule to compute the following sums without cubes:

    a. 5 + (-4) =   b. -6 + (-8) =   c. -6 + 4 =

OBJECTIVE: **Subtract integers using the take-away model**

You Will Need: Materials from Activity 1

1. These models show "take-away" subtractions. Try them with your cubes.

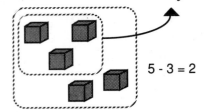   5 - 3 = 2   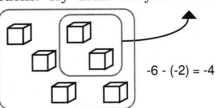   -6 - (-2) = -4

2. Use cubes to find these differences. Record by picture.

    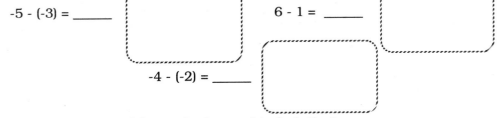

    -5 - (-3) = _____

    6 - 1 = _____

    -4 - (-2) = _____

3. The take-away model can also be used to find 5 - 8.
    Think of a plan to get enough black cubes to be able to take 8 of them away.

    Hint: Find another representation of 5.

    Record: 5 - 8 = _____

Use your method to find these differences. Record your pictures.

   a. 4 - 6 =

   b. 2 - 6 =

   c. 3 - 9 =

4. You can also use the take-away model to find -3 - 5.
   First : Count out 3 red cubes.

   Then : Put 5 black cubes and 5 red cubes with the 3 red cubes.

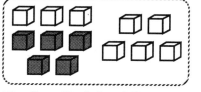

   What integer is represented here?_____

   (You now have enough black cubes to take away 5 black cubes.)

   Finally : Find the difference by taking away the 5 black cubes.   -3 - 5 =_____

5. Use cubes to find these differences. Record your pictures.

   a. 5 - (-2) =

   b. -3 - 2 =

   c. -3 - (-4) =

OBJECTIVE: **Show subtraction as adding the opposite**

You Will Need: Materials from Activity 1

1. Use red and black cubes to find -3 - 4 = _____
   Record your picture.

   Now find -3 + (-4) = _____ using cubes.
   Record your picture.

   Did you get the same answer both times?_____ Explain why this is so.

2. Verify these equations using cubes:

   a. -5 - 4 = -5 + (-4)

   b. 3 - (-2) = 3 + 2

Summary: In order to subtract two integers, you can rewrite the difference as the first integer plus the _____ of the second integer and follow the rules for addition.

OBJECTIVE: **Show subtraction with missing-addend addition**

You Will Need: Materials from Activity 1

1. Use some black cubes and 3 red cubes to represent 5. Record by picture.

   How many black cubes did you use?

   What number can be added to -3 to get 5?

2. Use some red cubes and 4 black cubes to represent -3. Record by picture.

   How many red cubes did you use?

   What number can be added to 4 to get -3?

3. Compute 5 - (-2) by using cubes to find the missing addend in the equation
   _____ + (-2) = 5. Record.

4. Compute -6 - 3 by using the missing-addend method.

   Hint: Ask yourself, "What can I add to 3 to get -6?"

   -6 - 3 = _____

5. Compute these differences by using the missing-addend model.
   Record your results:

   a. -7 - 3 =   b. 4 - (-1) =   c. -7 - 8 =

The last two activities in this chapter will present models for multiplication and division of integers.

 **OBJECTIVE:** **Use representations of 0 to multiply integers**

You Will Need: Materials from Activity 1

1. The equation $2 \times 3 = 6$ means $3 + 3 = 6$. If we start with a representation of 0 like this

   and then add 3 black cubes two times we get 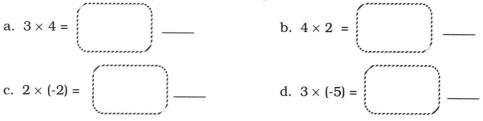 = 6.

   The problem 2×3 tells us we must *put in* 3 black cubes 2 times.

2. Use red or black cubes to compute these products:

   a. $3 \times 4 =$ _____

   b. $4 \times 2 =$ _____

   c. $2 \times (-2) =$ _____

   d. $3 \times (-5) =$ _____

   The problem $2 \times (-2)$ tells us we must _____2 red cubes 2 times.

3. We can also find products for problems of this type -2×3.

   To do this, we must use a different representation of 0.

   This problem tells us we must *take out* 2 groups of 3 black cubes. Therefore, we begin with this representation of 0.

   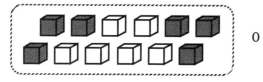 0

   Now *take out* 2 groups of 3 black cubes. What cubes remain?_____
   What integer is represented by the remaining cubes?_____

   Thus, $-2 \times 3 =$ _____

4. Use your cubes to find these products. Start with an appropriate representation of zero; in part (a) this has been done for you.

a. -4 × 2 =

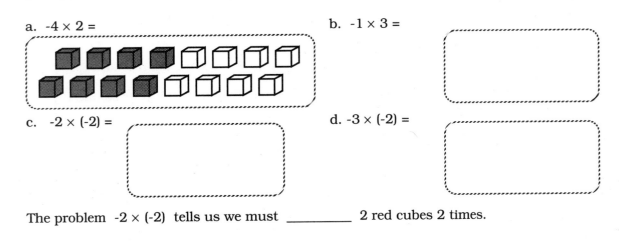

b. -1 × 3 =

c.   -2 × (-2) =

d. -3 × (-2) =

The problem -2 × (-2) tells us we must _____ 2 red cubes 2 times.

5. Use your answers to parts 2 and 4 to record these products:

a. 3 × 4 = _____

b. 4 × 2 = _____

c. 2 × (-2) = _____

d. 3 × (-5) = _____

e. -4 × 2 = _____

f. -1 × 3 = _____

g. -2 × (-2) = _____

h. -3 × (-2) = _____

State a shortcut for multiplying integers.

6. Use your pattern to compute these products without using cubes:

a. 3 × 6 = _____

b. -4 × 5 = _____

c. 7 × (-2) = _____

d. -3 × (-6) = _____

ACTIVITY 9

OBJECTIVE: **Divide integers**

You Will Need: Materials from Activity 1

1. To find the quotient $-8 \div 2$ we must find n such that $-8 = 2 \times n$, i.e. $n = -4$.

   Use the cubes and the multiplication model from Activity 8 to check your solution.

2. Compute these quotients by finding a value for n that makes each statement true.

   a. $6 \div 3 = $ _____
      $6 = n \times 3$ $n = $ _____

   b. $-10 \div 5 = $ _____
      $-10 = n \times 5$ $n = $ _____

   c. $8 \div (-4) = $ _____
      $8 = n \times (-4)$ $n = $ _____

   d. $-6 \div 6 = $ _____
      $-6 = n \times 6$ $n = $ _____

   Use cubes to check your answers.

   Look at the problems above. State a pattern for division of integers.

3. Find these quotients using your pattern:

   a. $15 \div (-3) = $ _____   b. $-12 \div 6 = $ _____   c. $-7 \div (-7) = $ _____   d. $153 \div 3 = $ _____

MENTAL MATH

Determine today's temperature at 5:00 P.M.

At 1:00 A.M. the temperature was 30°. By 5:00 A.M. it had dropped 13°. It then began to rise at the rate of 2° per hour. This rate continued until noon when the rate of increase changed to 3° per hour. At 4:00 P.M. it reached its peak and began dropping 2° per hour. What was the temperature at 5:00 P.M.? _____

EXERCISES

Why did the bike racer go to the psychiatrist?

Solve each problem. Place the letter preceding the problem above the solution at the bottom of the page. Be sure to put the letter above the solution each time it appears.

U 27 - (-8) = _____
T -18 - 5 = _____
H 18 + (-12) = _____
A -45 + (-30) = _____
F 60 + (-40) = _____
E -11 - 6 = _____
V -15 + 41 = _____
L -3 + 15 = _____
S -47 - (-77) = _____

W 4 + (-22) = _____
D 7 + (-20) = _____
O 15 - 45 = _____
I -1 - (-20) = _____
G -8 + 4 - (-9) = _____
C -78 + (-37) = _____
N 22 + (-9) = _____
Y 1 - 12 = _____

6 -17   -18 -75 30   6 -75 26 19 13 5

—

-115 -11 -115 12 -17   12 -30 5 19 -115 -75 12

!

-13 19 20 20 19 -115 35 12 -23 19 -17 30

Designing with Integers

Connect each problem number (BIG NUMERALS) to its solution (small numerals) in the circle following. Use a straightedge to draw the lines. Your finished work will make a lovely design.

1. $2 \times (-4) = $ ____
2. $-90 \div 9 = $ ____
3. $-36 + 76 = $ ____
4. $8 - 26 = $ ____
5. $-10 \times (-13) = $ ____
6. $65 - (-20) = $ ____
7. $75 \div (-5) = $ ____
8. $60 \div (-6) = $ ____
9. $34 + (-56) = $ ____
10. $90 \div (-5) = $ ____
11. $-15 - (-84) = $ ____
12. $6 \times (-6) = $ ____
13. $2 \times (-45) = $ ____
14. $-3 \times (-15) = $ ____
15. $-42 - (-7) = $ ____
16. $-4 \times (-18) = $ ____
17. $-11 + (-3) = $ ____
18. $-63 \div 9 = $ ____
19. $-11 + 3 = $ ____
20. $-225 \div (-5) = $ ____
21. $-20 \times (-2) = $ ____
22. $-24 - (-96) = $ ____
23. $-20 + 150 = $ ____
24. $105 \div (-3) = $ ____
25. $21 + (-36) = $ ____
26. $-13 \times (-3) = $ ____
27. $-3 - 19 = $ ____
28. $-53 - (-53) = $ ____
29. $-23 \times (-3) = $ ____
30. $-200 \div (-4) = $ ____
31. $-56 + (-34) = $ ____
32. $-23 - (-62) = $ ____
33. $26 + (-26) = $ ____
34. $56 \div (-4) = $ ____

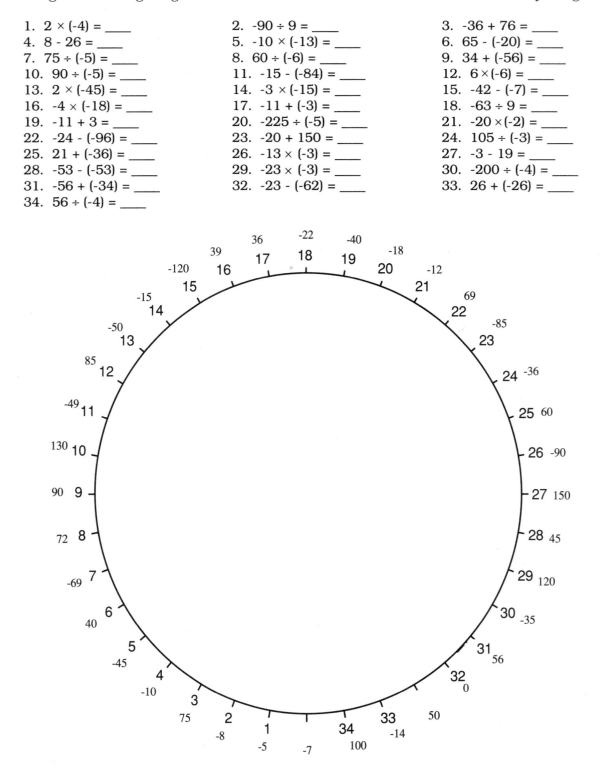

SELF-TEST

1. Which of the following is *false* ?

   a. The opposite of an integer is always negative.
   b. Every negative integer is the opposite of an integer.
   c. The opposite of a negative integer is always positive.
   d. None of a, b, or c.

2. B's are positive, R's are negative, and B + R is zero. What problem is illustrated here?

   R̶ R̶ R̶ R̶ R̶   a. 5 + (-9) = -4   b. 9 - 5 = 4
   B̶ B̶ B̶ B̶ B̶ B B B B   c. -5 + 9 = 4   d. None of a,b, or c.

3. Which of the following is the *adding-the-opposite* equivalent of -8 - 6 = _____?

   a. 8 + (-6) = _____   b. -8 + (-(-6)) = _____   c. 8 + (-(-6)) = _____   d. -8 + (-6) = _____

4. Which of the following is the *missing-addend* equivalent of (-9) - (-4) = _____?

   a. -9 + _____ = -4   b. -4 + _____ = -9   c. -(-4) + _____ = -9   d. -(-4) + _____ = 9

5. B's are positive, R's are negative, and B + R is zero. What problem is shown here?

   B̶ B̶ B̶ B̶ R R R R R   a. 4 - 10 = -6   b. 10 - 4 = 6
   B̶ B̶ B̶ B̶ B̶ B̶   c. -6 - (-4) = 10   d. -6 - 4 = 10

6. Which of these is true?

   a. $((a - b) - c)d = ((a - c) - b)(- d)$ b. $(a - b)(- c) = (b - a)(- c)$

   c. $(- a - b)c = (- b - a)c$ d. None of a , b , or c.

7. What can be concluded from the following "proof"?

   $$\mathbf{0} = -6(7 + (- 7)) = (-6)7 + (-6)(-7) = \mathbf{-42 + (-6)(-7)}$$

   a. 7 - 7 = 0   b. (-6)7 = -42   c. (-6)(-7) = 42   d. (-6)0 = 0

8. Which of the following is *not* a property of integers?

   a. distributivity   b. additive inverse

   c. multiplicative inverse   d. multiplicative identity

9. For integers a and b, $a < b$ if there is a positive integer c such that:

    a. $a - c = b$ b. $c = a + b$ c. $a - b = c$ d. $a + c = b$

10. If a, b, c are integers, which of the following is *false*?

    a. If $a < b$ and $b < c$, then $a + b < b + c$.   b. If $a < b$, then $a + c < b + c$.

    c. If $a < b$ and $c \geq 0$, then $ac \leq bc$.   d. If $a < b$ and $c < 0$, then $ac < bc$.

SOLUTIONS

Warm-up
60 students

Hands-on Activities

Activity 1
2. 8 black cubes, 7 red cubes, 4 black cubes, 3 red cubes, 5 red cubes

Activity 2
Answers can vary.

Activity 3
Each black cube cancels one red cube.

Activity 4
2. -3
3. a. 4   b. -7   c. -6
     Rule: The sum of 2 negatives or 2 positives is the sum of the whole numbers, the sign does not change; the sum of a positive and a negative is the whole number difference, the sign will be that of the greater whole number.
4. a. 1   b. -14   c. -2

Activity 5
2. -2, 5, -2
3. -3 (represent 5 as 8 black cubes and 3 red cubes);   a. -2   b. -4   c. -6
4. -3, -8
5. a. 7   b. -5   c. 1

Activity 6
1. -7, -7, Yes. Subtracting 4 is equivalent to adding -4
2. Opposite

Activity 7
1. 8 black cubes; 8
2. 7 red cubes; -7
3. 7
4. -9
5. a. -10   b. 5   c. -15

Activity 8
2. a. 12   b. 8   c. -4   d. -15; put in
3. 6 red cubes, -6, -6
4. a. -8   b. -3   c. 4   d. 6; take out
5. a. 12   b. 8   c. -4   d. -15   e. -8   f. -3   g. 4   h. 6
   A negative times a negative is a positive, a positive times a positive is a positive, a positive times a negative is a negative.
6. a. 18   b. -20   c. -14   d. 18

Activity 9
2. a. 2   b. -2   c. -2   d. -1
   Division with 2 negatives or with 2 positives gives a positive quotient, division with a positive and a negative gives a negative quotient.
3. a. -5   b. -2   c. 1   d. 51

Mental Math
41 degrees

Exercises

Why did the bike racer go to the psychiatrist?

U 35	W -18	T -23	D -13	H 6	O -30	A -75
I 19	F 20	G 5	E -17	C -115	V 26	N 13
L 12	Y -11	S 30				

HE WAS HAVING CYCLE-LOGICAL DIFFICULTIES !

Designing with Integers

1. -8	2. -10	3. 40	4. -18	5. 130	6. 85
7. -15	8. -10	9. -22	10. -18	11. 69	12. -36
13. -90	14. 45	15. -35	16. 72	17. -14	18. -7
19. -8	20. 45	21. 40	22. 72	23. 130	24. -35
25. -15	26. 39	27. -22	28. 0	29. 69	30. 50
31. -90	32. 39	33. 0	34. -14		

You should find a cardioid (heart-shaped) design.

Self-Test
1. a   2. c   3. d   4. b   5. a   6. c   7. c   8. c   9. d   10. d

RESOURCE ARTICLES

Battista, Michael T. "A Complete Model for Operations on Integers." *Arithmetic Teacher* 30 (May 1983): 26-31. *A concrete model for teaching the four basic operations on the set of integers.*

Chang, Lisa. "Multiple Methods of Teaching the Addition and Subtraction of Integers." *Arithmetic Teacher* 33 (December 1985): 14-19. *Relating operations with integers to real-world situations.*

Crowley, Mary L., and Kenneth A. Dunn. "On Multiplying Negative Numbers." *Mathematics Teacher* 78 (April 1985): 252-256. *The ideas involved in the multiplication of negative numbers.*

Dirks, Michael K. "The Integer Abacus." *Arithmetic Teacher* 31 (March 1984): 50-54. *Help in understanding the algebraic rule of signs.*

Sarver, Vernon Thomas, Jr. "Why Does a Negative Times a Negative Produce a Positive?" *Mathematics Teacher* 79 (March 1986): 178-180. *Provides an interesting concrete interpretation.*

Willy, W. Edward. "Addition of Antinumbers." *Mathematics Teacher* 78 (November 1985): 606-608. *A motivational technique for introducing addition of integers.*

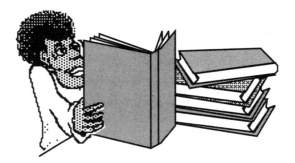

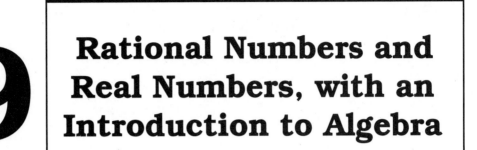

9 Rational Numbers and Real Numbers, with an Introduction to Algebra

THEME: Extending Number Systems

Strategy Review:
Use Properties of Numbers.
This strategy, introduced in Chapter 5, will help you solve this problem.

I'm thinking of a number. It is a prime number less than 100. The sum of its digits is 16. If you reverse the digits, the resulting number is also prime. What's the number?

HANDS-ON ACTIVITIES

The activities in this chapter will use the Pythagorean theorem to help you gain an understanding of irrational numbers. The geoboard, a useful classroom manipulative, will be utilized for these activities.

OBJECTIVE: **Find areas on the geoboard**

You Will Need: A geoboard (optional)

1. The geoboard is a 5 by 5 array of pegs. Rubber bands are used to form the shapes as illustrated:

This square will be our unit of area measure.

▢ = 1 square unit.

Construct this square on your geoboard.

Construct each of these shapes on your geoboard. What is the area of each shape? Hint: How many ▢ are in each shape?

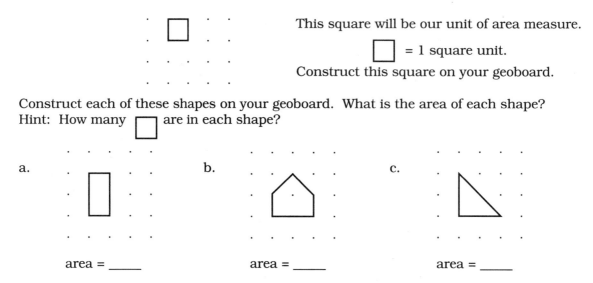

a.   area = _____   b.   area = _____   c.   area = _____

2. Now find the area of each of the square regions below:

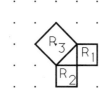

Area of R_1 = _____
Area of R_2 = _____
Area of R_3 = _____
Sum of R_1 & R_2 = _____

What do you notice about the area of R_3 and the sum of the areas of R_1 and R_2?_____

3. Now find the areas of these square regions given on a square lattice:

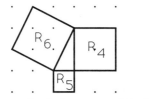

Area of R_4 = _____
Area of R_5 = _____
Their sum = _____

You can find the area of R_6 by finding the areas of the regions determined by the dashed lines as illustrated:

Area of R_6 = _____

Describe another way for finding the area of R_6.

OBJECTIVE: **Investigate the Pythagorean theorem**

You Will Need: Materials Card 9.2 and scissors

1. Cut out the figure on Materials Card 9.2.

2. Cut away the square on side x, the square on side y, and the square on side z.

3. Now cut the square with side y into 4 pieces as indicated by the dashed lines.

4. Arrange square x and the pieces of square y to fit exactly into square z. (It can be done!)

> What have you shown about the areas of the three squares?
> Interpret this in terms of the original right triangle given.

OBJECTIVE: **Develop the Pythagorean theorem algebraically**

You Will Need: Materials Card 9.3 and scissors

1. Cut out the four copies of the right triangle with sides x, y and z from Materials Card 9.3. Arrange them to form a square "donut" with a square hole as shown:

    Now answer these questions:

2. The length of any side of the donut is side _____ of the triangle plus side _____ of the triangle, or _____+_____ (in terms of x, y, and z).

    What is the area of the larger square?_____
    We will call this area A_1.

3. What is the length of any side of the donut hole?_____
    What is the area of the hole?_____ We will call this area A_2.

4. What is the area of each right triangle?_____
   (Remember that the area of a triangle is 1/2 the base times the height. This is easy to see here since two of the triangles can be fitted together to make a rectangle with dimensions x and y .)

5. What is the sum of the areas of the four right triangles?_____
   We will call this area S.

6. Write an equation involving A_1, A_2, and S. _____
   Now substitute the x , y , and z values for A_1, A_2, and S.
   Simplify your equation.

7. Explain your simplified equation in geometric terms that apply to the right triangle.

8. Using this equation, we know that 3, 4, and 5 could be the sides and hypotenuse of a right triangle because $3^2 + 4^2 = 5^2$. Which of the following triples could be the lengths of the sides and hypotenuse of a right triangle?

   a. 6, 8, 10   b. 5, 12, 13   c. 15, 112, 113   d. 7, 25, 26

We can now use our knowledge of right triangles and the lengths of their sides
and hypotenuse to explore real numbers. Again, we will use the geoboard.

OBJECTIVE: **Construct real number lengths**
                   on the geoboard

You Will Need: A geoboard (optional)

DEFINITION: If r is any nonnegative number, then $\sqrt{r}$, called the **square root** of r , is the nonnegative number whose square is r . In symbols, $\sqrt{r}$ satisfies the two properties:

$$\text{(i) } \sqrt{r} \geq 0 \qquad \text{and} \qquad \text{(ii) } (\sqrt{r})^2 = r$$

For example, $\sqrt{4} = 2,$ $\sqrt{9} = 3,$ $\sqrt{144} = 12$

1. In the given isosceles right triangle, the sides have length 1
    and the hypotenuse has length c.

    We can say $1^2 + 1^2 = c^2$, or $2 = c^2$.

    Therefore, the length of the hypotenuse $c = \sqrt{2}$.

2. Find the length of each hypotenuse below:

    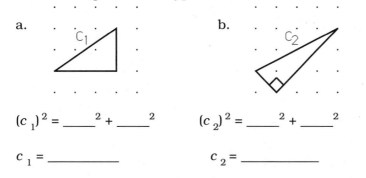

    a.

    b.

    $(c_1)^2 = \underline{\quad}^2 + \underline{\quad}^2$ $(c_2)^2 = \underline{\quad}^2 + \underline{\quad}^2$

    $c_1 = \underline{\hspace{2cm}}$ $c_2 = \underline{\hspace{2cm}}$

3. Determine which of the following can be represented on a 5 by 5 geoboard. Give your
    rationale by describing the right triangle whose hypotenuse has that length. Draw your
    triangles on the 5 by 5 arrays given below. For example, the right triangle with sides

    3 and 1 can be used to represent the length $\sqrt{10}$, because $3^2 + 1^2 = (\sqrt{10})^2$.

    a. $\sqrt{17}$ $\underline{\quad}^2 + \underline{\quad}^2 = (\sqrt{17})^2$

    b. $\sqrt{32}$ $\underline{\quad} + \underline{\quad} = \underline{\hspace{2cm}}$

    c. $\sqrt{18}$ $\underline{\quad} + \underline{\quad} = \underline{\hspace{2cm}}$

    d.   5 $\underline{\quad} + \underline{\quad} = \underline{\hspace{2cm}}$

    e. $\sqrt{28}$ $\underline{\quad} + \underline{\quad} = \underline{\hspace{2cm}}$

    f. $\sqrt{22}$ $\underline{\quad} + \underline{\quad} = \underline{\hspace{2cm}}$

MENTAL MATH

If 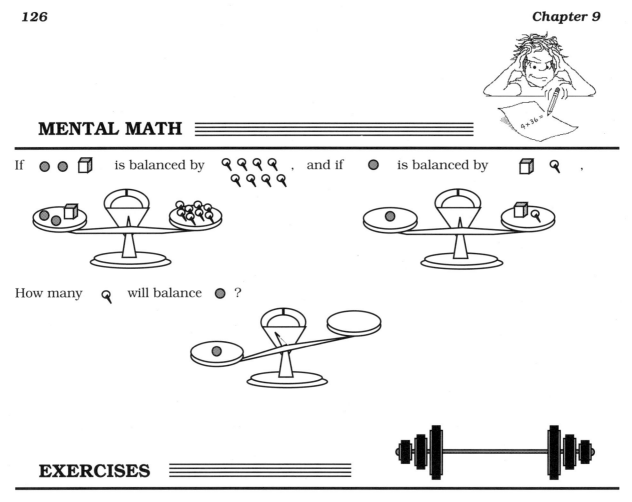 is balanced by ⚲⚲⚲⚲ ⚲⚲⚲⚲ , and if ● is balanced by ⬜ ⚲ ,

How many ⚲ will balance ● ?

EXERCISES

Just FOUR You!

Express each whole number from 1 to 10 using a number sentence that involves the number **four** exactly **four** times and at least one square root.

For example, $4 \times \sqrt{4} + 4 \times \sqrt{4} = 16$

_____	=	1	_____ = 6
_____	=	2	_____ = 7
_____	=	3	_____ = 8
_____	=	4	_____ = 9
_____	=	5	_____ = 10

What happens to frogs who double park?

Decide whether each number is rational or irrational. Circle the letter in the appropriate column at the right. When you are finished, print the circled letters above the appropriate blanks at the bottom of the page to solve the riddle.

		Rational	Irrational
1.	22/7	E	I
2.	π	W	T
3.	6.125	G	A
4.	0.571428571428 . . .	W	A
5.	$\sqrt{225}$	Y	S
6.	$\sqrt{49}$	Y	S
7.	$\sqrt{2}$	B	T
8.	-4/3	A	R
9.	3.1415925385 . . .	C	A
10.	0.060060006 . . .	A	H
11.	0.135135135 . . .	T	E
12.	-0.999199911999 . . .	R	A
13.	3.40764076 . . .	D	T
14.	-9.7071212212221 . . .	A	O
15.	$\sqrt{13}$	R	E

Letter Answer   _ _ _ _   _ _ _   _ _ _ _   _ _ _ _ !

Question Number   7 10 1 5   3 15 11   2 14 8 13   9 4 12 6

SELF-TEST

1. If W, F, I, and Q represent the whole numbers, fractional numbers, integers, and rational numbers, respectively, which of the following is false?

    a. $F \cup I = Q$ b. $W \subseteq I \subseteq Q$ c. $W \subseteq F \subseteq Q$ d. None of a, b, or c.

2. Which of the following properties, among others, make this computation easy?

    $$(-5/3 + 4/7 + 5/3) \times 7/4$$

    (i) additive inverse   (ii) distributive property   (iii) multiplicative inverse

    a. i only   b. i and ii only   c. i and iii only   d. i, ii, and iii

3. The decimal form of 2/7 is

    a. $.\overline{285714}$ b. $.2\overline{828}$ c. $.\overline{285713}$ d. $.\overline{28562749}$

4. If the fractional form of the rational number whose decimal form is $.\overline{45}$ is written in simplest form, the sum of the numerator and denominator is

    a. 16   b. 29   c. 145   d. 149

5. Which of the following is true about $6.\overline{360}$?

    (i) It is rational.   (ii) It is a terminating decimal.   (iii) It is an integer.

    a. i only   b. i and ii only   c. ii and iii only   d. i and iii only

6. .121221222. . . is

    a. rational and real
    c. rational but not real
    b. irrational and real
    d. irrational but not real

7. Which set contains only rational numbers?

    a. $\{ \sqrt{1},\ \sqrt{2},\ \sqrt{3} \}$ b. $\{ \sqrt{4},\ \sqrt{9},\ \sqrt{16} \}$

    c. $\{ \sqrt{4},\ \sqrt{5},\ \sqrt{9} \}$ d. None of a, b, or c.

8. What is the length of the diagonal on the geoboard shown?

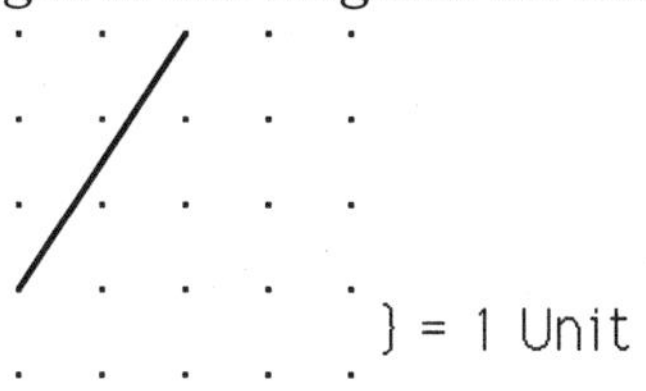

    } = 1 Unit

    a. 5   b. 6   c. 3 1/2   d. None of a, b, or c.

9. Which of the following orderings is correct?

    a. -3/8 < 2/-5 < 1/3 < 1/2   b. -2/7 < -3/11 < 2/5 < 3/8

    c. 3/-10 < -2/9 < 5/7 < 7/9   d. None of a, b, or c.

10. Solve the following equation, and write your answer in simplest form.

    $$(3/4)x - 4/5 = (2/3)x + 1/2$$

    What is the denominator?

    a. 4   b. 5   c. 3   d. 2

SOLUTIONS

Warm-up

79 or 97

Hands-on Activities

Activity 1
1. a. 2   b. 3   c. 2
2. 1, 1, 2, 2; equal
3. 4, 1, 5, 5, Find the sum of the areas of R_4 and R_5.

Activity 2
The sum of the areas of the squares on the sides of a right triangle is equal to the area of the square on the hypotenuse.

Activity 3
2. x, y, $x + y$, $(x + y)^2$
3. z, z^2
4. $xy/2$
5. $2xy$
6. $A_1 - A_2 = S$ $(x + y)^2 - z^2 = 2xy$; $x^2 + 2xy + y^2 - z^2 = 2xy$ or $x^2 + y^2 = z^2$
7. See Activity 2 solution
8. a, b, c

Activity 4
2. $2^2 + 3^2$, $\sqrt{13}$, $(\sqrt{2})^2 + (\sqrt{18})^2$, $\sqrt{20}$

3. a. $4^2 + 1^2$ b. $4^2 + 4^2 = (\sqrt{32})^2$ c. $3^2 + 3^2 = (\sqrt{18})^2$
     d. $3^2 + 4^2 = 5^2$ e. and f.   cannot be done

Mental Math
Three tacks will balance one marble.

Exercises
Just FOUR You !
- - answers will vary.

What happens to frogs who double park?
THEY GET TOAD AWAY !

Self-Test
1. a   **2.** c   **3.** a   **4.** a   **5.** b   **6.** b   **7.** b   **8.** d   **9.** c   **10.** b

RESOURCE ARTICLES

DiDomenico, Angelo S. "Pythagorean Triples from the Addition Table." *Mathematics Teacher* 78 (May 1985): 346-348. *An investigation using the addition table.*

Drysdale, Ron. "An Act of Creation in First-Year Algebra." *Mathematics Teacher* 78 (April 1985): 266-268. *A motivational technique for first-year algebra students.*

Giambrone, Tom M. "Challenges for Enriching the Curriculum: Algebra." *Mathematics Teacher* 76 (April 1983): 262-263. *Problems that require students to use techniques other than the known algorithms.*

Harder, Ken. "Algebra Tic-tac-toe." *Mathematics Teacher* 76 (January 1983): 34-36. *A game format for practice with factoring.*

Hawkins, Vincent J. "The Pythagorean Theorem Revisited: Weighing the Results." *Arithmetic Teacher* 32 (December 1984): 36-37. *Using Cuisenaire rods to investigate the Pythagorean theorem.*

Hollis, L. Y. "Teaching Rational Numbers— Primary Grades." *Arithmetic Teacher* 31 (February 1984): 36-39. *What can and should be taught in the primary grades.*

Jacobson, Marilyn Hall. "Teaching Rational Numbers— Intermediate Grades." *Arithmetic Teacher* 31 (February 1984): 40-42. *A model for the introduction of decimals.*

Kieren, Thomas E. "Helping Children Understand Rational Numbers." *Arithmetic Teacher* 31 (February 1984): 3. *A discussion of the mechanisms, images, and language needed for the development of rational-number ideas.*

Lester, Frank K., Jr. "Preparing Teachers to Teach Rational Numbers." *Arithmetic Teacher* 31 (February 1984): 54-56. *Suggestions for instruction in rational numbers for pre-service teachers.*

Levine, Deborah R. "Proof by Analogy: The Case of the Pythagorean Theorem." *Mathematics Teacher* 76 (January 1983): 44-46. *A special case involving the Pythagorean theorem.*

Marche, M. M. "A Pythagorean Curiosity." *Mathematics Teacher* 77 (November 1984): 611-613. *A method for finding integral values for the three sides of a right triangle.*

Ockenga, Earl. "Chalk Up Some Calculator Activities for Rational Numbers." *Arithmetic Teacher* 31 (February 1984): 51-53. *Create interest in the study of fractions by using the calculator.*

Payne, Joseph N. "Curricular Issues: Teaching Rational Numbers." *Arithmetic Teacher* 31 (February 1984): 14-17. *A discussion of the debate on relative emphasis to be given fractions and decimals.*

Prevost, Fernand J. "Teaching Rational Numbers - Junior High School." *Arithmetic Teacher* 31 (February 1984): 43-46. *Extending whole number operations to rational numbers.*

Ryden, Robert. "Nearly Isosceles Pythagorean Triples." *Mathematics Teacher* 76 (January 1983): 52-56. *The beauty of patterns in the Pythagorean triples.*

Skypek, Dora Helen B. "Special Characteristics of Rational Numbers." *Arithmetic Teacher* 31 (February 1984): 10-12. *Interpretations and coding conventions of rational numbers.*

Trafton, Paul R., and Judith S. Zawojewski. "Teaching Rational Number Division: A Special Problem." *Arithmetic Teacher* 31 (February 1984): 20-22. *Division of fractions and decimals.*

Usiskin, Zalman, and Max S. Bell. "Ten Often Ignored Applications of Rational-Number Concepts." *Arithmetic Teacher* 31 (February 1984): 48-50. *A look at the variety of contexts in which numbers appear in today's world.*

Wagner, Sigrid. "What Are These Things Called Variables?" *Mathematics Teacher* 76 (October 1983): 474-479. *Suggestions for overcoming difficulties related to variables for beginning algebra students.*

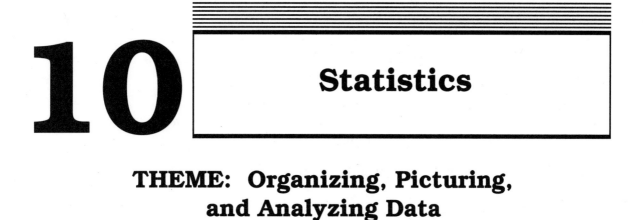

10 | Statistics

THEME: Organizing, Picturing, and Analyzing Data

Strategy Review:
Solve an Equation.
This strategy was
presented in
Chapter 9 of the text.

Each row, column, and diagonal has
the same sum.

-7	x	-8
$2y$	-5	-4
$x-2$	-10	y

What is that sum ?_____

$x =$ _____ $y =$ _____

HANDS-ON ACTIVITIES

The activities in this chapter will help you organize, represent, and analyze data using a variety of picturing techniques. Depending on the data, it may be appropriate to use a bar graph, line graph, pictograph, or circle graph. These are explored in the following activities.

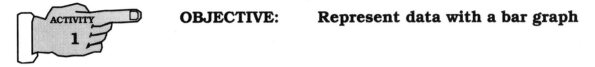

OBJECTIVE: Represent data with a bar graph

A **bar graph** can be used when you want to make comparisons between several quantities or make comparisons over a period of time.

1. Use this graph to record the birth month of 20 people. Color a square for each person.

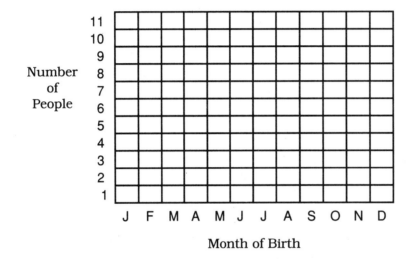

2. You can now use your graph to answer these questions:

During which month did the most births occur?_____
the least births?_____

During which quarter of the year did the most births occur?_____
the least?_____

What was the total number of births in 31-day months?_____
in months with less than 31 days?_____

3. Think of 3 more questions that could be answered by your graph.

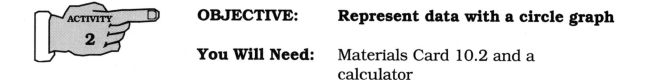

OBJECTIVE: **Represent data with a circle graph**

You Will Need: Materials Card 10.2 and a calculator

A **circle graph** can be used when you want to show the fractional parts into which a whole has been divided and to compare their relative sizes.

1. Fill in this chart based on how you spent your time yesterday and compute the percent of time spent in each activity. Remember, you can use a proportion to compute percent. For example, if you spent 8 hours sleeping, your proportion would be:

$$8/24 = n/100 \qquad n = \text{\_\_\_\_}$$

Time in Hours

Sleep	Eat	Travel	School	Work	Study	Exercise	Chores	TV	Other
___	___	___	___	___	___	___	___	___	___
___%	___%	___%	___%	___%	___%	___%	___%	___%	___%

Now construct a circle graph that represents your data. Remember to multiply each percent by 360° to find the measure of the central angle for each sector.

How I Spend My Time

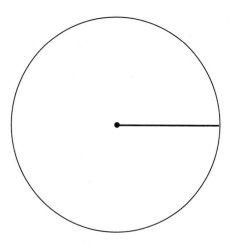

Be sure to label each sector of your graph.

2. Find the percent of time spent in recreational activities. _____%

Find the percent of time in work-related activities, including school. _____%

3. How might your graph be different if you kept track of your time for an entire week?

What factors might cause this graph to be a poor representation of how you usually spend your time?

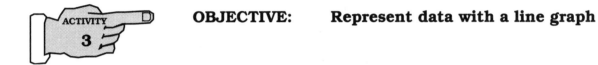

OBJECTIVE: Represent data with a line graph

A **line graph** is useful in plotting data over a period of time and in looking at trends.

The following table provides temperature data for two U.S. cities (M means data is missing). Drawing a line graph with a separate line for each city would allow us to compare the temperatures in the two cities.

Temperature on a day in July at two-hour intervals

Temperatures in Celsius

	12 Midnight	2	4	6 A.M.	8	10	12 Noon	2	4	6 P.M.	8	10 Midnight	12
Denver, CO	20	18	19	22	24	28	32	35	34	30	27	M	M
Washington, DC	25	24	23	25	28	30	32	33	32	30	28	M	M

1. In order to draw a line graph, we first need to determine the horizontal and vertical scales. The horizontal scale for time has already been drawn on the graph shown. What would be an appropriate scale for the vertical temperature axis? Hint: Remember it should start at zero.

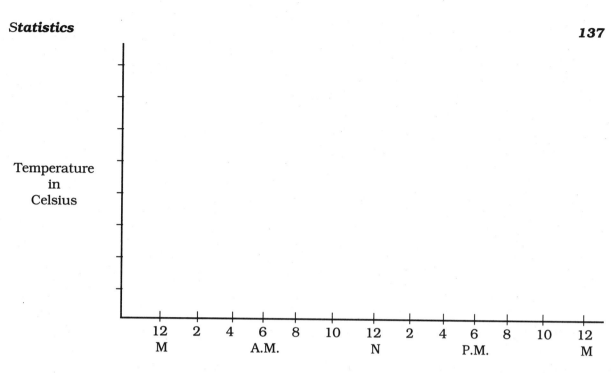

Temperature
in
Celsius

| 12 | 2 | 4 | 6 | 8 | 10 | 12 | 2 | 4 | 6 | 8 | 10 | 12 |

M   A.M.   N   P.M.   M

Time of Day in Two-Hour Intervals

2. Now mark dots corresponding to the numbers for each city. Connect the dots for Denver with solid line segments and the dots for Washington with dashed line segments.

3. Use your graph to answer the following questions.

   a. Which city reached the warmest temperature during the day? the coolest temperature?

   b. Which city was warmer at 10 a.m.? at 2 p.m.? at 8 p.m.?

   c. During which hours was Washington warmer than Denver?

   d. During which hours was Denver warmer than Washington?

   e. When were the temperatures in Denver and Washington the same?

   f. About what was the temperature at 9 a.m. in Washington? in Denver?

   g. When approximately was the temperature in Denver equal to 25° C?

   h. Assuming the trend of the temperatures since 6 p.m. continues, what would you estimate the temperatures to be at 12 midnight at the end of the day in Denver? in Washington?

OBJECTIVE: **Represent data with a pictograph**

A **pictograph** uses a small drawing to symbolize the quantities being represented. A pictograph can be used to make comparisons between similar situations or across time.

The following table provides data for the sales of a textbook in six selected states.

State	Number of books sold
New York	670,643
Massachusetts	231,506
Kentucky	163,114
Michigan	355,860
California	810,520
Montana	98,478

1. In order to draw a pictograph, you will need to decide how to label your axis. You will also need to choose a symbol and decide how many books it will represent.

   a. What symbol will you use?

   b. If you let each symbol represent 10,000 books, how many symbols would be needed to represent the smallest amount? the largest amount? Is this a reasonable choice?

   c. If you let each symbol represent 200,000 books, how many symbols would be needed to represent the smallest amount? the largest amount? Is this a reasonable choice?

   d. What might be a more reasonable choice to let each symbol represent?

   e. You also need to decide whether you want to round your data to use a whole number of symbols or to represent a fraction of your symbol. What will you do here?

2. On the axes provided, draw a pictograph using the given data.

3. Using your pictograph, answer the following questions.

   a. Which state had the largest sales? the smallest sales?

   b. In which states were fewer books sold than in Massachusetts?

   c. In which states were approximately twice the number of books sold as in Kentucky?

   d. In which states were approximately one-third as many books sold as in New York?

Numbers that provide information about the overall "average" of a group are called **measures of central tendency.** The following activity explores three of these measures and a measure of the overall spread of the data.

OBJECTIVE: Analyze data

1. Find the heights of 20 people (in centimeters). List the heights here in order from shortest to tallest:

2. a. The heights range from the shortest of _____ to the tallest of _____. The **range** of heights is the tallest minus the shortest or _____.

    b. The height shared by the most people is called the **mode**. What height is that?_____

    c. The height that is in the middle of the list is called the **median**. There are the same number of heights above and below this height. Since there is an even number of heights in this case, take the value midway between the two middle scores (add the two middle scores and divide by 2). What is the median height?_____

    d. The **mean** is determined by adding all of the heights together and then dividing by the number of people measured.   What is the mean height for your group of 20 people?_____

3. Using the graph paper given below, construct a bar graph that represents your data. What will be an appropriate scale for the horizontal axis? the vertical axis?

Number
of
People

Height in Centimeters

4. Draw a dashed line (-----) vertically through your graph to represent the mean height. Are there an equal number of people represented on your graph to the left and to the right of the mean?

   Draw a dotted line (. . . . .) vertically to represent the mode. Do you have an equal number of people to the left and to the right of the line?

   Draw a dot/dash line (._._._.) vertically to represent the median. Do you have an equal number of people to the left and to the right of the line?

5. a. Which of the three, mean, mode, or median, is most likely to divide your graph so that the same number of people are to the left and to the right of the line?

   b. What factors might cause the mode to be off-center?

   c. What factors might cause the mean to be off-center?

   d. Why will the median be most likely to divide your graph evenly?

In the last activity, you will use what you have learned in the first five activities to help you determine the best way to represent given data in graphical form.

OBJECTIVE: **Select appropriate graph for representation of data**

1. The students in Miss Kelly's math class received the following scores on their semester test: (85 points possible)   67, 42, 59, 80, 71, 67, 48, 53, 64, 73, 56, 77, 40, 35,

    78, 67, 59, 44, 76, 75, 42, 67, 65, 58, 31, 79, 56, 67

2. What is the range of scores?_____   What is the median?_____

   What is the mode?_____   What is the mean?_____

3. Miss Kelly asked the students to graph the test scores to assist her in preparing final grades. Which student's graph gives Miss Kelly the most useful representation of the data?

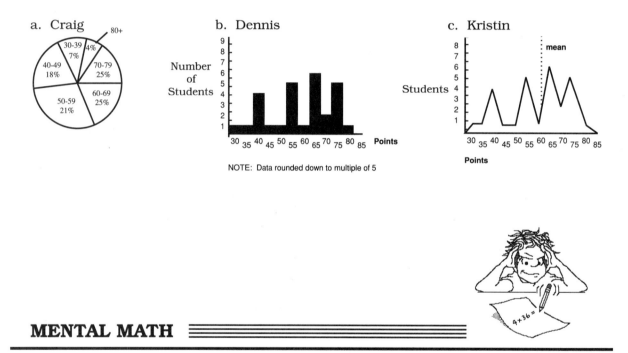

a. Craig   b. Dennis   c. Kristin

NOTE: Data rounded down to multiple of 5

MENTAL MATH

In a recent survey of 50 music lovers, 15 preferred rock music, 7 preferred classical music, 25 preferred country music, and 3 preferred jazz. Which graph most accurately represents this data?

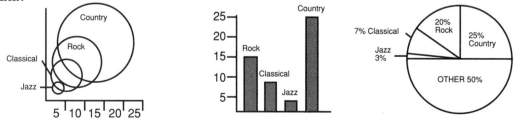

EXERCISES

What do you put on a sick pig?

Put the letter of the correct answer
on the appropriate line at the bottom
of the page.

1. What is the range of the recorded
   temperatures?
       A. 10°F   **O. 12°F**

2. What was the temperature at 4 A.M. ?
       I. -2°F   **B. 4°F**

3. When was the temperature 10°F?
       R. 2 PM   **N. Noon**

4. What is the median of temperatures
   recorded from 4 AM through noon?
       S. 3.5°F   **K. 4°F**

5. What is the mean of the temperatures
   recorded from noon through 6 PM?
       M. 6.7°F   **T. 10.3°F**

6. For how long was the temperature
   below 0°F?
       E. 5.5 hr.   **F. 7 hr.**

7. What was the temperature at 3 PM?
       G. -5°F   **N. 7°F**

8. What is the mean of the temperatures
   recorded from 1 AM through 6 PM?
       H. -1.3°F   **T. 4.2°F**

HOURLY TEMPERATURES
January 1

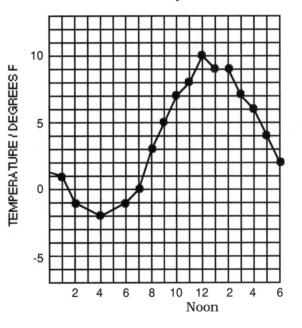

TIME

__ __ __ __ __ __ __ __ !
1   2   3   4   5   6   7   8

How is a sick bird like robbing a bank?

Put the letter of the correct answer on the appropriately-numbered line below.

The Pin Busters Bowling Team bowled 3 games.   Use their scores to answer these questions:

1. Who had the greatest range of scores?   S. Wally   O. Molly

2. Who had the lowest mean score?   R. Holly   H. Dolly

3. What was the mean score for the team
    (for all 15 games)?   L. 166   P. 171

4. Who bowled the median game score
    (for all 15 games)?   J. Pauly   R. Holly

5. What was the team mean for game 1?   Y. 171   G. 181

6. Who had the higher mean score?   C. Molly   B. Pauly

7. Whose mean was above the overall team mean?   I. Wally   K. Dolly

8. Who was nearest the team mean in game 3?   V. Pauly   S. Wally

9. For which game was the team mean lowest?   A. #2   U. #1

10. Is the team mean above or below the
    median game?   E. Below   F. Above

11. Who had the least range of scores?   L. Holly   G. Pauly

12. What was the team's total score?   T. 2491   W. 2563

	GAME 1	GAME 2	GAME 3	TOTAL PINS
Dolly	142	136	157	
Molly	173	131	209	
Pauly	169	171	180	
Wally	216	154	172	
Holly	153	167	161	
TEAM SCORES				

___ ___ ___ ___   ___ ___ ___   ___ ___ ___ ___   ___ ___ ___—___ ___ ___ ___ ___!
12 2 10 5   9 4 10   6 1 12 2   7 3 3   10 9 11 3 10 8

SELF-TEST

1. Which bar graph best represents the frequency table?

Frequency		
x	ΗΗ ΙΙΙΙ	
y	ΙΙΙ	
z	ΗΗ	

a. x ⊢———————— y ⊢———————— z ⊢——

b. x ⊢———— y ⊢————— z ⊢———————

c. x ⊢———————— y ⊢——— z ⊢————

d. x ⊢———————— y ⊢—— z ⊢—————

2. The third letter of the name of the graph that best illustrates relative amounts of chemicals in a substance is

   a. c   b. r   c. n   d. s

3. Which of the following is most affected by one extremely low score?

   a. mean   b. median   c. mode   d. All are equally affected.

4. Which is false for the data 2, 2, 5, 4, 2 ?

   a. The mode equals the median.   b. The mean is greater than the median.

   c. The median is 3.   d. The mode is less than the mean.

5. Find the median, standard deviation, mean and variance for the following data: 2, 8, 10, 14, 26. Add your answers together to obtain an answer below.

   a. 84   b. 124   c. 94   d. None of a, b, or c.

6. What is the sum of the mean and standard deviation of the following data: 0, 24, 32, 48, 96 ?

   a. 78   b. 40   c. 72   d. 32

7. The following test scores have been recorded by Ms. Burton. What is the z-score for the second to the highest score?
   Scores: 24, 72, 79, 83, 83, 86, 90, 123.

   a. 1.5   b. 1   c. 2   d. 1.25

8. Which is true when comparing two sets of scores?

   (i) The larger standard deviation comes from the set with the larger mean.

   (ii) If the means are equal, so are the variances.

   a. i only   b. ii only   c. i and ii   d. Neither is true.

9. Given 12, 14, 14, 20, which number has a z-score of -1 ?

   a. 12   b. 14   c. 20   d. None of a, b, or c.

10. Which of the following is false about a normal distribution?

   (i) Mean = median

   (ii) The higher the standard deviation, the higher the "peak".

   (iii) The interval from 2 standard deviations below the mean to 2 standard deviations above
         the mean contains about 68% of the measurements.

   a. i and ii only   b. i and iii only   c. ii and iii only   d. None of a, b, or c.

SOLUTIONS

Warm-up
Sum -15, $x = 0$, $y = -3$

Hands-on Activities

Activity 1
Answers will vary.

Activity 2
Answers will vary.
3. More representative; may have been a week-end, a day with no classes, you might have
   been ill or worked overtime, etc.

Activity 3
1. Let each mark represent 5° C.
3. a. Denver;   Denver
   b. Washington; Denver;   Washington
   c. 12 midnight to 12 noon and after 6 p.m.
   d. 12 noon to 6 p.m.
   e. 12 noon and 6 p.m.
   f. 29° C; 26° C
   g. 8:30 a.m.
   h. 21° C; 24° C

Activity 4
1. a. A drawing of a book would be one possibility
   b. About 10, about 81, probably not
   c. Less than 1/2 a symbol, about 4, probably not
   d. Probably something between 50,000 and 100,000
   e. For example, if you let each symbol represent 100,000 you could round to the nearest 25,000 and draw quarters of the symbol.
3. a. California, Montana
   b. Kentucky, Montana
   c. Michigan
   d. Massachusetts

Activity 5
Answers will vary.
5. a. Median   b. A small group of tall or short people in the sample
   c. A few very tall or very short people   d. It is the middle height.

Activity 6
2. Range = 49 points; mode = 67; median = 64.5; mean = 60.57
3. Dennis' graph is the most accurate even though he grouped the data. The sectors in Craig's graph are the wrong size and Kristin's graph suggests scores that do not exist (between 35 and 40 for example).

Mental Math
The bar graph is most accurate. The area of the circles in the pictograph is misleading. The percentages in the circle graph are inaccurate.

Exercises

What do you put on a sick pig?   OINKMENT!

How is a sick bird like robbing a bank?   THEY ARE BOTH ILL-EAGLES!

Self-Test
1. d   **2.** b   **3.** a   **4.** c   **5.** c   **6.** c   **7.** d   **8.** d   **9.** a   **10.** c

RESOURCE ARTICLES

Bruni, James V., and Helene J. Silverman. "Developing Concepts in Probability and Statistics - and Much More." *Arithmetic Teacher* 33 (February 1986): 34-37. *A four-step approach using manipulatives to develop statistics concepts.*

Collis, Betty. "Teaching Descriptive and Inferential Statistics Using a Classroom Microcomputer." *Mathematics Teacher* 76 (May 1983): 318-322. *A framework for integrating a microcomputer into a statistics unit.*

Dickinson, J. Craig. "Gather, Organize, Display: Mathematics for the Information Society." *Arithmetic Teacher* 34 (December 1986): 12-15. *Activities for organizing and displaying data.*

Kelly, Margaret. "Elementary School Activity: Graphing the Stock Market." *Arithmetic Teacher* 33 (March 1986): 17-20. *Graphing activities based on the stock market.*

Kimberling, Clark. "Mean, Standard Deviation, and Stopping the Stars." *Mathematics Teacher* 77 (November 1984): 633-636. *Generating data on the spot with computers for early experiences with the study of statistics.*

Kissane, Barry V. "'Easy' Statistical Exercises." *Mathematics Teacher* 76 (February 1983): 101-104. *Exercises with "nice" numbers for initial experience with statistical computations.*

Klitz, Ralph H., Jr., and Joseph F. Hofmeister. "Statistics in the Middle School." *Arithmetic Teacher* 26 (February 1979): 35-36, 59. *Getting students involved with data sets that are of genuine interest and concern to the students.*

Landwehr, James M., and Ann E. Watkins. "Stem-and-Leaf Plots." *Mathematics Teacher* 78 (October 1985): 528-532, 537-538. *A method for displaying data.*

Ryoti, Don E. "Computer Corner." *Arithmetic Teacher* 34 (April 1987): 42-44. *Use of computer to process data.*

Saltinski, Ronald. "Graphs and Microcomputers: A Middle School Program." *Arithmetic Teacher* 31 (October 1983): 17-20. *Using the computer to teach about making and reading graphs.*

Shaw, Jean. "Let's Do It: Making Graphs." *Arithmetic Teacher* 31 (January 1984): 7-11. *Organizing data and interpreting results by gathering data from classmates.*

Shaw, Jean. "Let's Do It: Dealing with Data." *Arithmetic Teacher* 31 (May 1984): 9-15. *Experiences with collecting and handling data.*

Shulte, Albert P. "A Case for Statistics." *Arithmetic Teacher* 26 (February 1979): 24. *A rationale for teaching statistics in the elementary and middle school.*

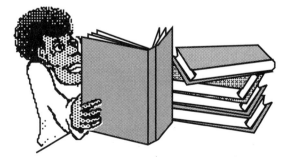

11 Probability

THEME: Using Mathematics to Predict

WARM-UP

Strategy Review:
Use Direct Reasoning.
This strategy was
presented in
Chapter 3.

Guess how this grid is colored.
Row 1 has a yellow, a blue, and a red.
Column 2 has 2 yellows and a red.
Row 2 has 2 greens and a red.
Column 3 has a red, a green, and a blue.
One of the diagonals has 2 reds and a yellow.

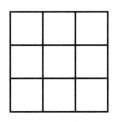

HANDS-ON ACTIVITIES

Probability has useful applications in the sciences, in business, and in sports because it indicates the likelihood of uncertain events. The first few activities introduce you to the concept of probability.

ACTIVITY 1

OBJECTIVE: **Compute experimental and theoretical probability**

You Will Need: Materials Card 11.1

1. One kind of probability is called **experimental probability**. The experimental probability of an event is found by actually performing the experiment several times and then comparing the number of outcomes favorable to the event to the total number of outcomes. In other words, the experimental probability (denoted Pr) of an event E is

$$Pr(E) = \frac{\text{number of outcomes favorable to E}}{\text{total number of outcomes}}$$

For example, cut out one block each of those labeled blue, red, and yellow from Materials Card 11.1. Place them face down on the table and mix them up. Draw one, record its color, and return it to the table face down. Draw a block from the table 10 times, tallying your results below.

BLUE   **RED**   **YELLOW**

The experimental probability of drawing a blue block is

$$Pr(\text{blue}) = \frac{\text{number of times blue was drawn}}{\text{total number of draws}} = \frac{}{10}$$

Determine the following.

a. Pr(red) = _____   b. Pr(yellow) = _____

2. Repeat part 1 and compute the experimental probabilities again.

a. Pr(blue) = _____   b. Pr(red) = _____   c. Pr(yellow) = _____

Do you get the same experimental probabilities?

3. The **theoretical probability** of an event, if all outcomes are equally likely, is found by considering an ideal experiment and comparing the total possible outcomes of an event to the total number of outcomes in the sample space. Consider the blue, red, and yellow blocks again. To determine the theoretical probability (denoted P) of drawing a blue block, we consider how many blocks satisfy the condition "blue" out of the total number of blocks. Since there is one blue block and three blocks altogether, P(blue) = 1/3. Determine the following.

a. P(red) = _____   b. P(yellow) = _____

4. Using all the cubes from Materials Card 11.1, perform the experiment of selecting a cube. Repeat 10 times and compute the following probabilities.

   a. Pr(blue) = ＿＿＿＿ b. Pr(red) = ＿＿＿＿ c. Pr(yellow) = ＿＿＿＿

   d. P(blue) = ＿＿＿＿ e. P(red) = ＿＿＿＿ f. P(yellow) = ＿＿＿＿

 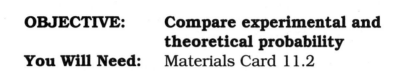

OBJECTIVE: **Compare experimental and theoretical probability**

You Will Need: Materials Card 11.2

1. Look at the circle below. Compute the theoretical probability of landing in each area.

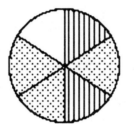

   a. P(plain) = ＿＿＿＿ b. P(striped) = ＿＿＿＿ c. P(dotted) = ＿＿＿＿

2. Now, using the spinner as directed on Materials Card 11.2, spin 10 times and record your spins here.

Plain	
Striped	
Dotted	

   Compute your experimental probability after 10 spins.

   a. Pr(plain) = ＿＿＿＿ b. Pr(striped) = ＿＿＿＿ c. Pr(dotted) = ＿＿＿＿

   Continue spinning and recording 40 more times, then compute the experimental probability again, based on 50 spins.

   d. Pr(plain) = ＿＿＿＿ e. Pr(striped) = ＿＿＿＿ f. Pr(dotted) = ＿＿＿＿

   Which experimental probability most closely resembles the theoretical probability?

OBJECTIVE: **Explore properties of probability**

1. Suppose that a box contains blue, red, and yellow blocks. An experiment consists of drawing a block from the box and recording its color. Suppose that the experiment is repeated 10 times.

    a. What is the fewest number of times that the blue block could have been chosen? _____

        What is the smallest possible value for Pr(blue)? _____

    b. What is the greatest number of times that the blue block could have been chosen? _____

        What is the largest possible value for Pr(blue)? _____

    c. Fill in the blanks.   _____ $\leq$ Pr(blue) $\leq$ _____

2. Suppose that a box contains only red blocks. Compute the following.

    a. Pr(green) = _____   b. Pr(red) = _____

    The event of selecting a green block is an **impossible** event. The event of drawing a red block is a **certain** event.

3. Suppose that a box contains 2 blue blocks, 4 red blocks, and 6 yellow blocks. Compute the following.

    a. P(blue) = _____   b. P(red) = _____   c. P(yellow) = _____

    d. P(blue) + P(red) + P(yellow) = _____

4. Suppose that a box contains 3 blue blocks, 5 green blocks, and 2 red blocks. In how many ways can you select a blue block or a green block? _____

    a. What is P(blue or green)? _____

    Compute the following.

    b. P(blue) = _____   c. P(green) = _____   d. P(blue or green) = _____

    e. In this case, the event of drawing a blue block is disjoint from the event of drawing a green block. Is the following true? _____

        P(blue or green) = P(blue) + P(green)

5. Suppose that a box contains 2 blue blocks, 3 yellow blocks, and 4 red blocks. The event of "not selecting a blue block" is called the **complement** of the event of "selecting a blue block." Compute the following.

   a. P(blue) = _____   b. P(not blue) = _____

   c. P(yellow) = _____   d. P(not yellow) = _____

   e. P(red) = _____   f. P(not red) = _____

   g. How is the probability of the complement of an event related to the probability of the event?

Summarize the properties of probability.

   a. For any event E, _____ $\leq$ P(E) $\leq$ _____

   b. P(impossible event) = _____

   c. P(certain event) = _____

   d. If A and B are disjoint events, then P(A or B) = _____

   e. If $\overline{A}$ denotes the complement of event A, then P($\overline{A}$) = _____

Now that you have computed probabilities for some simple experiments, let's consider some more complicated situations. The next few activities introduce some useful tools for computing probabilities.

OBJECTIVE: **Compute probabilities when tossing dice**

You Will Need: Materials Card 11.4 or a pair of dice

1. Toss your pair of dice 20 times, and tally the sum each time in the table below.

2	3	4	5	6	7	8	9	10	11	12

Compute the probabilities of getting the following sums.

a. Pr(7) = ____   b. Pr(3) = ____   c. Pr(12) = ____

d. Pr(less than 5) = ____   e. Pr(more than 6) = ____

2. Now let's analyze all the outcomes in another way. Fill in the sums in the chart.

Die #1

+	1	2	3	4	5	6
1						
2						
3						
4						
5						
6						

Die #2 (rows 3)

Summarize the number of ways of getting each possible outcome in the table.

Sum	2	3	4	5	6	7	8	9	10	11	12
Number of ways											

This table will come in handy in dice-tossing experiments.

3. Compute the following probabilities.

a. P(7) = ____   b. P(3) = ____   c. P(12) = ____

d. P(less than 5) = ____   e. P(more than 6) = ____

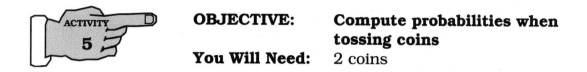

OBJECTIVE: **Compute probabilities when tossing coins**

You Will Need: 2 coins

1. Two coins are tossed 10 times. If there is a match (two heads or two tails), Player 1 gets a point. If there is no match (one head and one tail), player 2 gets 2 points.

    Toss both coins 10 times and record each toss below:

Toss #	1	2	3	4	5	6	7	8	9	10
Match										
No Match										

    Total Matches _____

    Total No Matches _____

    Who won the game?_____

    Based on your experiment, compute the following.

    a. Pr(match) = _____   b. Pr(no match) = _____

2. Now let's compute the theoretical probability of "match" or "no match." First we must count the possible outcomes. A **tree diagram** can be used to represent all possible outcomes when tossing coins.

    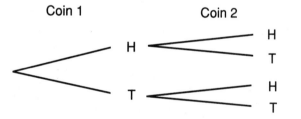

    By following the branches of our tree we see that there are four possible outcomes: { (H,H), (H,T), (T,H), (T,T) } .

    Now compute the theoretical probabilities:

    a. P(match) = _____   b. P(no match) = _____

3. Is this a fair game?_____ How can we make it fair?

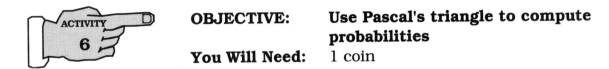

OBJECTIVE: **Use Pascal's triangle to compute probabilities**

You Will Need: 1 coin

1. Toss your coin three times and record how it landed (HTH for example).
    Perform 9 more sets of three tosses until you have recorded ten outcomes. Compute the
    following probabilities.

    a. Pr(exactly 1 head) = ____   b. Pr(at least one head) = _____

    c. Pr(all tails) = _____   d. Pr(less than two tails) = _____

2. Again, a tree diagram is useful in representing all possible outcomes.

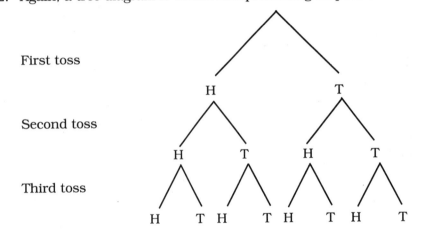

First toss

Second toss

Third toss

List all possible outcomes:

Compute the following probabilities.

    a. P(exactly 1 head) = _____   b. P(at least one head) = _____

    c. P(all tails) = _____   d. P(less than 2 tails) = _____

3. Extend the tree from part 2 to illustrate all the outcomes for tossing the coin 4 times. Complete the following tables.

Toss a coin

	1 time			2 times				3 times					4 times		

Number of H's	0	1		0	1	2		0	1	2	3		0	1	2	3	4
Number of ways	1	1		1	2	1											

4. The lower rows of the tables in part 3 can be arranged to show an array called **Pascal's triangle**. See if you can discover the pattern that yields each row from the entries in the previous row. Hint: Consider the lines drawn.

Pascal's Triangle

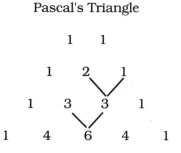

Extend the triangle to the row that begins 1 8 . . . and ends . . . 8 1.

Give an interpretation of that row in terms of a coin-tossing experiment.

5. Using Pascal's triangle, compute the following probabilities.

   a. P(4 heads when tossing 6 coins) = _____

   b. P(at least 5 heads when tossing 8 coins) = _____

   c. P(at least 1 head when tossing 5 coins) = _____
       Hint: Consider the complement.

OBJECTIVE: **Analyze a game using probabilities**

You Will Need: Your dice from Activity 4 and a coin

1. Dennis the delivery boy delivers sandwiches for the local Deli. His boss tells Dennis that he can keep all of the tips from businesses A, B, D and W, Y, Z. He must give his boss all of the tips from businesses C and X. Is the boss making Dennis a fair offer?

A	B	C	D	DELI	W	X	Y	Z

Place your coin on the square marked DELI . The destination of each delivery is determined by rolling a die 4 times. If the roll is odd, move the coin one space to the left. If the roll is even, move the coin one space to the right. Repeat this procedure for four rolls of the die. Record where Dennis made the delivery at the end of 4 rolls (or if he returned to the deli for directions and no tip). This constitutes one turn. Take 10 turns.

NOTE: Always place the coin back on the square marked DELI after a turn of 4 rolls is completed.

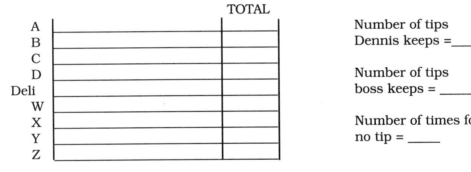

TOTAL

Number of tips
Dennis keeps =_____

Number of tips
boss keeps = _____

Number of times for
no tip = _____

Is this a fair deal for Dennis? _____   Why or why not?

2. Let's list all the possible outcomes of 4 rolls of the dice:

No Evens	1 Even	2 Evens	3 Evens	4 Evens
OOOO	EOOO	EEOO	EEEO	EEEE
	OEOO	EOEO	EEOE	
	OOEO	EOOE	EOEE	
	OOOE	OEEO	OEEE	
		OEOE		
		OOEE		

To compute the theoretical probability of landing on each business, follow each possible turn and place a tally mark where the delivery was made (i.e. the square you land on at the end of 4 rolls). Compute the following probabilities.

a. P(keeping tip) =_____   b. P(giving tip to boss) =_____   c. P(no tip) = _____

Is Dennis's boss fair? ____ Explain.

OBJECTIVE: **Compute expected value**

You Will Need: Your dice from Activity 4

1. In a certain gambling casino, a player rolls two dice. He wins $5 if he rolls a 7 or an 11 and loses $1 if he throws anything else. Play the game for 36 throws to see who has the advantage, the player or the casino. Record your throws here:

    [grid with columns labeled: 2 3 4 5 6 7 8 9 10 11 12]

    a. The total number of 7's and 11's
       _____ × $5 = Player's winnings
       _____

    b. The total number of all other
       throws = Casino's winnings
       _____

    Based on your experiment, who will come out ahead?_____

2. Using the chart you made in Activity 4, compute the following probabilities.

    a. P(7) = _____   b. P(11) = _____   c. P(7 or 11) = _____

3. Complete the following table.

	Win (7 or 11)	Lose
Outcome	$5.00	-$1.00
Probability		

    Compute: (Amount won) × P(win) + (Amount lost) × P(lose) = _____

    This is called the **expected value** of the payoff. Do you, the player, come out ahead, or does the casino? How is this related to the expected value of the payoff?

4. Repeat part 3, assuming that a loss costs $2.00. Who comes out ahead now?

OBJECTIVE: **Do a simulation**

You Will Need: A coin and a die

1. Frank and Hazel are lost in the University Library. Frank likes history and Hazel likes poetry. They must stay together since only Hazel has a library card. The library is set up like a maze because Franny, the librarian loves to play tricks on people. Frank and Hazel are now at Point A. At points A, B, C, and D, all choices are equally likely.

   Where do you predict Frank and Hazel will end up - in the history section or the poetry section?

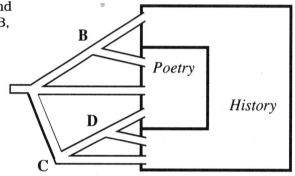

2. To simulate this experiment, roll the die at point A. If it lands with 1 or 2, go up; if it lands 3 or 4, go straight; if 5 or 6, go down. At points B, C, and D, flip the coin. Go up if head, down if tail. Perform this simulation 10 times. Record the destination each time.

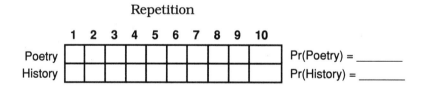

Repetition

	1	2	3	4	5	6	7	8	9	10	
Poetry											Pr(Poetry) = _____
History											Pr(History) = _____

3. We can use a tree diagram to determine the theoretical probability of ending in the poetry or history section.

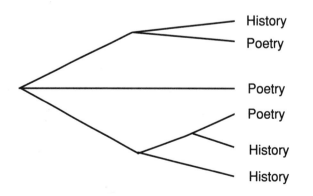

History
Poetry
Poetry
Poetry
History
History

Place the appropriate probabilities along each branch of the tree. To find the probability of following any particular path, multiply the probabilities of the branches covered.

a. How many of the paths end in the history section? ____

    What is the sum of the probabilities for those paths? ____

b. How many of the paths end in the poetry section? ____

    What is the sum of the probabilities for those paths? ____

c. Which destination is more likely?

MENTAL MATH

Fern, the school cook, surveyed 20 students to determine their favorite lunch. The results of her survey were:

HAMBURGERS	10
HOT DOGS	5
PIZZA	3
FISHWICH	2

She wants to please everyone once in a while. What is the probability that a student will be smiling when he comes through the lunch line on Hot Dog Day? _____

on Hamburger Day? _____   on Fishwich Day? _____

What is the probability he will *not* be smiling on Pizza Day? _____

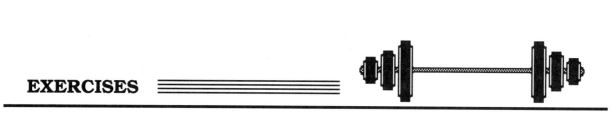

EXERCISES

What do you get when you cross an owl with an oyster?

For each problem below, find the correct answer. Write the letter of that answer on the line above the problem number it matches at the bottom of the page.
Use the answers below to complete problems 1 - 4.

B 1/2   **V** 1/4   **A** 1/3   **C** 7/12   **L** 2/3   **J** 3/4   **F** 1/6   **U** 5/12

Look at this spinner. If the arrow is spun, what is the probability that it will stop on a number that is

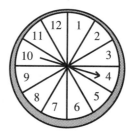

1. a multiple of 2?
2. a multiple of 3?
3. a multiple of 2 *and* a multiple of 3?
4. a multiple of 2 *or* a multiple of 3?

Use the answers below to complete problems 5 - 18.

H 7/15   **O** 1/3   **I** 2/5   **W** 1/15

T 2/15   **P** 3/5   **S** 4/15   **K** 11/15

R 2/3   **M** 8/15   **E** 1/5   **D** 4/5

G 1   **Y** 1/2   **N** 0   **Q** 1/4

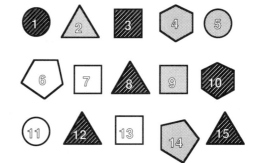

If a card is picked at random from the group of cards above, what is the probability that the card

5. is hexagonal (six-sided)?
6. is dotted?
7. has more than 4 sides *and* is not white?
8. is striped?
9. is triangular?
10. is a multiple of 3 *or* square?
11. is not dotted?

12. is even *or* dotted?
13. is odd?
14. is dotted *and* pentagonal (five-sided)?
15. is not circular?
16. is not triangular?
17. is dotted *or* striped *or* white?
18. is odd *and* a multiple of 2?

— — — — —   — — — —
2   1 8 11 15   5 10 2 5

— — — — —   — — — — — — — —   — — — — — —
16 7 7 12 9   15 11 6 12 12 8 18 17   12 7 2 11 4 9

— — — — — — — — !
6   3   14 8 9 15 6 13

SELF-TEST

1. If you have 3 sweaters, 4 skirts, and 5 pairs of shoes, how many different sweater/skirt/ (pairs of) shoes combinations can you wear?

   a. 60   b. 12   c. $(3^4)^5$ d. None of a, b, or c.

2. The sample space of the experiment "tossing 3 coins" consists of how many elements?

   a. 6   b. 27   c. 8   d. 9

3. Which of the following is the tree diagram for the experiment "toss 4 coins"?

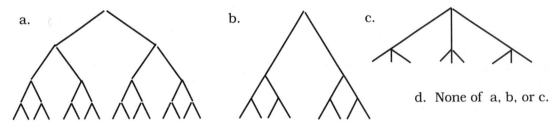

   d. None of a, b, or c.

4. Which of the sample spaces for the following experiments consists of an odd number of elements?

   a. Tossing 3 dice.   b. Tossing 7 coins.
   c. Drawing a card from a 52-card deck.   d. None of a, b, or c.

5. The probability of tossing at least two heads if six coins are tossed is:

   a. 27/32   b. 15/16   c. 57/64   d. None of a, b, or c.

6. Find the probability of getting exactly 2 heads and a number greater than 8 when tossing 3 coins and 2 dice.

   a. 13/44   b. 5/12   c. 5/48   d. 13/36

7. What is the probability of getting 100% on a multiple choice (a,b,c,d) math quiz? There are 12 questions and you guess on all 12 of them.

   a. $\dfrac{1}{12^4}$ b. $\dfrac{1}{4^{12}}$ c. $\dfrac{1}{4}$ d. $\dfrac{1}{48}$

8. There are 26 names in a hat, 13 girls' names, and 13 guys' names. What is the probability that 2 girls' names will be drawn?

   a. 4/25   b. 1/4   c. 6/25   d. 1/3

9. If two cubes have the numbers 1, 2, 3, and 4 on each of four sides leaving the other two sides with 0, what is the probability of getting an even number as a sum on the two cubes?

   a. 1   b. 5/9   c.   1/3   d. None of a, b, or c.

10. The odds that the horse Apollo 1000 wins Race 1 are 4 : 5, and the odds that he wins Race 6 are 11 : 3. What is the probability that he wins Race 1 and comes back to win Race 6 also?

   a. $\frac{4}{5} + \frac{3}{11}$ b. $\frac{4}{5} \times \frac{3}{11}$ c. $\frac{4}{9} \times \frac{11}{14}$ d. $\frac{4}{9} + \frac{3}{14}$

SOLUTIONS

Warm-up

B Y R
G R G
Y Y B

Hands-on Activities

Activity 1
1. Answers will vary.
2. Anwers will vary and may differ from results in part 1.
3. a. 1/3   b. 1/3
4. Experimental probabilities will vary.   d. 1/2   e. 3/8   f. 1/8

Activity 2
1. a. 1/6   b. 1/3   c. 1/2
2. Answers will vary. Generally, experimental probability will be closer to theoretical probability after more repetitions.

Activity 3
1. a. Zero times, 0   b. 10 times, 1   c. 0, 1
2. a. 0   b. 1
3. a. 1/6   b. 1/3   c. 1/2   d. 1
4. 8 ways   a. 4/5   b. 3/10   c. 1/2   d. 4/5   e. yes
5. a. 2/9   b. 7/9   c. 1/3   d. 2/3   e. 4/9   f. 5/9
   g. P(complement of event E) = 1 - P(event E)
   Summarize: a. 0, 1   b. 0   c. 1   d. P(A) + P(B)   e. 1 - P(A)

Activity 4

1. Answers will vary.
2. Usual addition table
   1 2 3 4 5 6 5 4 3 2 1
3. a. 6/36 = 1/6   b. 1/18   c. 1/36   d. 1/6   e. 7/12

Activity 5

1. Answers will vary.
2. a. 1/2   b. 1/2
3. No. Give an equal number of points for match and no match.

Activity 6

1. Answers will vary.
2. HHH, HHT, HTH, HTT, THH, THT, TTH, TTT   a. 3/8   b. 7/8   c. 1/8   d. 1/2
3. 1, 3, 3, 1; 1, 4, 6, 4, 1
4. Add the two elements of the row above.
   Next rows: 1, 5, 10, 10, 5, 1; 1, 6, 15, 20, 15, 6, 1;
   1, 7, 21, 35, 35, 21, 7, 1; 1, 8, 28, 56, 70, 56, 28, 8, 1;
   There is 1 way of getting no heads, 8 ways of getting 1 head and 7 tails, 28 ways of getting 2 heads and 6 tails, etc. when tossing 8 coins.
5. a. 15/64   b. 93/256   c. 31/32

Activity 7

1. Answers will vary.
2. a. 1/8   b. 1/2   c. 3/8
   No. Dennis will only keep the tip for 2 out of 16 deliveries.

Activity 8

1. Answers will vary.
2. a. 1/6   b. 1/18   c. 2/9
3. 2/9, 7/9, (2/9) × (5) + (7/9) × (-1) = 1/3 = \$0.33
   The player comes out ahead by an average of \$0.33 per game.
4. (2/9) × (5) + (7/9) × (-2) = -4/9 = - \$0.44; The casino gains an average of \$0.44 per game.

Activity 9

1. Answers will vary.
2. Answers will vary.
3. a. 3 paths, 5/12   b. 3 paths, 7/12   c. Poetry

Mental Math

Hot Dog = 1/4; Hamburger = 1/2; Fishwich = 1/10; Not smiling on Pizza = 17/20

Exercises

What do you get when you cross an owl with an oyster?
A bird that keeps dropping pearls of wisdom!

Self-Test

1. a   **2.** c   **3.** a   **4.** d   **5.** c   **6.** c   **7.** b   **8.** c   **9.** b   **10.** c

RESOURCE ARTICLES

Bruni, James V., and Helene J. Silverman. "Developing Concepts in Probability and Statistics - and Much More." *Arithmetic Teacher* 33 (February 1986): 34-37. *A four-step approach using manipulatives to develop probability concepts.*

Ernest, Paul. "Introducing the Concept of Probability." *Mathematics Teacher* 77 (October 1984): 524-525. *An intuitive approach to probability.*

Fennell, Francis (Skip). "Ya Gotta Play to Win: A Probability and Statistics Unit for the Middle Grades." *Arithmetic Teacher* 31 (March 1984): 26-30. *Relating probability, statistics, and particularly gaming to the curriculum in grades 5-8.*

Haigh, William E. "Using Microcomputers to Solve Probability Problems." *Mathematics Teacher* 78 (February 1985): 124-126. *Using the computer to simulate or imitate probability problems.*

Horak, Virginia M., and Willis J. Horak. "Let's Do It: Take a Chance." *Arithmetic Teacher* 30 (May 1983): 8-15. *Introducing children to the basic ideas of probability.*

Jones, Graham. "A Case for Probability." *Arithmetic Teacher* 26 (February 1979): 37, 57. *A rationale for inclusion of probability in the mathematics curriculum.*

Ott, Jack A. "Who's Going to Win the Playoff?" *Mathematics Teacher* 78 (October 1985): 559-563. *A real world probability activity.*

Santulli, Tom. "Playing with Probability." *Mathematics Teacher* 76 (October 1983): 494-496. *An introductory probability activity.*

Shulte, Albert P. "Research Report: Learning Probability Concepts in Elementary School Mathematics." *Arithmetic Teacher* 34 (January 1987): 32-33. *Research findings concerning elementary school student's understanding of probability.*

Swift, Jim. "Challenges for Enriching the Curriculum: Statistics and Probability." *Mathematics Teacher* 76 (April 1983): 268-269. *A series of challenge problems for junior high and high school.*

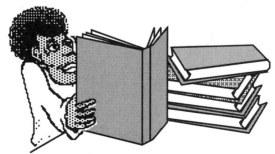

12 | Geometric Shapes

THEME: Analyzing Geometric Shapes

Strategy Review:
Use Direct Reasoning.
This strategy was
introduced in
Chapter 3 of the text.

Guess My Number!
$n > 25$
n is odd
n is not prime
$n < 75$
Sum of digits = 9
The tens digit is a multiple
of the ones digit.

What is the number?_____

HANDS-ON ACTIVITIES

The activities in this chapter will help you recognize, reason about, and analyze
geometric shapes. This first activity is a warm-up to sharpen your skills in
visual thinking.

OBJECTIVE: **Use visual cues to reason about shapes**

1. Each set of dots below can be connected to form these two shapes:

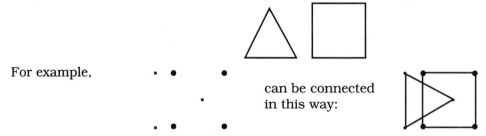

For example,   can be connected in this way:

Connect each set of dots to form these two shapes. (They must be the same size as the examples.)

a.

b.

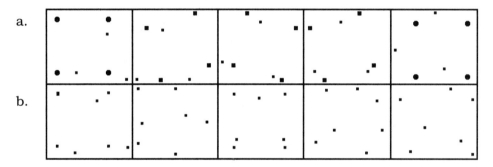

You should have found a square and a triangle in each box.

2. Each shape given below was built from two puzzle pieces.

For example:

Shade part of each shape to show how the pieces fit together.

a.

b.

c.

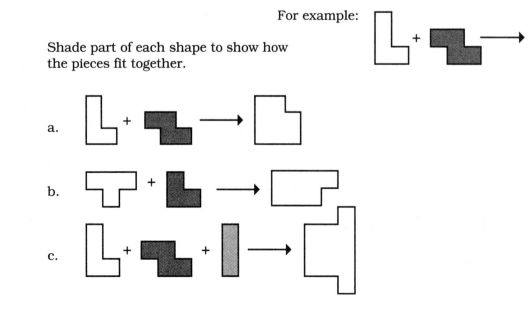

3. In each of these pictures a mirror line has been drawn. Everything on one side of the mirror will appear to be on the other side, too, but in reverse or mirror image. Put in everything exactly as it would appear in the mirror. For example:

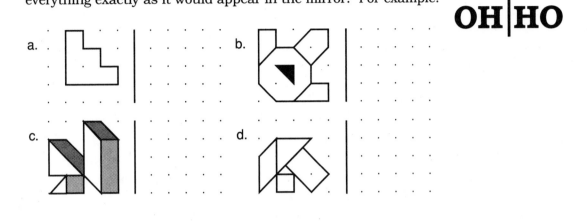

The next two activities involve constructing geometric shapes on a geoboard or on dot paper.

OBJECTIVE: **Construct triangles on a geoboard**

You Will Need: A geoboard (optional)

1. A triangle that has two or more sides the same length is called an **isosceles** triangle. This triangle is an isosceles triangle:

   Using your geoboard, make 5 different isosceles triangles.
   Record them here:

2. A triangle that has no two sides the same length is called a **scalene** triangle. This is a scalene triangle:

   Use your geoboard to construct 5 different scalene triangles.
   Record them here:

3. A triangle that has one right angle is a **right** triangle.   right angle
    This is a right triangle:

    Construct 5 different right triangles. Record them here:

ACTIVITY 3

OBJECTIVE: **Construct quadrilaterals on a geoboard**

You Will Need: Materials Card 12.3

1. A **quadrilateral** is a polygon with four sides. A **square** is a special quadrilateral with four sides the same length and four right angles.   How many squares of different sizes can you construct on a 5 by 5 geoboard?_____

    Use Materials Card 12.3 to record your squares.

2. A **rectangle** is a quadrilateral with four right angles. How many rectangles of different sizes can you construct on a 5 by 5 geoboard?_____ (Don't forget to include your squares from part 1.) Record your rectangles on Materials Card 12.3.

3. A quadrilateral with its opposite sides parallel is a **parallelogram**. How many parallelograms of different sizes can you construct on a 5 by 5 geoboard? _____ Record your parallelograms on Materials Card 12.3. Can you include the squares from part 1 and the rectangles from part 2? Why or why not?

4. A **rhombus** is a quadrilateral with four sides the same length. Construct a rhombus on your geoboard. Record it here:

    Construct each of these figures on your geoboard. Mark an X on each rhombus.

    a.   b.   c.   d.   e.

5. A **kite** is a quadrilateral with 2 pairs of adjacent nonoverlapping sides the same length. Figure (d) in part 4 is a kite. Construct a kite on your geoboard. Record it here:

6. A **trapezoid** is a quadrilateral with exactly one pair of parallel sides. This is a trapezoid: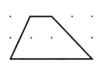

Construct each of these figures on your geoboard. Mark an X on each figure that is a trapezoid.

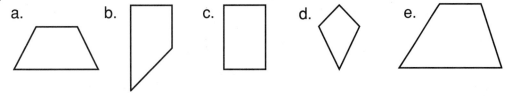

a. b. c. d. e.

The first activities helped you recognize shapes. In this next activity you will be looking at specific attributes of various shapes.

OBJECTIVE: **Analyze shapes**

You Will Need: Materials Card 12.4

1. Cut out the shapes on Materials Card 12.4. Find all of the shapes that are triangles. Draw them here:

2. Find all of the shapes that are quadrilaterals. Draw them here:

3. Find all of the shapes that have one or more pairs of sides congruent (same length). Draw them here:

4. Find all of the shapes that have at least one right angle. Draw them here:

5. Find all the shapes that have at least two congruent angles (same measure). Draw them here:

6. A figure that can be reflected across a mirror line so that one side of its outline exactly fits on the other side has **reflection symmetry**. This figure has reflection symmetry:

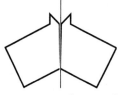

Find all of the figures that have one or more lines of reflection symmetry. Draw them here. Hint: You can fold to check. Draw the line of symmetry on each figure.

Do some figures have more than one line of reflection symmetry? _____ Draw them here:

Which figure has the most lines of reflection symmetry? _____
Explain why.

The tangram puzzle serves as the basis of the next activity
which asks you to explore a variety of shapes.

   **OBJECTIVE:**   **Use tangram pieces to form
                                        polygons**
            You Will Need: Materials Card 12.5

1. Cut out the tangram puzzle on Materials Card 12.5. Use the pieces to complete the chart
    below. For example, you can construct a square from 3 tangram pieces as illustrated in the
    chart already.

NUMBER OF TANGRAM PIECES USED	TRIANGLE	SQUARE	RECTANGLE	PARALLELOGRAM	TRAPEZOID	PENTAGON *	HEXAGON *
1							
2					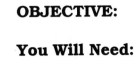		
3		▧				⌂	
4							
5							
6							
7							

*These might not be regular polygons (congruent sides and congruent vertex angles).

Are some boxes impossible to fill using the tangram pieces? You might check with other
students and compare your findings.

The next activity will help you gain insight about the measure of the vertex angles of regular polygons. A **regular polygon** has all sides and all vertex angles congruent.

OBJECTIVE: **Determine the sum of the vertex angles of polygons**

You Will Need: Materials Card 12.6

1. Cut out the triangle on Materials Card 12.6. Tear off the 3 corners (vertex angles) of the triangle as indicated by the dotted lines. Arrange them side by side as illustrated.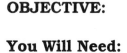

   Notice that the sides of angles 1 and 3 form a straight line. What does this tell you about the sum of the angles?

2. Use the upper right portion of Materials Card 12.6 to draw and then cut out a different triangle. Repeat part one. Describe the result.

3. Now draw any quadrilateral using the bottom portion of Materials Card 12.6. Tear off the vertex angles and arrange as above. Draw your findings here.

   What does this tell you about the sum of the angles?

4. You have found that the sum of the vertex angles of a triangle is 180°. Notice that the diagonal from one vertex of a quadrilateral to the non-adjacent vertex divides the quadrilateral into two triangles. The sum of the angles of these two triangles is 360°, which is also the sum of the vertex angles of the quadrilateral.

   We can use this technique to determine the sum of the vertex angles of any polygon. First draw all possible diagonals from the vertex marked by the arrow to all non-adjacent vertices.

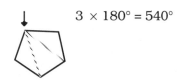

          $3 \times 180° = 540°$ $4 \times 180° = 720°$

Then, find the number of triangles formed. Multiply the number of triangles by 180° to find the sum of the angle measures.

Find the sum of the angle measures for each of these polygons:

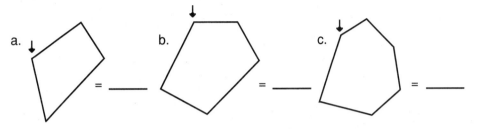

a. = _____   b. = _____   c. = _____

A **tessellation** is a covering of the plane with one or more shapes so that there are no gaps and no overlaps. In the next two activities, we will investigate tessellations with regular polygons of the same size.

OBJECTIVE: **Form tessellations with regular polygons**

You Will Need: Materials Card 12.7, scratch paper

1. Cut out the models of the regular polygons on Materials Card 12.7. Take the triangle and try to tessellate a plain sheet of paper. Trace around the model, making sure the sides of the polygons meet exactly.

   permitted   not permitted

   Remember that the page must be covered completely with no gaps or overlappings (the borders do not matter). Can this be done with the triangle? _____

2. Try the same thing with the square, pentagon, hexagon, octagon, decagon, and dodecagon. Will all of the polygons tessellate? _____
   Which ones will? Which will not?

You have discovered that certain regular polygons tessellate. Using that information in the next activity, we will investigate tessellations with other triangles and quadrilaterals.

OBJECTIVE: **Investigate other tessellations**

You Will Need: Materials Card 12.8, scratch paper

1. Cut out the isosceles triangle on Materials Card 12.8. Will it tessellate? Do the same with each of the other shapes.

2. Which of the shapes will tessellate?

Which will not?

Write a statement that summarizes tessellating with triangles or quadrilaterals.

The last activity in this chapter deals with three-dimensional shapes called polyhedra.

OBJECTIVE: **Build models of polyhedra**

You Will Need: Materials Card 12.9, plain paper, scissors, and paper clips or tape.

1. Cut out the circle patterns on Materials Card 12.9. Find the pattern that has a square on it. Make 6 copies of this pattern. Fold each circle on the dotted lines as illustrated.

Cube

Put the 6 squares together to form a cube. The flaps will be on the outside so that you can paper clip or tape the squares together. Notice that every face of the cube is a square.

2. A **regular polyhedron** (plural is polyhedra) is one in which all faces are identical regular polygonal regions and each vertex is surrounded by the same arrangement of polygons. Use the other polygon patterns to make the following regular polyhedra.

Make 2 polyhedra with triangular faces (one with 4 triangles and one with 8 triangles).

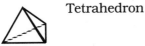 Tetrahedron

 Octahedron

Make a polyhedron with 12 pentagonal faces.

 Dodecahedron

3. A **semiregular polyhedron** is one constructed from regular polygonal regions of more than one type such that each vertex is surrounded by the same arrangement of polygons.

Make the following polyhedron with 8 triangles and 6 squares. Each vertex is surrounded by a triangle-square-triangle-square arrangement.

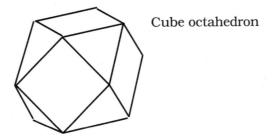 Cube octahedron

4. An interesting relationship exists between the number of faces, vertices, and edges of a polyhedron. Using the models you have made, complete the following table.

	Faces (F)	Vertices (V)	Edges (E)
Cube			
Tetrahedron			
Octahedron			
Dodecahedron			
Cube octahedron			

What relationship do you observe? Hint: Add another column with F + V.

MENTAL MATH

It is possible to make one straight cut in each of these shapes so that the two pieces will form a square.

For example:

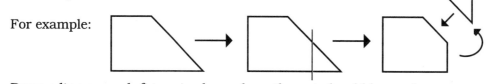

Draw a line on each figure to show where the cut should be made:

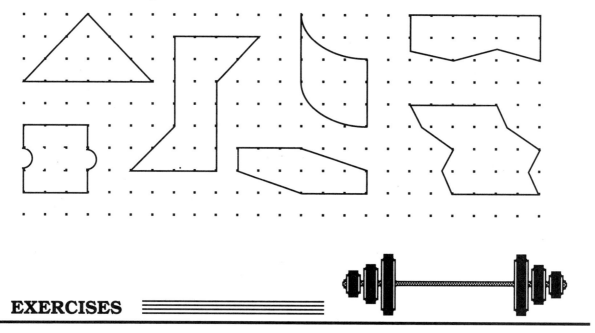

EXERCISES

Crossword Geometry

ACROSS

2. Consists of all points between A and B on line $\overleftrightarrow{AB}$, together with A and B.
5. A quadrilateral with four sides the same length.
7. Given two lines and a transversal, the angles on opposite sides of the transversal and interior to the lines are called _____ interior angles.
10. The set of points in three-dimensional space equidistant from a fixed point.
12. A quadrilateral with two pairs of parallel sides.
15. Formed by connecting each point of a circle to a point in space.
16. A quadrilateral that is both a rectangle and a rhombus.
17. Given two points in the plane, there is a unique _____ that contains them.
19. Three or more points that lie on the same line are called_____.
20. Union of two line segments or rays with a common endpoint.
21. Angle $\angle POQ$ of a polygon where P and Q are consecutive vertices and O is the center.

24. Polyhedron with two parallel opposite faces that are identical polygons and rectangular lateral faces.
26. A polygon has _____ _____ if there is a point within the polygon around which the polygon can be turned, less that 360° so that the turned image matches the original polygon perfectly.

DOWN

1. The sum of the measures of the vertex angles in a triangle is 180 _____.
3. A polygon with 3 straight sides.
4. A pentagon has _____sides.
6. Set of all points in the plane that are a fixed, constant distance from a given point.
8. Angles formed by 2 intersecting lines that have only a vertex in common.
9. A triangle with 2 or 3 sides of the same length.
10. A triangle with sides of unequal lengths.
11. The angle that forms a straight angle with the vertex angle of a polygon.
13. A quadrilateral with 4 right angles.
14. A tool, marked from 0° to 180°, that is useful in measuring angles.
18. Union of line segments forming a closed figure, where two segments intersect only at endpoints.
19. Analogous to prism, except has circular bases.
22. A location in the plane that has no size.
23. An angle measuring less than 90°.
25. Part of line $\overleftrightarrow{CD}$ that consists of point C and all points on the same side of C as point D.

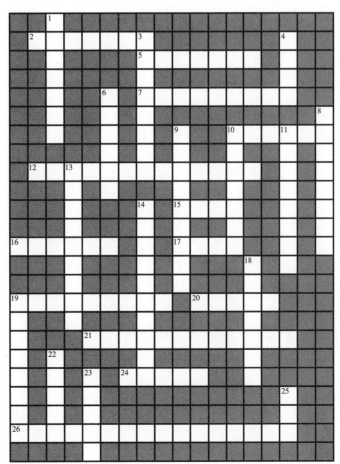

Plane Slices

Each figure below is sawed in two by the plane indicated. Match the figure with the resulting cross section. Put the letter from the answer in the blank below that is numbered the same as the problem.

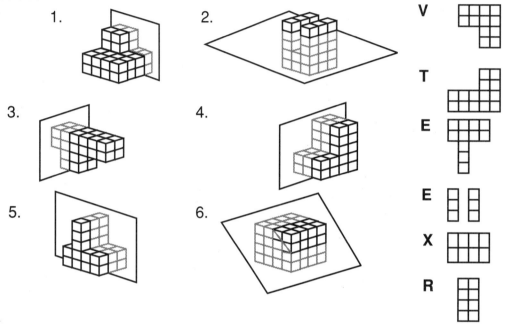

What the heroine said when the cowboy rescued her just as she was about to be sawed in two.

If it weren't ___ ___ ___ ___ ___ ___ I would have been bisected!
　　　　　　　1　2　3　4　5　6

SELF-TEST

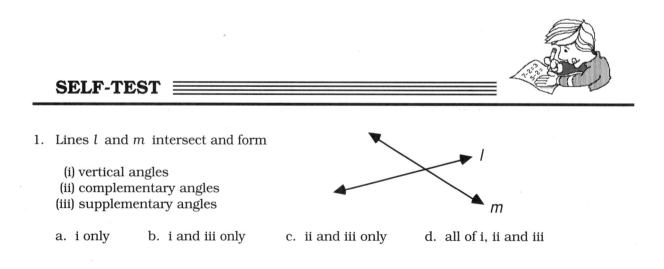

1. Lines *l* and *m* intersect and form

   (i) vertical angles
   (ii) complementary angles
   (iii) supplementary angles

   a. i only　　　b. i and iii only　　　c. ii and iii only　　　d. all of i, ii and iii

2. Add up the number of lines of reflection symmetry and the number of centers of rotation symmetry for this regular polygon.

   a. 5   b. 6   c. 10   d. 11

3. A certain parallelogram has congruent diagonals (same length). Which of the following must it be?

   a. rectangle   b. rhombus   c. kite   d. None of a, b, or c.

4. Which of the following is (are) true?

   (i) If a figure is a rectangle, then it is also a parallelogram.
   (ii) If a figure is a rhombus, then it is also a square.
   (iii) If a figure is a square, then it is a rectangle and a rhombus.

   a. i and ii only   b. i and iii only   c. ii and iii only   d. i, ii, and iii

5. Which of the following regular polygons could *not* be used to tile a floor?

   a. 3-gon   b. 4-gon   c. 5-gon   d. 6-gon

6. Which of these polygons always has rotational symmetry (through an angle less than 360°)?

   (i) parallelogram   (ii) rectangle   (iii) trapezoid

   a. i and ii only   b. i and iii only   c. ii and iii only   d. None of a, b, or c.

7. Which of the following is the largest?

   a. Measure of a vertex angle of a regular 5-gon.
   b. Measure of a vertex angle of a regular 10-gon.
   c. Measure of a central angle of a regular 3-gon.
   d. Measure of a central angle of a regular 6-gon.

8. Which regular polygon has a vertex angle sum of 900°?

   a. 5-gon   b. 7-gon   c. 9-gon   d. None of a, b, or c.

9. How many faces in total does a hexagonal prism have?

   a. 6   b. 7   c. 8   d. None of a, b, or c.

10. How many edges in total does a pentagonal pyramid have?

   a. 7   b. 10   c. 15   d. None of a, b, or c.

SOLUTIONS

Warm-up
63

Hands-on Activities

Activity 1

1. a.
    b.

2. a.   b.   c.

3. a.   b.   c.   d.

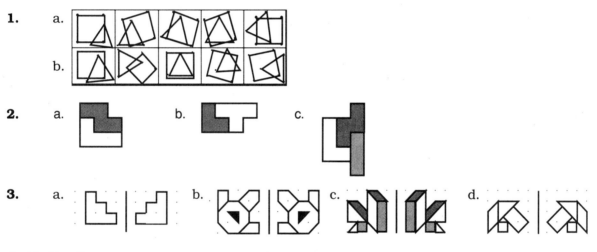

Activity 2
Answers may vary.

Activity 3
1. 8

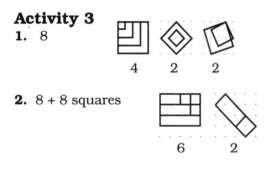

    4   2   2

2. 8 + 8 squares

    6   2

3. 31 + 8 squares and 8 rectangles

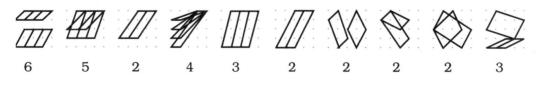

    6   5   2   4   3   2   2   2   2   3

Yes, they have parallel opposite sides .

4. a, b, e
5. Answers may vary.
6. a, b, e

Activity 4

1. a, d, e, g, v
2. b, c, f, h, o, s, t, w, y
3. a, b, c, e, f, h, j, k, m, n, o, q, s, t, u, w, x
4. e, f, g, h, q, t, u, y
5. a, b, c, e, f, h, j, k, m, n, o, q, s, t, u, w, y
6. a, b, c, e, f, h, i, j, k, l, m, n, p, q, r, s, u, w, x, z; Yes, a, b, f, h, i, j, k, m, n, p, r, w, z
    The circle has an infinite number of lines of symmetry.

Activity 5

Answers may vary.

Activity 6

1. Sum is 180°.
2. Sum is also 180°.
3. 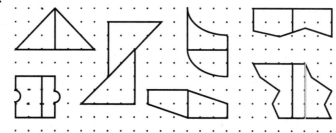   Sum is 360°.

4. a. 360°   b. 540°   c. 720°

Activity 7

1. Yes
2. No; square, hexagon will; the rest will not

Activity 8

1. Yes
2. They all tessellate the plane.
    It is possible to tessellate the plane with any triangle or quadrilateral.

Activity 9

4. Cube   6   8   12
    Tetrahedron   4   4   6
    Octahedron   8   6   12
    Dodecahedron   12   20   30
    Cube octahedron   14   12   24
    F + V = E + 2   This is called Euler's Formula (pronounced "oiler's")

Mental Math

Exercises
Crossword Geometry

```
            D
    S E G M E N T                    F
      G         R H O M B U S        I
      R         I                    V
      E     C   A L T E R N A T E    E
      E     I   N                    V
      S     R   G       S P H E R E  E
            C   L       C        X   R
    P A R A L L E L O G R A M    T   T
      E     E   S       L        E   I
      C   P   C O N E   R        I   C
      T     R   E       N        O   A
    S Q U A R E O L I N E    P   R   L
            A   T   E        R   O
            N   R   S        O
    C O L L I N E A R   A N G L E
    Y     E     C           Y
    L   C E N T R A L A N G L E
    I   P         O           O
    N   O   A   P R I S M     N
    D   I   C               R
    E   N   U               A
    R O T A T I O N S Y M M E T R Y
            E
```

Plane Slices
VERTEX

Self-Test
1. b   2. b   3. a   4. b   5. c   6. a   7. b   8. b   9. c   10. b

RESOURCE ARTICLES

Bledsoe, Gloria. "Guessing Geometric Shapes." Mathematics Teacher 80 (March 1987): 178-180. Activity focusing on distinguishing features of geometric figures.

Brown, Susan A. "Drawing Altitudes of Triangles." Mathematics Teacher 78 (March 1985): 182-183. Using graph paper to develop the concept of altitude of a triangle.

Burger, William F. "Geometry." Arithmetic Teacher 32 (February 1985): 52-56. How to develop geometric reasoning through the study of two-dimensional shapes.

Butzow, John W. "Y is for Yacht Race: A Game of Angles." Arithmetic Teacher 33 (January 1986): 44-48. Game approach for teaching concept of angle.

Campbell, Patricia F. "Cardboard, Rubber Bands, and Polyhedron Models." *Arithmetic Teacher* 31 (October 1983): 48-52. *Constructing three-dimensional models.*

Clements, Douglas C., and Michael Battista. "Geometry and Geometric Measurement." *Arithmetic Teacher* 33 (February 1986): 29-32. *Illustrates use of manipulatives in geometry.*

Esbenshade, Donald H., Jr. "Adding Dimension to Flatland: A Novel Approach to Geometry." *Mathematics Teacher* 76 (February 1983): 120-123. *Expanding students' perceptions of geometry.*

Hollingsworth, Caroline. "Perplexed by Hexed." *Mathematics Teacher* 77 (October 1984): 560-562. *An exploration with pentominoes.*

Hollingsworth, Caroline. "Polyominoes: An Unsolved Problem." *Mathematics Teacher* 78 (May 1985): 364-365. *Looking for patterns using polyominoes.*

Horak, Virginia M., and Willis J. Horak. "Let's Do It: Using Geometry Tiles As a Manipulative for Developing Basic Concepts." *Arithmetic Teacher* 30 (April 1983): 8-15. *Developing and extending beginning geometric concepts.*

Kennedy, Leonard M. "Geometry— More Than a Holiday Prelude." *Arithmetic Teacher* 33 (September 1985): 2. *Expanding elementary teachers' notion of geometry instruction.*

Kerr, Donald R., Jr. "A Case for Geometry: Geometry is Important, It is There, Teach It." *Arithmetic Teacher* 26 (February 1979): 14. *A rationale for the teaching of geometry.*

Kolnowski Linda, W., and Joann King Okey. "Ideas: See Shapes Book, What's Your Shape? and Puzzling Polygons." *Arithmetic Teacher* 34 (April 1987): 26-31. *Activities exploring shapes.*

Lappan, Glenda, Elizabeth A. Phillips, and Mary Jean Winter. "Spatial Visualization." *Mathematics Teacher* 77 (November 1984): 618-625. *Activities improving students' ability to visualize by building, drawing, and evaluating three-dimensional shapes.*

Maletsky, Evan M. "Generating Solids." *Mathematics Teacher* 76 (October 1983): 499-500, 505-507. *Activities for visualizing, identifying, and describing the solids generated by rotating polygons about axes.*

Mansfield, Helen. "Projective Geometry in the Elementary School." *Arithmetic Teacher* 32 (March 1985): 15-19. *Developing spatial skills and understanding.*

Mathematics Teacher 78 (September 1985). A special issue focusing on geometry. Includes the following articles: "Geometry in the Junior High School." by Fernand J. Prevost; "Spadework Prior to Deduction in Geometry." by J. Michael Shaughnessy and William F. Burger; "Sharing Teaching Ideas." by Catherine Folio, Andrew A. Zucker, Steven R. Lay; "How Well Do Students Write Geometry Proofs?" by Sharon L. Senk; "Logic for Algebra: New Logic for Old Geometry." by Kenneth A. Retzer; "A Piagetian Approach to Transformations Geometry via Microworlds." by Patrick W. Thompson; "Microworlds: Options for Learning and Teaching Geometry." by Joseph F. Aieta; "The Shape of Instruction in Geometry: Some Highlights from Research." by Marilyn N. Suydam; " Geometry in the '90's." by Jay Greenwood; "Informal Geometry— More is Needed." by Philip L. Cox.

Moser, James M. "How Many Triangles?" *Mathematics Teacher* 78 (November 1985): 598-604. *A geoboard exploration.*

Ockenga, Earl, and Joan Duea. "Ideas." *Arithmetic Teacher* 31 (January 1984): 28-32. *Activities with shapes.*

Olson, Melfried, and Judith Olson. "Triangles, Rectangles, and Parallelograms." *Mathematics Teacher* 76 (February 1983): 112-117. *Activities for observing relationships between triangles and quadrilaterals.*

Renshaw, Barbara S. "Symmetry the Trademark Way." *Arithmetic Teacher* 34 (September 1986): 6-12. *Teaching line and rotational symmetry using familiar trademarks.*

Silverman, Helene. "Geometry in the Primary Grades: Exploring Geometric Ideas in the Primary Grades." *Arithmetic Teacher* 26 (February 1979): 15-16. *Introducing geometric concepts in the primary grades.*

Troccolo, Joseph A. "The Rhombus Construction Company." *Mathematics Teacher* 76 (January 1983): 37-42. *Activities exploring properties of symmetry of geometric figures.*

Turner, Sandra. "Windowpane Patterns." *Mathematics Teacher* 76 (September 1983): 411-413, 428. *A computerized challenge in finding rectangles.*

Usiskin, Zalman. "Enrichment Activities for Geometry." *Mathematics Teacher* 76 (April 1983): 264-266. *Activities which instruct about mathematics as they instruct in mathematics.*

Van de Walle, John, and Charles S. Thompson. "Let's Do It: Cut and Paste for Geometric Thinking." *Arithmetic Teacher* 32 (September 1984): 8-13. *Use of simple materials to present geometric activities.*

Willcutt, Bob. "Triangles on a Grid." *Mathematics Teacher* 78 (November 1985): 608, 611-614. *Searching for right triangles on a grid.*

Zurstadt, Betty K. "Tessellations and the Art of M. C. Escher." *Arithmetic Teacher* 31 (January 1984): 54-55. *Introducing the art of tessellating to children.*

13 Measurement

THEME: Using Real Numbers to Analyze Geometric Shapes

WARM-UP

**Strategy Review:
Guess & Test.**
You can review this strategy in Chapter 1 of the text.

These math problems appeared on a worksheet on the comet Computo. Can you describe the mathematical operation they call *cometication* ?

4   5 = 29

2   12 = 38

3   6 = 27

How do you perform cometication?
Hint: Two of our operations are necessary to cometicate.

HANDS-ON ACTIVITIES

The first activities in this chapter will help you describe the measurement process and create your own system of measurement to determine measures of length.

OBJECTIVE: **Use body parts to measure length**

1. Early measurements were often reported in terms of body parts such as thumbs, hands, and feet. For this activity, you will use your thumbs, spans, and hands.

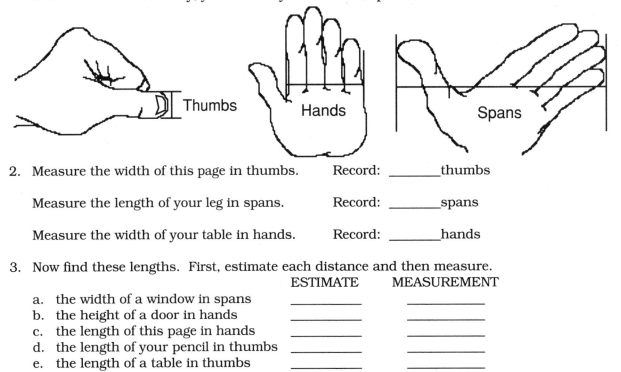

2. Measure the width of this page in thumbs.   Record: _____thumbs

   Measure the length of your leg in spans.   Record: _____spans

   Measure the width of your table in hands.   Record: _____hands

3. Now find these lengths. First, estimate each distance and then measure.

	ESTIMATE	MEASUREMENT
a. the width of a window in spans	_____	_____
b. the height of a door in hands	_____	_____
c. the length of this page in hands	_____	_____
d. the length of your pencil in thumbs	_____	_____
e. the length of a table in thumbs	_____	_____

4. Can you think of a more appropriate unit to use in (e) above?

   Why might spans or hands be a better unit for measuring the length of a table?

   Why might a unit such as foot or pace be better for measuring distances like the width of a room?

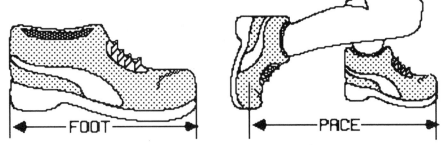

   When might you choose to use a smaller unit?

OBJECTIVE: **Develop a non-standard measurement system**

1. Often, you must use fractional parts of a unit to report the measure of an object. For example, measure the length of this page from top to bottom in spans.
   Record: _____spans

   What special problems do we encounter with this measurement?

2. It is helpful to have smaller units to help in reporting measures of this type. Let's use your pencil to create a system for measuring the length of this page.

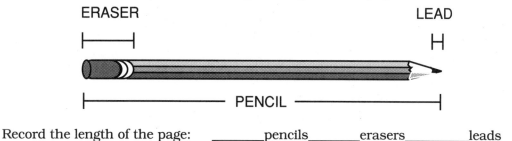

   Record the length of the page: _____pencils_____erasers_____leads

   Compare your measure of the length of this page with another person's. What factors might cause your measures to be different?

3. Find another object such as a shoe or book that can be used to create a measurement system similar to the "pencil system." Measure the following objects:

   a. height of your table   _____(whole) _____(part) _____(part)

   b. width of your chair seat   _____ _____ _____

   c. your height   _____ _____ _____

4. Now measure the same objects using the "pencil system."

   a. _____pencils_____erasers_____leads

   b. _____pencils_____erasers_____leads

   c. _____pencils_____erasers_____leads

5. Compare your measurements in part 3 and part 4. Why might it be difficult for you to communicate these lengths to someone who has not seen your measuring device?

The next two activities will help you use the metric system for linear measures by developing mental images of the units.

OBJECTIVE: **Use body parts to estimate metric measures**

You Will Need: Materials Card 13.3

1. Certain body measures correspond very closely to metric units of measure. For example, the width of the little finger is approximately one **centimeter**.
   Check your little finger.

   1 cm   ┝━━━┥

   Your hand (including your thumb) may be close to one **decimeter** in width. Check with your hand as illustrated:

   1 Decimeter

   A **meter** is approximately the distance from your navel to the floor or the distance from your nose to the end of the hand when the head is turned to the opposite direction (see illustration).

2. This information is very useful when no metric measuring device is available or when an estimate of the metric length is all that is needed.

   Use your "personal" metric references to estimate these measures. When you have completed your estimates, construct the metric tape on Materials Card 13.3 and measure the metric length.

	ESTIMATE	MEASUREMENT
Height of the door	_____	_____
Height of the chair back	_____	_____
Distance from window to floor	_____	_____
Length of your pencil	_____	_____
Width of the room	_____	_____
Length of your foot	_____	_____

The next activity is best done in a group setting where participants can form 3-person teams.

OBJECTIVE: **Estimate and measure metric lengths in a Mini-Metric Olympics**

You Will Need: Materials Card 13.4 and metric tape from Activity 3

EVENT #1

1. The discus (paper circle from Materials Card 13.4) will be sailed like a frisbee.

    First, estimate how far your discus will go. Record:_____
    Then, stand at a starting line taped on the floor. Throw the discus three times and record the distance each time using your metric tape to measure. (See scorecard below.)

	Distance	Score = Difference between estimate and distance
First Trial	_____	_____
Second Trial	_____	_____
Third Trial	_____	_____

2. To compute your score on each trial, find the difference between the estimate and the actual measurement. (Subtract the smaller from the larger in each case.)

    The Team Score is the sum of each team member's best (lowest) score:

    _____ + _____ + _____ = _____
    Player A's Best   Player B's Best   Player C's Best   Team Score

EVENT #2

1. The javelin (paper cylinder from Materials Card 13.4) will be thrown by holding the cylinder on one end only.

    First, estimate how far you can throw the javelin. Record:_____
    Now, throw the javelin three times using the starting line from Event #1. Measure and record the distance of each throw. Compute your score as you did in the first event.

	Distance	Score = Difference between estimate and distance
First Trial	_____	_____
Second Trial	_____	_____
Third Trial	_____	_____

2. Now compute your Team Score as before:

    _____ + _____ + _____ = _____
    Player A's Best   Player B's Best   Player C's Best   Team Score

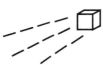

EVENT #3

1. The cube put (cube from Materials Card 13.4) is done by laying the cube in the palm of the hand. The cube is then propelled by an upward and outward motion (this is called a put).

    First, estimate how far you can put the cube. Record:_____
    Now, put the cube three times, using the starting line from Event #1. Measure and record the distance of each put. Compute your score as in previous events.

	Distance	Score = Difference between estimate and distance
First Trial	_____	_____
Second Trial	_____	_____
Third Trial	_____	_____

2. Now compute your Team Score as before:

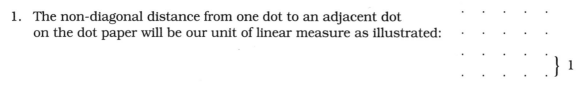

    _____   +   _____   +   _____   =   _____
    Player A's Best   Player B's Best   Player C's Best   Team Score

GO FOR THE GOLD:

   Record team scores for each individual event and for the total team score (sum of all three events). The team with the *smallest* score wins.

   Recognize GOLD, SILVER, and BRONZE winners for individual events and for the all-around title.

In the next two activities you will measure perimeter and
area of two-dimensional shapes.

OBJECTIVE: **Use dot paper to find perimeter and area of geometric shapes**

You Will Need: Materials Card 13.5

1. The non-diagonal distance from one dot to an adjacent dot
    on the dot paper will be our unit of linear measure as illustrated:

2. The perimeter is determined by counting the units around the figure.

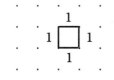

      Each side has a length of one. The sum of the lengths
      of the four sides gives us the perimeter of 4 units.

3. Find the perimeter of each of these figures:
   a.   b.   c.

   _____units   _____units   _____units

4. While linear units are useful for measuring one-dimensional measures such as length, width, height, or perimeter, they are not sufficient for reporting the two-dimensional measure of area.

   For the next activity, our two-dimensional unit will be the smallest square that can be formed on the dot paper with a dot at each vertex, as illustrated:

   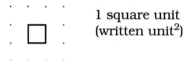

   1 square unit
   (written unit^2)

   The area of a figure is determined by counting the number of square units contained within it. The square to the left has an area of 4 square units.

   Area = 4 square units

5. Find the area of each of these figures:
   a.   b.   c.   d.

   _____ square units   _____ square units   _____ square units   _____square units

6. Let's look at a method for finding the area of a right triangle.

   To find the area of this triangle, we can draw another congruent triangle as illustrated:

   What is the area of the resulting rectangle?_____square units

   The area of the triangle is 1/2 the area of the rectangle, or _____square units.

   Determine the area of each of these triangles:
   a.   b.   c.   d.

   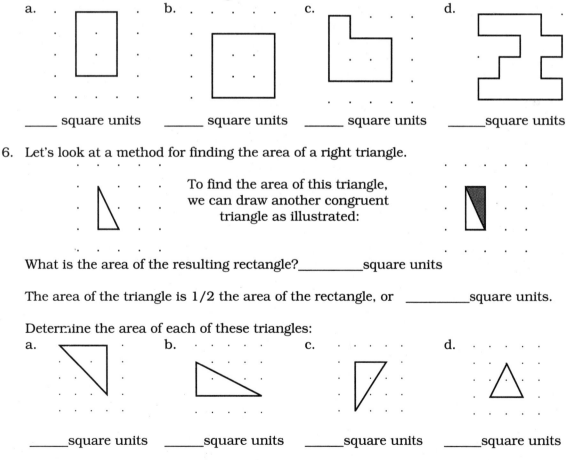

   _____square units   _____square units   _____square units   _____square units

   What special problem is presented by triangle (d) above?

7. You can find the area of a parallelogram by a similar method as illustrated:

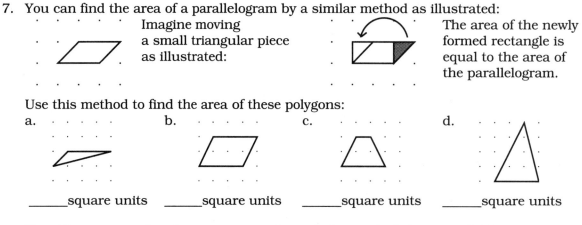

Imagine moving a small triangular piece as illustrated: The area of the newly formed rectangle is equal to the area of the parallelogram.

Use this method to find the area of these polygons:

a.   b.   c.   d.

_____square units   _____square units   _____square units   _____square units

Hint: You may need to draw two rectangles to help you find the area of (d).

8. Find both the perimeter and area of each of these figures:

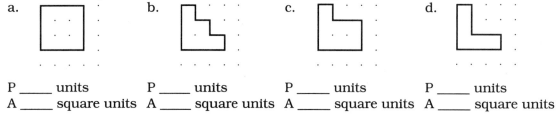

a.   b.   c.   d.

P _____ units   P _____ units   P _____ units   P _____ units
A _____ square units   A _____ square units   A _____ square units   A _____ square units

What do you notice about the perimeters of the four figures?

What do you notice about the areas of the four figures?

9. Use the dot paper on Materials Card 13.5 to draw examples of all the different rectangles that have an area of 36 square units. Find the perimeter of each rectangle.

The area of each rectangle is 36 square units; what do you notice about the perimeters?

10. A 6th grade student says that if the perimeters of two figures are the same, the areas of these figures must also be the same. How might you respond to this?

Another student says if areas are equal, then the perimeters are also equal? How might you respond to this?

OBJECTIVE: **Find the area of an irregular shape**

You Will Need: Materials Card 13.6

1. Look at the map of Blackhawk County on Materials Card 13.6. Each square on the grid is equal to 1/100 of a square mile. Estimate the area of the county in square miles.
   Record your estimate here:_____

2. Now, let's look at a method for improving our estimate of the area.

   First, find the number of squares completely inside the county.
   Record the number here:_____

   Then, find the number of squares partially inside the county.
   Record that number here:_____

3. To determine your approximation of the area of Blackhawk County, add the number of squares completely inside the county to 1/2 of the number of squares partially inside the county. The sum is your approximate area in 1/100 square miles.

   _____   +   (_____ ÷ 2)   ≈   _____
   Squares inside   Squares partially inside   Area in 1/100 square miles

   To convert this to square miles, divide by 100.   Record the quotient:_____

   Quotient = _____ square miles ≈ Area of Blackhawk County

   _____

   The next activity also deals with area, but introduces the concept
   of surface area of three-dimensional objects.

   _____

OBJECTIVE: **Use grid paper to determine surface area**

You Will Need: Materials Card 13.7

1. Each face of this cube has an area of 1 square unit. The **surface area** is the sum of the areas of all the faces.

   If we open the cube out into a flat pattern (we will call this pattern a **net**), we can see that it has 6 of these 1-square unit faces, or a surface area of 6 square units.

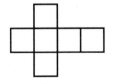

Surface area = 6 square units

2. Cut out figure 1 on Materials Card 13.7. Fold as directed and tape in place to form a rectangular prism.

    Count the number of square units on each face. The sum of the areas of the faces is the surface area of this figure.

    Your prism should look like this:

    What is the surface area of this rectangular prism?_____square units

    Hint: Open the net and lay it flat to count the square units on the surface if you are unsure.

3. Cut out figure 2 on Materials Card 13.7. Fold and tape as directed to form another rectangular prism.

    Your prism should look like this:

    What is the surface area of this prism?   _____square units

4. Cut out figure 3 on Materials Card 13.7. First, find the area of the square base (B). Use the method in Activity 5 to find the area of the triangular faces (T_1, T_2, T_3, T_4).
    Record the areas here:

    Area of B = _____ square units   The sum of the areas of:
    Area of T_1= _____ square units $B + T_1 + T_2 + T_3 + T_4$ = ____square units
    Area of T_2= _____ square units   This is the surface area of the prism
    Area of T_3= _____ square units   formed by this net.
    Area of T_4= _____ square units

    Now, fold and tape your net to form a pyramid like this:

    This pyramid is called a square pyramid.
    Record the surface area here:
                                SA = _____ square units

5. Describe how you could find the surface area of this prism:

    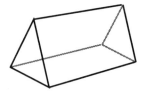

    Draw a sketch of the net for this prism.

The final activities in this chapter will explore the concept of volume. This is also an activity using three-dimensional objects.

ACTIVITY 8

OBJECTIVE: **Find the volume of rectangular prisms**

You Will Need: Materials Card 13.8 and centimeter cubes (optional)

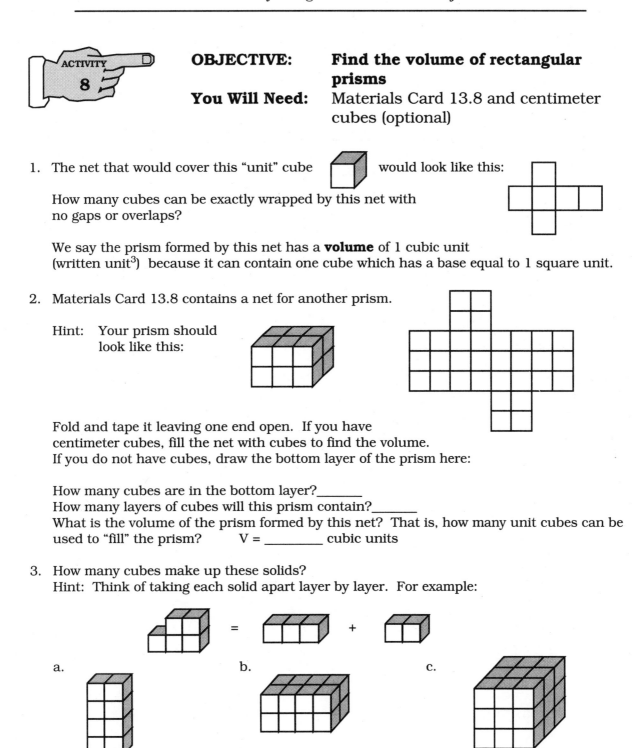

1. The net that would cover this "unit" cube would look like this:

   How many cubes can be exactly wrapped by this net with no gaps or overlaps?

   We say the prism formed by this net has a **volume** of 1 cubic unit (written unit^3) because it can contain one cube which has a base equal to 1 square unit.

2. Materials Card 13.8 contains a net for another prism.

   Hint: Your prism should look like this:

   Fold and tape it leaving one end open. If you have centimeter cubes, fill the net with cubes to find the volume. If you do not have cubes, draw the bottom layer of the prism here:

   How many cubes are in the bottom layer?_____
   How many layers of cubes will this prism contain?_____
   What is the volume of the prism formed by this net? That is, how many unit cubes can be used to "fill" the prism?   V = _____ cubic units

3. How many cubes make up these solids?
   Hint: Think of taking each solid apart layer by layer. For example:

   a.   b.   c.

   _____cubic units   _____cubic units   _____cubic units

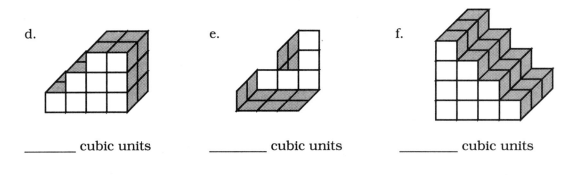

d.

e.

f.

_____ cubic units _____ cubic units _____ cubic units

The last activity in this chapter requires special materials. It may be done best in a lab setting, but can be accomplished on your own using rice or dry cereal.

OBJECTIVE: **Compare the volumes of a cylinder and a cone**

You Will Need: Materials Card 13.9, rice, tape and scissors

1. Cut out the 2 rectangles on Materials Card 13.9. Roll rectangle A into a cylinder and tape as directed.

Now roll rectangle B into a cone, using point C as the apex (tip) of the cone. Tape the tip only to maintain shape. Place the cone into the cylinder so that the tip of the cone touches the table in the center of the base as illustrated:

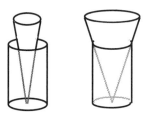

Spread out the cone to fit the top of the cylinder exactly and tape in place inside the cone.

Mark a line all the way around the cone at the top of the cylinder. Remove the cone and tape the outside securely in place. Cut along the mark as illustrated:

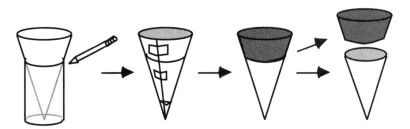

You have constructed a cone that has the same height and radius as the cylinder.

2. Predict how many cones full of rice will fill the cylinder. _____cones

3. Place the cylinder in a container such as a box lid to catch the spillage.

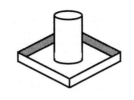

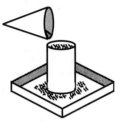

Now fill the cone with rice and pour into the cylinder. Record how many times you must fill the cone and pour it into the cylinder in order to completely fill the cylinder.

_____ cones

Write a ratio that compares the volume of the cone to the volume of the cylinder.
_____ : _____ = Volume of cone : Volume of cylinder

MENTAL MATH

Draw lines connecting figures whose areas are most nearly the same. You must connect a numbered figure to a lettered figure.

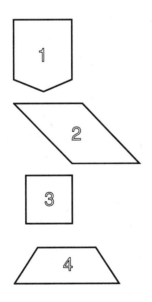

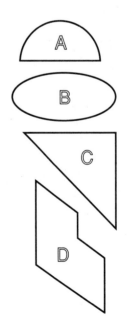

EXERCISES

Where do you send a cat who has lost its tail?

For each shape below, one dimension is missing. Determine the measure of the missing dimension. Find that measure in the set of dimensions listed below. Place the letter that is paired with that dimension on the line or lines at the bottom of the page that match the problem number for which that dimension is a solution.

DIMENSIONS:

L = 12   O = 3   I = 24   S = 1   A = 4   R = 6   E = 5   T = 27

1. L = 2 units
    W = 2 units
    H = ___ units
    V = 12 unit^3

2. L = 2 units
    W = 2 units
    H = 3 units
    V = ___ unit^3

3. L = 4 units
    W = 3 units
    H = 1 unit
    V = ___ unit^3

4. L = ___ units
    W = 3 units
    H = 4 units
    V = 60 unit^3

5. L = 4 units
    W = ___ units
    H = 2 units
    V = 8 unit^3

6. L = 3 units
    W = 2 units
    H = 4 units
    V = ___ unit^3

7. L = 4 units
    W = 2 units
    H = ___ units
    V = 16 unit^3

8. L = 3 units
    W = 3 units
    H = 3 units
    V = ___ unit^3

$$\frac{\quad}{8}\frac{\quad}{1}\quad\frac{\quad}{2}\quad\frac{\quad}{7}\frac{\quad}{4}\frac{\quad}{8}\frac{\quad}{2}\frac{\quad}{6}\frac{\quad}{3}\quad\frac{\quad}{5}\frac{\quad}{8}\frac{\quad}{1}\frac{\quad}{7}\frac{\quad}{4}!$$

Milli-Golf

Estimate the distance in millimeters from the tee to hole #1 and record it on the appropriate blank in the score card below. Now use a metric ruler to mark off your estimate from the tee (within the boundaries). Record that as one stroke. If your line ended in the hole, proceed to tee #2. If you missed the hole, estimate from your current position to hole #1 and record a second stroke. Continue until the ball is in the hole, then proceed to tee #2. If you land in a sand trap or water hazard, add one stroke to your score. You must stay within the boundaries for each hole. Continue until you have completed all 6 holes of the **Milli-Golf Course**.

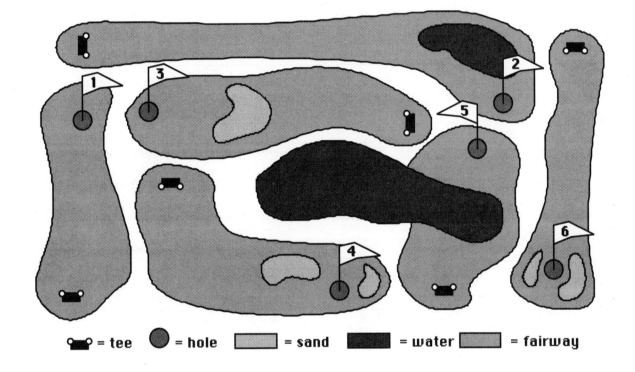

= tee   = hole   = sand   = water   = fairway

SCORE CARD:

	Estimate	Strokes	Par			Estimates	Strokes	Par
1.	_____	_____	2		4.	_____	_____	3
	_____					_____		
	_____					_____		
2.	_____	_____	3		5.	_____	_____	4
	_____					_____		
	_____					_____		
3.	_____	_____	2		6.	_____	_____	3
	_____					_____		
	_____					_____		

SELF-TEST

1. Order these:

   (i) 3 m   (ii) 300 mm   (iii) 3 cm   (iv) 0.03 km

   a. iii < ii < i < iv
   c. iv < i < ii < iii

   b. ii < iii < i < iv
   d. None of a, b, or c.

2. Which of the following areas is equivalent to 40,000 m^2 ?

   a. 4 hectares   b. 4 ares   c. 40 km^2 d. None of a, b, or c.

3. A sheet of plywood is 2.4 m long, 1.2 m wide, and 1.5 cm thick. What is its volume in cm^3?

   a. 43,200 cm^3 b. 420 cm^3 c. 43.2 cm^3 d. 420,000 cm^3

4. The water in a jug weighs 4.7 kg. What is the capacity of the jug in milliliters?

   a. 4.7   b. 0.0047   c. 470   d. 4700

5. The length of an average city block is closest to:

   a. 1/10 km   b. 10 km   c. 10 m   d. 1000 cm

6. Suppose you know that figure ABCD is a rhombus and M is the midpoint of side AD. Which of these equations is correct?

   a. $a^2 + (a/2)^2 = h^2$
   b. $a^2 + a^2 = h^2$
   c. $(a/2)^2 + h^2 = a^2$
   d. Not enough information is given.

7. Find the area of triangle ABC in square units.

   a. 4
   b. 5
   c. 8
   d. None of a, b, or c.

8. If the area of a circle is twice the radius, then the circumference of the circle is:

   a. 4   b. 8   c. 16   d. None of a, b, or c.

9. Imagine cutting out the square corners of this rectangular sheet of paper. Then fold up on the dotted lines to make a box. Which value of x will lead to the box of greatest volume?

   a. $x = 1$ b. $x = 2$
   c. $x = 3$ d. $x = 4$

10. The largest possible cone is cut from a wooden rectangular prism 1 by 1 by 2 units. Similarly, the largest possible sphere is cut from a wooden cube 1 by 1 by 1. Which has the larger volume?

   a. sphere   b. cone
   c. they're equal in volume   d. impossible to determine

SOLUTIONS

Warm-up
Product + Sum

Hands-on Activities
Activity 1
1-3. Answers will vary.
4. One of the longer units is more appropriate because it is less tedious to perform the measurement. Larger units are more convenient for measuring large measures. Smaller units are usually more appropriate for measuring small measures.

Activity 2
1. There are no fractional parts of a span.
2. Different length pencils will give different measures.
3-4. Answers will vary.
5. There is no standard size for a shoe or a pencil, so it is difficult to communicate the measure to someone else.

Activity 3
Answers will vary.

Activity 4
Answers will vary.

Activity 5

3. 8, 12, 12
5. 6, 9, 7, 11
6. 2, 1, 4.5, 4, 3, 2 The rectangle must be formed by two smaller triangles each equal to 1/2 of the original triangle.
7. 1.5, 6, 4, 6
8. 12, 9; 12, 6; 12, 7; 12, 5. The perimeters are all the same. The areas are different.
9. You should have found the following rectangles: 1 by 36, 2 by 18, 3 by 12, 4 by 9, 6 by 6 with perimeters 74, 40, 30, 26, and 24 units respectively. The perimeters are different.
10. Use examples such as in part 8 to demonstrate that while the perimeters stay constant the areas may vary. You might use the example as in 9 to demonstrate that while the perimeters vary, the area can be constant.

Activity 6

The area of Blackhawk County is approximately 5.5 square miles.

Activity 7

2. 10
3. 32
4. 25, 12.5, 12.5, 12.5, 12.5, 75, 75
5. Find the area of each rectangular face and the area of each triangular base. The sum of the areas is the surface area of the prism.

Activity 8

1. 1
2. 6, 2, 12
3. 8, 16, 27, 18, 10, 30

Activity 9

2. Answers may vary.
3. 3, 1:3

Mental Math

1 to C   2 to D   3 to A   4 to B

Exercises

Where do you send a cat who has lost its tail?
     1. 3   2. 4   3. 12   4. 5   5. 1   6. 24   7. 6   8. 27
To a retail store!

Milli-Golf
Answers will vary.

Self-Test

1. a   **2.** a   **3.** a   **4.** d   **5.** a   **6.** c   **7.** b   **8.** a   **9.** c   **10.** c

RESOURCE ARTICLES

Bazik, Edna F., and Benny F. Tucker. "Ideas." *Arithmetic Teacher* 30 (May 1983): 19-24. *Activity pages for teaching measurement.*

Blake, Rick N. "The Spider and the Fly: A Geometric Encounter in Three Dimensions." *Mathematics Teacher* 78 (February 1985): 98-104. *Helping students visualize three-dimensional problems.*

Bright, George. "Ideas." *Arithmetic Teacher* 33 (November 1985): 27-32. *Activities to develop concept of measuring length.*

Clemens, Stanley R. "Applied Measurement— Using Problem Solving." *Mathematics Teacher* 78 (March 1985): 176-180. *A view of the skills needed for proficiency in measurement.*

Cunningham, Trudy B. "Landmark Mathematics." *Arithmetic Teacher* 33 (September 1985): 16-19. *Problem solving involving measurement.*

Gill, Steve. "Making Boxes." *Mathematics Teacher* 77 (October 1984): 526-530. *Developing measurement skills using metric units.*

Harrison, William B. "How to Make a Million." *Arithmetic Teacher* 33 (September 1985): 46-47. *Making a model of a million.*

Harrison, William R. "What Lies Behind Measurement?" *Arithmetic Teacher* 34 (March 1987): 19-21. *Activities to develop understanding of the concept of a standard unit.*

Hart, Kathleen. "Which Comes First— Length, Area, or Volume?" Arithmetic Teacher 31 (May 1984): 16-18, 26-27. *A heirarchy of measurement skills.*

Hawkins, Vincent J. "Ring-Around-a-Trapezoid." *Mathematics Teacher* 77 (September 1984): 450-451. *An exercise in determining the area of a trapezoid.*

Hiebert, James. "Why Do Some Children Have Trouble Learning Measurement Concepts?" *Arithmetic Teacher* 31 (March 1984): 19-24. *Research on teaching the concept of measurement.*

Jensen, Rosalie. "Multilevel Metric Games." *Arithmetic Teacher* 32 (October 1984): 36-39. *Improvement of skills in comparison, estimation, and linear measurement.*

Kolnowski, Linda W., and Joann King Okey. "Ideas: Area and Perimeter." *Arithmetic Teacher* 34 (April 1987): 28, 32-33. *Activity exploring area and perimeter on dot grid.*

Litwiller, Bonnie H., and David R. Duncan. "Areas of Polygons on Isometric Dot Paper: Pick's Formula Revised." *Arithmetic Teacher* 30 (April 1983): 38-40. *Applying Pick's formula to simple closed polygons drawn on isometric dot paper.*

Lyon, Betty Clayton. "How Is Area Related to Perimeter?" *Mathematics Teacher* 76 (May 1983): 360-363. *Using rectangles to study the relation between area and perimeter.*

Martin, W. Gary, and Joao Ponte. "Measuring the Area of Golf Greens and Other Irregular Regions." *Mathematics Teacher* 78 (May 1985): 385-389. *A stimulating "true-life" problem to solve.*

McGinty, Robert. "Current Status of the Metric System." *Arithmetic Teacher* 32 (October 1984): 3-4. *A report on current surveys about use of metrics.*

Nelson, Rebecca S., and Donald R. Whitaker. "Another Use for Geoboards." *Arithmetic Teacher* 30 (April 1983): 34-37. *An area model that is both consistent and complete for the sequential development of all rational-number concepts.*

Shaw, Jean M. "Ideas." *Arithmetic Teacher* 32 (December 1984): 20-24. *Practice in metric measuring skills.*

Shaw, Jean M. "Let's Do It: Exploring Perimeter and Area Using Centimeter Squared Paper." *Arithmetic Teacher* 31 (December 1983): 4-11. *Using graph paper as a concrete aid for exploring concepts of area and perimeter.*

Shaw, Jean M. "Let's Do It: Student-made Measuring Tools." *Arithmetic Teacher* 31 (November 1983): 12-15. *Students produce their own measuring devices to use in measuring experiences.*

Szetela, Walter, and Douglas T. Owens. "Finding the Area of a Circle: Use a Cake Pan and Leave Out the Pi." *Arithmetic Teacher* 33 (May 1986): 12-18. *Several different methods for approximating the area of a circular region.*

Thompson, Charles S., and John Van de Walle. "Let's Do It: Learning about Rulers and Measuring." *Arithmetic Teacher* 32 (April 1985): 8-12. *A developmental sequence of activities that introduce children to linear measurement and the use of rulers.*

Van de Walle, John, and Charles S. Thompson. "Let's Do It: Estimate How Much." *Arithmetic Teacher* 32 (May 1985): 4-8. *Activities designed to help young children learn the basic notion of "about how much."*

Willcutt, Bob. "Triangular Tiles for Your Patio?" *Arithmetic Teacher* 34 (May 1987): 43-45. *Creative spatial problem-solving activities.*

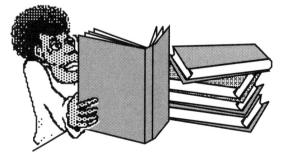

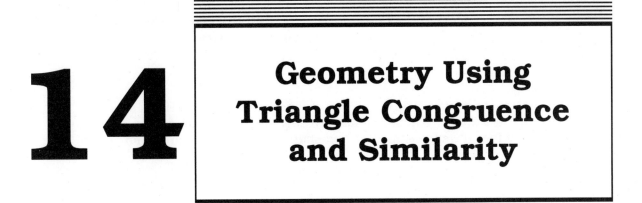

14 Geometry Using Triangle Congruence and Similarity

THEME: Exploring Triangle Congruence and Geometric Constructions

Strategy Review:
Make a List.
This strategy, presented in Chapter 1, will be useful in solving these problems.

How many squares of all sizes can you find in this array?

How many triangles can you find?

HANDS-ON ACTIVITIES

The first activity of this chapter will help you understand the meaning of congruent triangles and the correspondence between parts.

OBJECTIVE: **Recognize correspondences between congruent triangles**

You Will Need: Tracing paper

1. Two triangles are **congruent** if there is a correspondence between vertices such that all corresponding sides are congruent and all corresponding angles are congruent. Visually, that means that they have the same size and shape. Two triangles are given below. Trace Δ TOM.

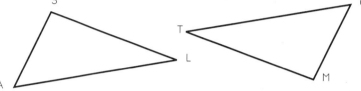

   Can you fit the copy of Δ TOM on top of Δ SAL?

2. When Δ TOM fits on top of Δ SAL you can identify the correspondence of points. Indicate that correspondence.

   T ⟷ __   O ⟷ __   M ⟷ __

3. In writing a statement of congruence, you want to list the points in corresponding order. Complete these statements:

   Δ TOM ≅ Δ ____   Δ MTO ≅ Δ ____   Δ MOT ≅ Δ ____

4. In the triangles pictured below, identify the correspondence and complete the congruence statements.

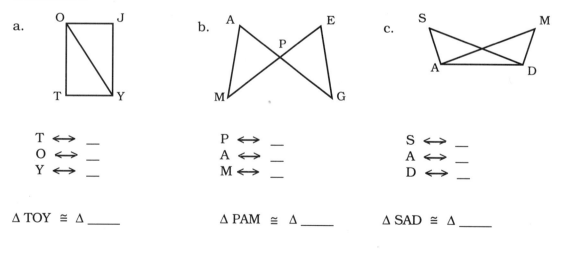

   a.
   T ⟷ __
   O ⟷ __
   Y ⟷ __

   b.
   P ⟷ __
   A ⟷ __
   M ⟷ __

   c.
   S ⟷ __
   A ⟷ __
   D ⟷ __

   Δ TOY ≅ Δ ____   Δ PAM ≅ Δ ____   Δ SAD ≅ Δ ____

The next activities investigate conditions that lead to congruence of triangles.

OBJECTIVE: **Investigate the SSS Congruence Property**

You Will Need: Scratch paper, compass, straightedge, and tracing paper

1. Given below are three segments. Follow the steps below to construct a triangle having sides congruent to these three segments.

    a : _____

    b : _____

    c : _____

    a. Lay off one side, for example, side *a*.

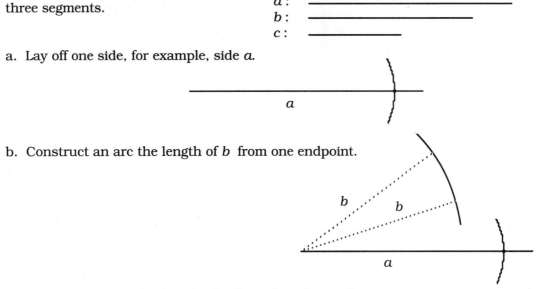

    b. Construct an arc the length of *b* from one endpoint.

    c. Construct an arc the length of *c* from the other endpoint.

    d. Where the two arcs meet is the third vertex of the triangle. Complete your triangle.

2. Construct another triangle using these three sides.   For example, you might want to use sides in a different order.

3. Trace one of the triangles. Does it fit exactly on top of the other one by some combination of flipping, turning or sliding? Are the triangles congruent?

> Write a sentence that summarizes what you found.

OBJECTIVE: **Investigate the SAS Congruence Property**

You Will Need: Scratch paper, compass, straightedge, and tracing paper or protractor (See Materials Card 10.2)

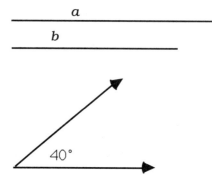

1. Given are two segments and a 40° angle. Draw a triangle having an angle with the same measure, using a protractor or tracing paper, and putting the segments along the rays of the angle. Connect the endpoints of the segments to find the third side.

2. Draw another triangle using these given components. For example, switch the segments on the sides of the angle.

3. Trace one of the triangles. Does it fit exactly on top of the other one? Are they congruent?

> Write a sentence that summarizes what you found.

OBJECTIVE: **Determine if there is an SSA Congruence Property**

You Will Need: Scratch paper, compass, straightedge, and tracing paper or protractor (See Materials Card 10.2)

1. Using the angle and sides given in Activity 3, follow the steps below.

   a. Using a protractor or tracing paper, make a copy of the angle. Call the vertex point A. Extend one side of the angle at least 8 cm.

b. On the other side of the angle, mark off a segment with the length of *a*.
    Call its endpoint B.

c. Set your compass to the length of *b*. From point B swing an arc towards the longer
    side of the original angle. It should intersect that side in two places. Call one point C
    and the other D.

2. You have formed two triangles, Δ ABC and Δ ABD. Are these triangles congruent?

3. If two triangles have a correspondence of vertices such that two pairs of corresponding
    sides and the pair of corresponding angles opposite one of the pairs of sides are congruent,
    are the triangles necessarily congruent?

4. Is there an SSA Congruence Property?

The next activities explore the construction of regular *n*-gons. These involve
applications of the basic construction techniques with compass,
straightedge, and Mira.

OBJECTIVE: **Construct regular *n*-gons of the
                   family *n* = 4**

You Will Need: Compass, straightedge, scratch paper

1. Recall that a **square** is any quadrilateral that has four
    congruent sides and four right angles. Using this
    definition, apply your construction techniques to   A _____ B
    construct a square on the scratch paper whose sides
    are congruent to segment $\overline{AB}$.

    How many times did you construct a right angle?

2. It can be shown that a rhombus with at least one right angle is a square. Based upon this
    information, can you refine the construction procedure you used in part 1 above?

3. The diagonals of a square are perpendicular bisectors of each other. Use this fact to construct a square inscribed in the given circle.

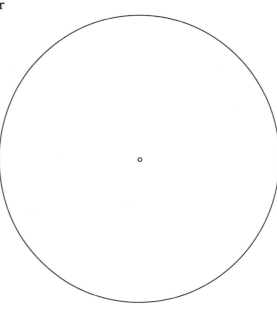

4. Using the square constructed in the previous part, bisect the central angles with other diameters. Connect the consecutive points on the circle (including those found previously).

    What regular *n*-gon does this form?

5. How could you proceed to construct a regular 16-gon?   32-gon?

 **OBJECTIVE:**   **Construct regular *n*-gons of the family *n* = 5**

You Will Need: Compass, straightedge, scratch paper

1. The construction of the following regular polygon is accomplished via a series of intermediate constructions. Use great care in each step. Do your work on scratch paper.

    a. Taking AB as a unit length, construct a segment $\overline{CD}$ of length $\sqrt{5}$. Hint: Use the Pythagorean theorem.   A _____ B

    b. Using AB and CD, construct a segment $\overline{EF}$ of length $\sqrt{5} - 1$.

    c. Bisect segment $\overline{EF}$ forming segment $\overline{EG}$. What is the length of segment $\overline{EG}$?

    d. Construct a circle whose radius is AB.

    e. With the compass open a distance equal to EG, make marks around the circle (starting from any point). Connect the consecutive points. What regular polygon did you form?

2. How could you utilize the polygon you have just constructed to construct a regular pentagon?

3. How could you construct a regular 20-gon?

The last activity investigates some special points and a special line of a triangle.

 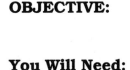

OBJECTIVE: **Construct the circumcenter, centroid, and orthocenter of a triangle and find the Euler line**

You Will Need: Mira, or compass and straightedge

The triangle given will be used for each of the following constructions. Using a Mira for the constructions, instead of a compass and straightedge, will eliminate many extraneous marks. Also, using a different colored pencil or pen for each step may be helpful.

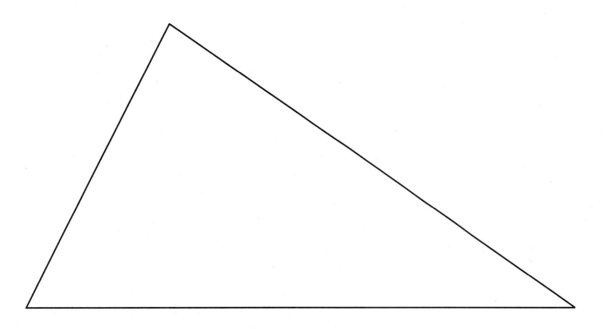

1. Construct the perpendicular bisectors of each side. These meet at a single point, called the **circumcenter** of the triangle. This point is the center of the **circumscribed circle** which contains all the vertices of the triangle. Label the circumcenter C.

2. The segment connecting a vertex with the midpoint of the opposite side is called a **median** of the triangle. Construct the median from each vertex of the triangle (Hint: You found the midpoints in part 1 above). The medians meet at a single point, called the **centroid**. This point is the center of gravity or point of balance of a triangle. Label the centroid D.

3. The segment from a vertex that is perpendicular to the line containing the opposite side is called an **altitude** of the triangle. Construct the altitude from each vertex. The altitudes also meet at a single point, called the **orthocenter**. Label the orthocenter O.

4. Connect the circumcenter, the centroid, and the orthocenter. Do these points appear to be collinear? _____ (They should.) The line containing these three points is called the **Euler line**, named for the Swiss mathematician Leonard Euler.

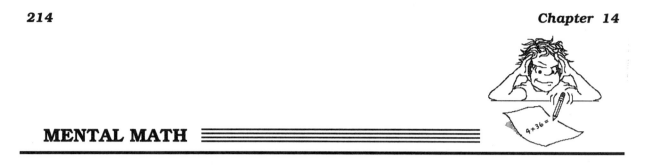

MENTAL MATH

For each figure below, make one cut that creates two congruent halves. The cut does not have to be straight, but it must be one continuous cut.

For example:

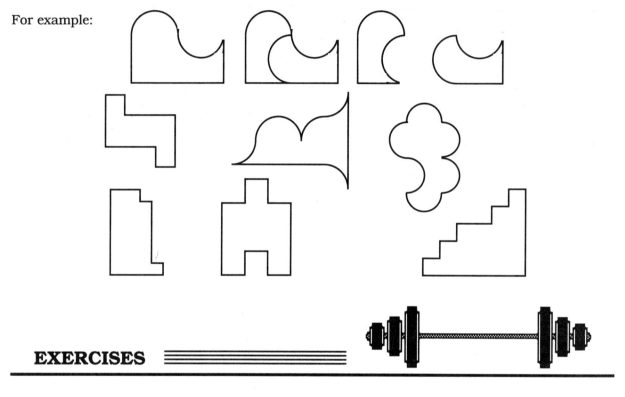

EXERCISES

Treasure Hunt

Given below are the instructions to find the treasure hidden on an exotic island. The only tools you have available are a compass (the kind that draws circles) and a straightedge. Where is the treasure located?

You land at the midpoint of segment $\overline{AB}$. The distance from your landing point to point A is one league. From your landing point head straight inland (making a right angle with the shore) for one league. Make a path parallel to the shore and travel eastward for two leagues. Turn toward the north and travel along a path that makes a 60° angle with your previous path. Your stopping point will be where a path through point P intersects your current path at a right angle. Turn and proceed on the path through P for three leagues. Turn toward the north again traveling along a path that makes a 45° angle with your previous path. Travel for three leagues. Proceed to the circumcenter of △ KLM. From your current path turn 75° and cross the same side of △ KLM you already crossed. Proceed for one and a half leagues and start digging.

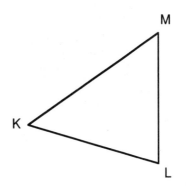

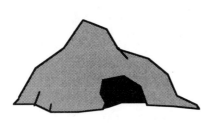

P

A

B

Constructible Designs

The following designs can be constructed using only compass and straightedge. How many of these designs can you construct? Hint: It may be easier to construct versions larger than those shown.

A.

B.

C.

D.

E.

F.

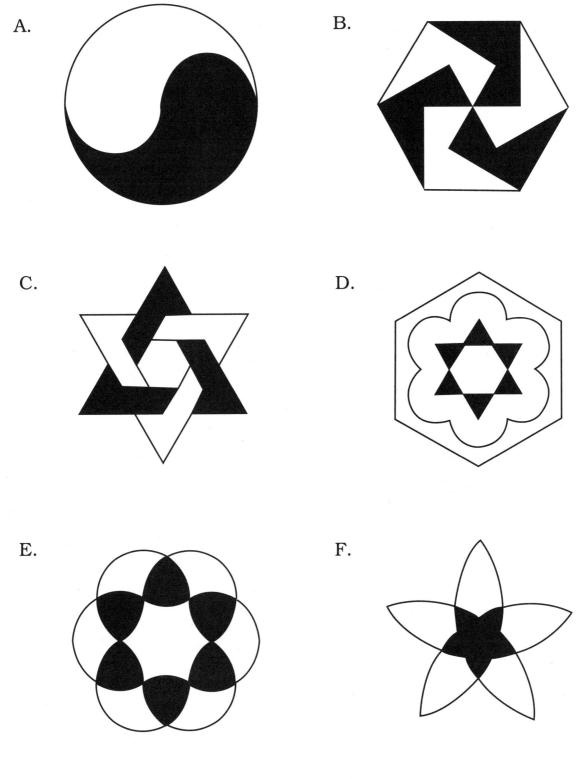

SELF-TEST

1. Which of the following is *not* an appropriate congruence relation for showing that triangles are congruent?

   a. ASA   b. SSS   c. SAS   d. AAA

2. In the diagram at the right, you can say that $\triangle$ DEF is actually a copy of $\triangle$ ABC because by construction they

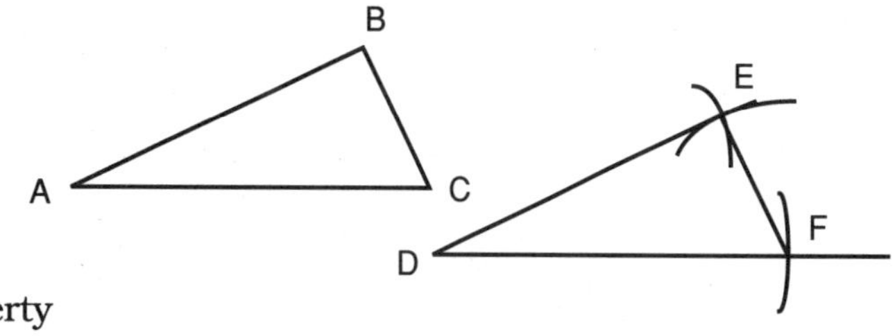

   a. have the same shape
   b. satisfy the SSS Congruence Property
   c. have the same size   d. satisfy the SAS Congruence Property

3. Given: Rectangle RSTU with diagonals meeting at point W.
   Which of the following statements could be shown to be true?

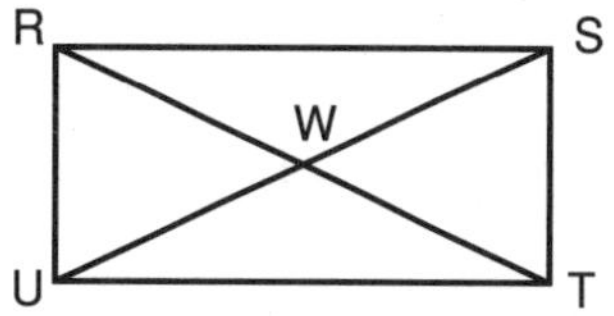

   (i) $\triangle$ RUT $\cong$ $\triangle$ STU   (ii) $\triangle$ RWU $\cong$ $\triangle$ SWT   (iii) $\triangle$ RWS is isosceles

   a. only i and ii   b. only i and iii   c. only ii and iii   d. i, ii, and iii

4. Given: Kite ABCD with diagonal $\overline{BD}$.
   In order to show that the diagonal divides the kite into two congruent triangles, each of the following statements is *justifiable* and *useful except*

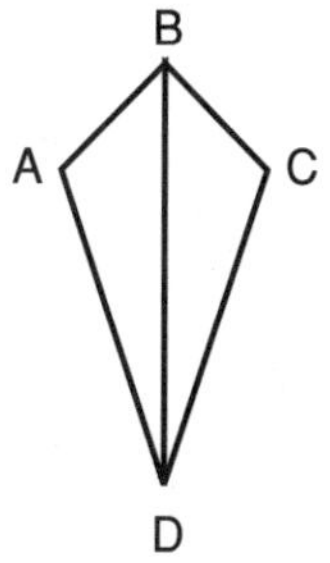

   a. $\angle$ A $\cong$ $\angle$ C   b. $\overline{AB} \cong \overline{CB}$ c. $\overline{BD} \cong \overline{BD}$ d. $\overline{DA} \cong \overline{DC}$

5. Given the figure at the right, complete the following statement:
   $\triangle$ LMN $\cong$ _____

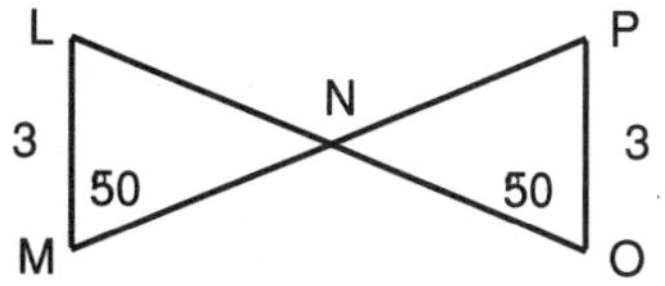

   a. $\triangle$ OPN
   b. $\triangle$ PON
   c. $\triangle$ NOP
   d. Insufficient given information.

6. Which of the following points associated with a triangle is the center of the circle that contains all three vertices of the triangle?

   a. centroid   b. circumcenter   c. incenter   d. orthocenter

7. Which of the following regular polygons cannot be constructed with a compass and straightedge?

    a. 36-gon   b. 85-gon   c. 60-gon   d. 64-gon

8. To construct the circle inscribed in a given triangle, each of the following construction steps would be applied *except*

    a. perpendicular bisector   b. perpendicular to a line through a point not on the line
    c. angle bisector   d. circle

9. Given $\overline{UV} \parallel \overline{WX}$, find $\overline{WX}$.

    a. 12   b. 20
    c. 18   d. 16

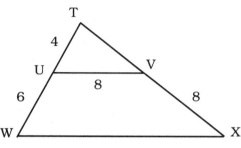

10. At a certain time of day, a flag pole casts a shadow 21 meters long on horizontal ground. At the same time, a vertical pole 4 meters high casts a shadow 6 meters long. How tall is the flag pole?

    a. 10 meters   b. 11.6 meters   c. 14 meters   d. 31.5 meters

SOLUTIONS

Warm-up
14 squares   16 triangles

Hands-on Activities
Activity 1
1. Yes
2. L, A, S
3. LAS, SLA, SAL
4. a. J, Y, O, JYO   b. P, E, G, PEG   c. M, D, A, MDA

Activity 2
3. Yes, Yes
    If two triangles have a correspondence of vertices such that all three pairs of corresponding sides are congruent, then the triangles are congruent.

Activity 3

3. Yes, Yes

If two triangles have a correspondence of vertices such that two pairs of corresponding sides and the pair of corresponding included angles are congruent, then the triangles are congruent.

Activity 4

2. No   **3.** Not necessarily   **4.** No

Activity 5

1. One, two, three or four
2. You should be able to construct a square by only constructing one right angle. Construct the angle first and mark off lengths on two sides of the angle. With the same compass setting, construct arcs from these endpoints that meet to form the fourth vertex.
3. Construct any diameter. Then construct another diameter perpendicular to the first one. Connect the endpoints of these diameters to form a square.
4. An octagon
5. Bisect central angles of a regular octagon; bisect central angles of a regular 16-gon.

Activity 6

1. a. Construct a right triangle with sides of length 2 and 1.
   b. Subtract length AB from CD   c. $(\sqrt{5} - 1)/2$ e. A decagon
2. Connect every other vertex of the decagon.
3. Bisect central angles of a regular decagon.

Activity 7

4. Yes

Mental Math

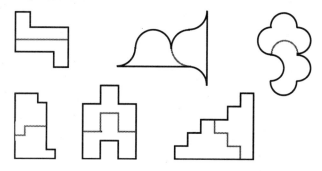

Exercises

Treasure Hunt
   Dig at the western edge of the hut.

Self-Test

1. d **2.** b **3.** d **4.** a **5.** b **6.** b **7.** a **8.** a **9.** b **10.** c

RESOURCES ARTICLES

Brown, Susan A. "Drawing Altitudes of Triangles." *Mathematics Teacher* 78 (March 1985): 182-183. *Introducing altitudes of triangles on graph paper.*

Ellington, Bee. "Star Trek: A Construction Problem Using Compass and Straightedge." *Mathematics Teacher* 76 (May 1983): 329-332. *Students perform a series of constructions to find Spock, who is lost in space.*

Horak, Virginia M., and Willis J. Horak. "Let's Do It: Using Geometry Tiles As a Manipulative for Developing Basic Concepts." *Arithmetic Teacher* 30 (April 1983): 8-15. *Using tiles to help children construct and visualize basic geometric shapes.*

Roberti, Joseph V. "Some Challenging Constructions." *Mathematics Teacher* 79 (April 1986): 283-287. *A game of geometric solitaire.*

Yeshurun, Shraga. "An Improvement of the Congruent Angles Theorem." *Mathematics Teacher* 78 (January 1985): 53-54. *A proof involving similar triangles.*

Yeshurun, Shraga, and David C. Kay. "An Improvement on SSA Congruence for Geometry and Trigonometry." *Mathematics Teacher* 76 (May 1983): 364-367, 347. *Discussions of investigations involving the SSA theorem.*

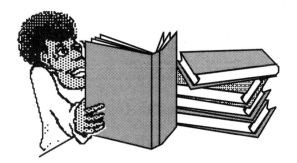

15

Geometry Using Coordinates

THEME: Using Coordinates in Geometry

**Strategy Review:
Identify Subgoals.**
This strategy,
presented in
Chapter 14,
will help solve
the given problem.

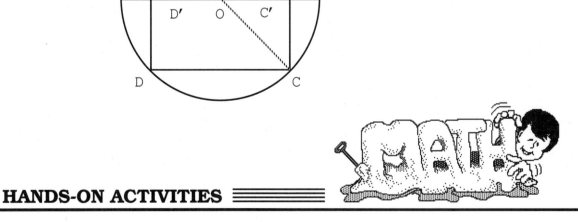

The area of the square ABCD inscribed
in circle O is 30 cm². What is the area
of square A'B'C'D' inscribed in a
semicircle of circle O?

HANDS-ON ACTIVITIES

The first activities of this chapter will help you become familiar with a
coordinate system in the plane.

OBJECTIVE: **Illustrate a coordinate system on a square lattice**

1. In previous chapters you have worked with a geoboard or with a square lattice. The points in an array like the one pictured can also be identified using coordinates.

    First, number the columns from left to right.

    Then, number the rows beginning with the bottom row.

    A point can be identified by giving its column number and its row number, in that order.

    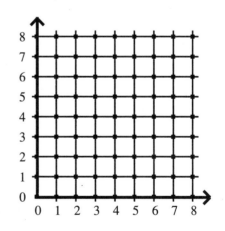

    For example, point A has coordinates (2, 5).

    Find the coordinates of the following points.

    a. B   b. C   c. D   d. E

2. Connecting the dots in each row and column yields the grid pattern to the right. The grid could be extended to include more points as illustrated.

    a. Plot the points A (2, 1), B (6, 1), C (6, 2), D (5, 3), E (5, 6), F (4, 8), G (3, 6), H (3, 3), and I (2, 2).

    b. Connect A to B, B to C, ... , and I to A. What type of polygon have you drawn?

3. Point A has coordinates (0, 5).

We could extend the grid to the
left and label with integers.
Then we see point B has coordinates
(-3, 6).

A similar extension of the
grid allows us to find coordinates
for points such as C and D.

What are the coordinates of
points C and D?

C = (,   )   D = (,   )

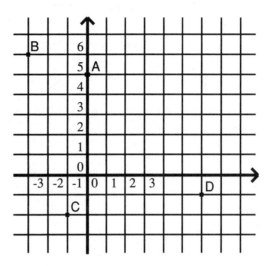

4. The grid system we now have is called the **Cartesian coordinate system**, in honor of the
mathematician René Descartes.

The two darkened lines that are
perpendicular to each other are
called the **axes** (singular is axis).
Here we call the horizontal line
the **x-axis** and the vertical line
the **y-axis.** They meet at the point
called the **origin**, which has
coordinates (0, 0).

a. Plot the points A (5, 2), B (3, -1),
C (-2, 5), D (1, -4), E (-3, -4),
and F (-6, -2).

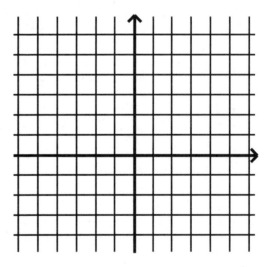

b. The axes divide the plane into 4 regions, called **quadrants**. These are numbered I to
IV, counterclockwise, beginning in the upper right-hand region. Identify the quadrant
that each of the points A through F is in.

c. In quadrant I all coordinates are positive. What do the coordinates of all the points in
quadrant II have in common? in quadrant III? in quadrant IV?

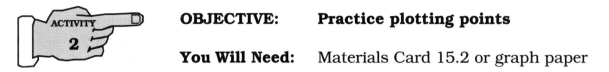

OBJECTIVE: **Practice plotting points**

You Will Need: Materials Card 15.2 or graph paper

1. Place the origin at the lower left corner.

2. Locate these points on your coordinate plane.

   A (12, 12)   B (12, 20)   C (20, 20)   D (20, 12)
   E (16, 24)   F (24, 24)   G (24, 16)   H (16, 16)

   Make solid line segments $\overline{AB}$, $\overline{AD}$, $\overline{AH}$, $\overline{BE}$, $\overline{EF}$, $\overline{EH}$, $\overline{DG}$, $\overline{FG}$, $\overline{GH}$. Make dashed line
   segments $\overline{BC}$, $\overline{CF}$, $\overline{CD}$. Do you see a cube? _____
   Which face looks closer to you, face ABCD or face EFGH?

3. Divide each coordinate in A, B, C, D, E, F, G, H by 2 to get new points A', B', C', D', E', F',
   G', H'. Complete the following.

   A' (6, 6)   B' (,   )   C' (,   )   D' (,   )

   E' (,   )   F' (,   )   G' (,   )   H' (,   )

4. Locate A', B', C', D', E', F', G', H' on your graph. Make similar solid and dashed lines as you
   did in part 2. Do you see a cube? _____

5. Now divide the coordinates in A', B', C', D', E', F', G', H', by 2 to get points A", B", C", D",
   E", F", G", H". Complete the following.

   A" (3, 3)   B" (,   )   C" (,   )   D" (,   )

   E" (,   )   F" (,   )   G" (,   )   H" (,   )

6. Locate the points in part 5 on your graph. Make similar solid and dashed lines as you did
   in parts 2 and 4.

7. Draw a straight line connecting B, B', and B". Draw another line connecting C, C', and C".
   Draw another line connecting D, D', and D". Extend your three lines so that they intersect.
   Do they meet at the origin? _____

8. Turn your paper half-way around. What do you see? Would the title "The Shrinking Cube"
   be appropriate for this activity?

9. Can you draw another cube that lines up with the three you have drawn and is smaller
   than all the others? Draw it.

The next activities explore the concepts of **distance** and **slope**
in the Cartesian coordinate system.

OBJECTIVE: **Develop the idea of distance in the plane**

1. a. Points A and B are shown
        to the right on a portion of a
        square lattice. What are their
        coordinates?
        A (,)   B (,)

    b. Form a right triangle with segment
        AB as the hypotenuse. Draw the
        vertical line through A and the
        horizontal line through B. Name the
        point where these lines intersect
        point C. What are the coordinates
        of point C?   C (,)

    c. What is the length of segment $\overline{AC}$? of $\overline{BC}$?

    d. Use the Pythagorean theorem to find the length of segment $\overline{AB}$; AB = _____

2. On the following coordinate grid, points A and B are given with their coordinates.

    a. Point C is located at the
        intersection of the horizontal
        line through A and vertical line
        through B. What are the
        coordinates of C? _____

    b. What is the distance
        between A and C? _____
        between B and C?_____

    c. Use the Pythagorean theorem to find
        the distance between A and C.

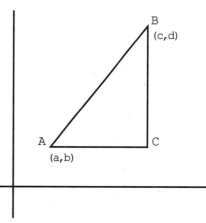

Summarize: If A is the point (a, b) and B is the point (c, d), then the distance
from A to B is

(This result is known as the **coordinate distance formula**.)

OBJECTIVE: **Investigate the slope of a line**

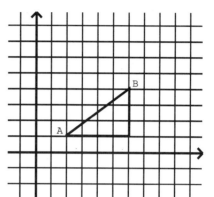

1. The **slope** of a line segment $\overline{AB}$ is defined as the ratio rise/run where rise is the vertical change from A to B and run is the horizontal change from A to B.

    Imagine that segment $\overline{AB}$ is a road up a hill.

    a. What is the vertical change from A to B? _____

    b. What is the horizontal change from A to B? _____

    c. What is the ratio of rise/run?

2. Sometimes, the 'rise' may be negative.

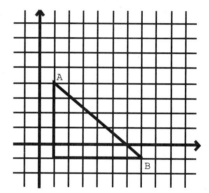

    a. What is the vertical change from A to B? _____

    b. What is the horizontal change from A to B? _____

    c. What is the slope of segment $\overline{AB}$? _____

3. On the grid to the right are points A and B with their coordinates (a, b) and (c, d), respectively.

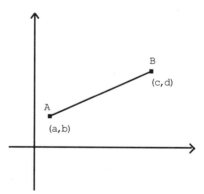

    a.   What is the vertical change from A to B? _____

    b.   What is the horizontal change from A to B? _____

    c.   What is the slope of segment $\overline{AB}$? _____

    d.   What is the vertical change from B to A? _____

    e.   What is the horizontal change from B to A? _____

    f.   What is the slope of the segment $\overline{BA}$? _____

    g.   Compare your results in parts (c) and (f). What to you observe?

Summarize: If A is the point (a, b) and B is the point (c, d), then the slope
of line segment $\overline{AB}$ (where $a \neq c$) is

This result is known as the **slope formula** for a line segment.

---

4. A line *l* is given on the grid to the right.
    Points A (-4, -1), B (0, 1), C (2, 2), and
    D (6, 4) are on the line *l*. Find the
    slopes of segments $\overline{AB}$, $\overline{AC}$, and $\overline{BD}$.
    What is the slope of line *l*?

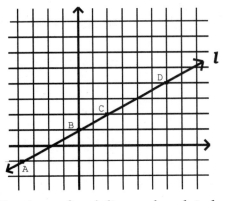

5. The following pairs of lines are parallel. Find the slope of each line and explain how the
    slopes of parallel lines are related.

a.   b.

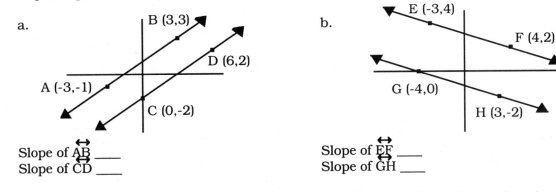

Slope of $\overleftrightarrow{AB}$ ____   Slope of $\overleftrightarrow{EF}$ ____
Slope of $\overleftrightarrow{CD}$ ____   Slope of $\overleftrightarrow{GH}$ ____

The following pairs of lines are perpendicular. Find the slope of each line and explain how
the slopes of perpendicular lines are related. Hint: Consider their product.

c.   d.

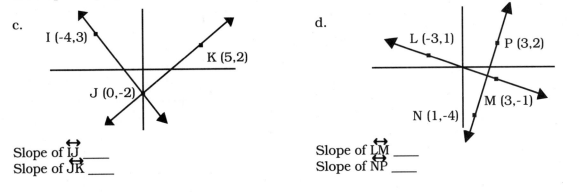

Slope of $\overleftrightarrow{IJ}$ ____   Slope of $\overleftrightarrow{LM}$ ____
Slope of $\overleftrightarrow{JK}$ ____   Slope of $\overleftrightarrow{NP}$ ____

Summarize:
If two nonvertical lines are parallel, then their slopes are _____.

If two nonvertical lines are perpendicular, then the product of their slopes
is _____.

The final activity explores the relationship between points in the plane and
algebraic equations.

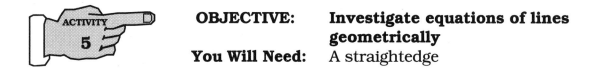

OBJECTIVE: **Investigate equations of lines geometrically**

You Will Need: A straightedge

1. Consider the equation $y = 2x - 3$.

    a. We want to find points of the form (x, y) that satisfy this equation. For the points below, an x-coordinate has been chosen. By substituting x into the equation, find the corresponding y-coordinate.

    $(0, \ \ )$ $(2, \ \ )$ $(4, \ \ )$ $(1, \ \ )$ $(3, \ \ )$ $(-1, \ \ )$

    b. On the coordinate grid to the right, plot the points you found in part (a). Connect these points to form a line.

    What is the slope of this line? _____
    Does that number appear in the
    equation? _____ Where? _____

    What is the y-coordinate of the point where
    the line crosses the y-axis? _____ This is called
    the **y-intercept**. Does this value appear in the
    equation? _____ Where? _____

    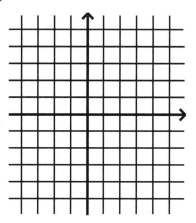

    c. Repeat parts (a) and (b) with the equation $y = -(2/3)x + 4$.

    d. In general, the equation of a nonvertical line may be written in the form $y = mx + b$.
    What does the value of m represent? _____
    What does the value of b represent? _____

2. a. On the coordinate grid to the right, graph the following points: $(0, 0)$, $(1, 2)$, $(2, 4)$, $(3, 6)$, $(-1, -2)$, $(-2, -4)$, and $(-3, -6)$.

    b. Connect the points to form a straight line. What do you observe about the x- and y-coordinates of the points on this line?

    c. If (x, y) is a general point on this line, express the relationship you found as an equation.

    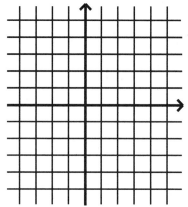

    Note: Any line in the plane can be represented by an algebraic equation.
            However, not all equations will be as easy to find as the example here.

3. a. On the coordinate grid to the right,
        graph the vertical line through (3, 2).

        Does this line have a slope? _____
        Does it have a y-intercept? ____
        What do you observe about the
        x-coordinates of the points on this
        line? _____

        Write an equation to express this.

Summarize:
A nonvertical line can be represented by an equation of the form $y = mx + b$.
What does m represent? _____
What does b represent? _____

A vertical line has no slope. A vertical line through the point (a, b) can be represented
by the equation _____ .

MENTAL MATH

Identify the line or circle on the graph
that is described below.

A. $y = 2x + 1$

B. $x = -2$

C. $(x - 3)^2 + (y - 2)^2 = 13$

D. $y = (-2/3)x + 1$

E. $(x + 3)^2 + (y + 2)^2 = 4$

F. a line parallel to $y = (1/4)x + 5$

G. a line whose slope is zero

H. a line perpendicular to
    $y = (-2/3)x - 3$

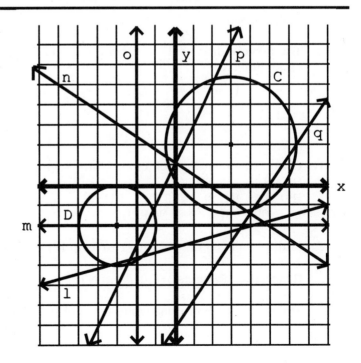

EXERCISES

SYMMETRY THROUGH COORDINATES

A. 1. Graph the points and form △ ABC.
A(3, 5)　　　B(4, 1)　　　C(2, -1)

2. Multiply each *x*-coordinate by -1.
A'(　, 5)　　B'(　, 1)　　C'(　, -1)

3. Graph △ A'B'C'.

4. The two triangles *together* have
what kinds of symmetry?

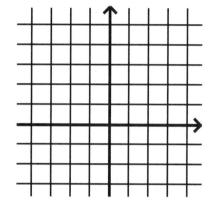

B. 1. Graph the points and form quadrilateral ABCD.
A(-2, 4)　　　B(2, 5)　　　C(5, 1)　　　D(-4, 0)

2. Multiply each *y*-coordinate by -1.
A'(-2,　)　　B'(2,　)　　C'(5,　)　　D'(-4,　)

3. Graph quadrilateral A'B'C'D'.

4. The two quadrilaterals *together* have what kinds
of symmetry?

C. 1. Graph the following points and form segments
$\overline{HI}$, $\overline{IJ}$, . . . , $\overline{NH}$.
H(0, 4)　　I(1, 2)　　J(3, 2)　　K(1, 0)
L(-1, 0)　　M(-3, 2)　　N(-1, 2)

2. Multiply all coordinates by -1 to form H', I', J', . . . , N'.

3. Graph the segments $\overline{H'I'}$, $\overline{I'J'}$, ..., $\overline{N'H'}$.

4. The resulting figure has what kinds of symmetry?

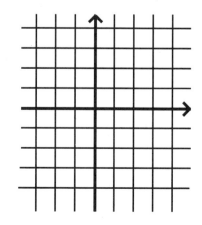

GEOMETRIC TRAINING

Dave likes to build model trains. However he has not completed the one pictured below. Follow the directions given to complete his model.

1. For a window, draw the rectangle whose sides are on the lines $x = -1$, $y = 2$, $x = -8$, $y = 7$.

2. For the top, draw the parallelogram whose sides are on lines $y = 8$, $y = 10$, $y = -2x + 8$, $y = -2x - 18$. Hint: To find one corner, determine where the lines $y = 8$ and $y = -2x + 8$ intersect.

3. For the back wheel, shade the region between the circle $(x + 4)^2 + (y + 6)^2 = 25$ and the circle $(x + 4)^2 + (y + 6)^2 = 16$.

4. For the front wheel, shade the region between the circle $(x - 9)^2 + (y + 7)^2 = 16$ and the circle $(x - 9)^2 + (y + 7)^2 = 9$.

5. For the smokestack, draw the trapezoid whose sides are on $y = 4$, $y = 6$, $y = -2x + 22$, $y = 2x - 18$ and the rectangle whose sides are on $x = 8$, $x = 12$, $y = 6$, $y = 8$. Look for intersection points.

6. For the cowcatcher, draw the right triangle with the vertex of the right angle at $(15, -11)$, one vertical leg, and the hypotenuse on the line $y = (-3/2)x + 17.5$. Again, look for intersection points.

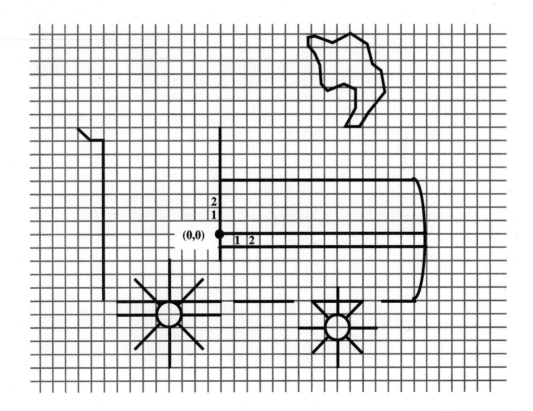

SELF-TEST

1. The distance from the origin to the point A (-3, 4) is

   a. 25   b. 5   c. $\sqrt{7}$ d. None of a, b, or c.

2. The equation of the vertical line through (6, -4) is

   a. $y = -4$ b. $y + 6 = 0$ c. $x - 6 = 0$ d. $x + 6 = 0$

3. An equation of the line passing through the point (-4, 5) with slope -3/2 is

   a. $3x + 2y = -2$ b. $2y - 2x = 3$ c. $2y - 3x = 2$ d. $3x - 2y = -2$

4. If the points A (-1, 1) and B (5, -7) are the endpoints of the diameter of a circle, find the equation of the circle.

   a. $(x - 2)^2 + (y + 3)^2 = 25$ b. $(x + 3)^2 + (y + 4)^2 = 100$
   c. $(x + 2)^2 + (y - 3)^2 = 5$ d. $(x - 2)^2 + (y + 3)^2 = 49$

5. The equation of the line passing through the point (-2, 3) that is perpendicular to the line $3x + y = 0$ is

   a. $3y + x = 11$ b. $y = (1/3)x + 3$ c. $3y + x = 7$ d. $3y - x = 11$

6. Which set of points below are the vertices of a right triangle?
   a. (1, 2), (3, 5), (6, 3)   b. (1, 5), (3, 7), (5, 9)
   c. (3, 1), (2, 6), (4, 7)   d. (4, -3), (2, 1), (4, 8)

7. Which of the following statements is *true* regarding the two lines whose equations are given to the right? $2x - y + 1 = 0$
   $-2x - y + 1 = 0$

   a. The lines are parallel.   b. The lines are perpendicular.
   c. The lines intersect at a point on the y-axis.   d. The lines coincide.

8. Find the y-intercept of the line that contains the points (2, 7) and (4, -1).
   a. -15   b. 15   c. 23   d. 30

9. Which one of the following points is collinear with the points (1, -2) and (6, 1)?
   a. (4, -1)   b. (5, 0)   c. (12, 4)   d. (-4, -5)

10. Given is △ ABC with vertices A (-3, 5), B (1, 7), and C (5, -1). Find the equation of the circle that circumscribes △ ABC.

   a. $(x + 1)^2 + (y + 2)^2 = 5$ b. $(x - 2)^2 + (y - 1)^2 = 41$
   c. $(x - 1)^2 + (y - 2)^2 = 25$ d. None of a, b, or c.

SOLUTIONS

Warm-up

A subgoal would be to find the radius of the circle.

$AD^2 + DC^2 = (2r)^2$ $(B'C')^2 + (OC')^2 = (OB')^2$

$2AD^2 = 4r^2$ $(B'C')^2 + ((1/2)B'C')^2 = r^2$

$2(30) = 4r^2$ $(5/4)(B'C')^2 = 15$

$15 = r^2$ $(B'C')^2 = 12$ The area is 12 cm².

Hands-on Activities

Activity 1

1. a. (4, 5)   b. (3, 2)   c. (5, 1)   d. (1, 3)   **2.** b. A 9-gon resembling a rocket

3. C (-1, -2), D (6, -1)

4. b. A in I, C in II, E & F in III, B & D in IV   c. A negative x-coordinate, positive
y-coordinate; negative x- and y-coordinates; positive x-coordinate, negative y-coordinate

Activity 2

2. You should. EFGH

3. B' (6, 10), C' (10, 10), D' (10, 6), E' (8, 12), F' (12, 12), G' (12, 8), H' (8, 8)

4. You should.   **5.** B" (3, 5), C" (5, 5), D" (5, 3), E" (4, 6), F" (6, 6), G" (6, 4), H" (4, 4)

7. Yes

Activity 3

1. a. A (2, 5), B (5, 1)   b. (2, 1)   c. 4, 3   d. 5

2. a. (c, b)   b. $c - a$, $d - b$ c. $\sqrt{(c - a)^2 + (d - b)^2}$

$\sqrt{(c - a)^2 + (d - b)^2}$

Activity 4

1. a. 3 units   b. 4 units   c. 3/4   **2.** a. -5 units   b. 6   c. -5/6

3. a. $d - b$ b. $c - a$ c. $(d - b)/(c - a)$ d. $b - d$ e. $a - c$ f. $(b - d)/(a - c)$

g. The results are equal. It does not matter which endpoint is used first, as long as you
are consistent in the numerator and denominator.
$(d - b)/(c - a)$

4. 1/2, 1/2, 1/2; The slope of l is equal to the slope of any line segment of l, here 1/2.

5. a. 2/3, 2/3   b. -2/7, -2/7   The slopes are equal.
c. -5/4, 4/5   d. -1/3, 3   The product of the slopes is -1.
equal, -1

Activity 5

1. a. -3, 1, 5, -1, 3, -5   b. 2; It is multiplied by x;   -3; Yes, it is added to the x-term.
c. The slope is -2/3. The y-intercept is 4.   d. slope; y-intercept

2. b. The *y*-coordinate is 2 times the *x*-coordinate.   c. $y = 2x$
3. No; no, always equal to 3; $x = 3$
Slope; *y*-intercept, $x = a$

Mental Math
A. p   B. o   C. Circle C   D. n   E. Circle D   F. l   G. m   H. q

Exercises

Symmetry Through Coordinates
A. Reflection symmetry in the *y*-axis   B. Reflection symmetry in the *x*-axis
C. Reflection symmetry in the *x*-axis and *y*-axis, rotational symmetry in the origin

Self-Test
1. b   **2.** c   **3.** a   **4.** a   **5.** d   **6.** a   **7.** c   **8.** b   **9.** d   **10.** c

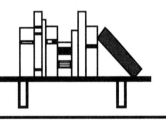

RESOURCE ARTICLES

Burger, William F. "Graph Paper Geometry." In *Mathematics for Middle Grades* (1982 NCTM Yearbook). Reston, VA: National Council of Teachers of Mathematics, 1982. *Collection of introductory coordinate geometry activities.*

Cangelosi, James S. "A 'Fair' Way to Discover Circles." *Arithmetic Teacher* 33 (November 1985): 11-13. *Discovering the attributes of circles.*

Hastings, Ellen H., and Daniel S. Yates. "Microcomputer Unit: Graphing Straight Lines." *Mathematics Teacher* 76 (March 1983): 181-186. *Investigations involving slope.*

Kroll, Diana L. "Ideas." *Arithmetic Teacher* 33 (December 1985): 27-32. *Activities to develop the coordinate system.*

Smith, Robert F. "Let's Do It: Coordinate Geometry for Third Graders." *Arithmetic Teacher* 33 (April 1986): 6-11. *Developing children's ability to name and locate coordinates.*

Terc, Michael. "Coordinate Geometry--Art and Mathematics." *Arithmetic Teacher* 33 (October 1985): 22-24. *Early experience with plotting coordinate points.*

Tucker, Benny F. "Secret Codes and Systems of Equations." *Mathematics Teacher* 79 (April 1986): 256-258. *Finding solutions to systems of equations graphically.*

16 | Geometry Using Transformations

THEME: Using Geometric Transformations

Strategy Review:
Use Symmetry.
This strategy is
presented in
Chapter 16 of
the text.

Imagine that you are looking in a mirror and
you see a clock behind you. What time does
the real clock show for the following *mirror*
images?

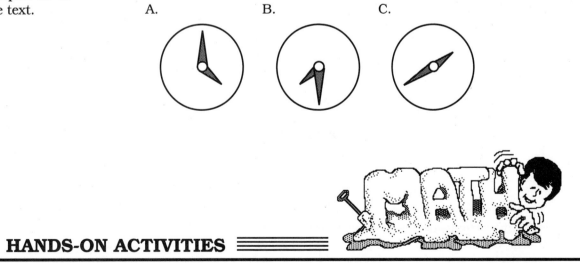

A.   B.   C.

HANDS-ON ACTIVITIES

A **geometric transformation** is a 1-1 correspondence between points in the
plane. The first few activities will investigate some basic transformations and
their properties.

OBJECTIVE: **Investigate translations and their properties**

You Will Need: Tracing paper

1. A **translation** is a transformation associated with a sliding motion of a specified distance and direction, without any turning. The distance and direction can be indicated with an arrow or **directed line segment**. Follow the given steps to translate the indicated point.

    a. The arrow indicates a translation. Extend the arrow by drawing a dashed line $\overleftrightarrow{AB}$.

    b. Lay a piece of tracing paper on the figure and trace the dashed line, point A (the tail of the arrow), and the point P you want to translate.

    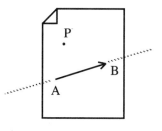

    c. Slide the tracing paper until point A is at the head of the arrow (on top of point B). Be sure that the dashed line is still on top of itself.

    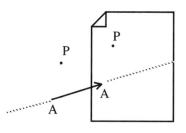

    d. With your pencil, press an indentation through the tracing paper at point P. Remove the tracing paper and at the mark, label the point P'. The point P' is the translation image of point P.

    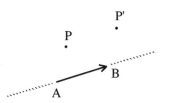

2. Using tracing paper, find the images of points X, Y and Z under the translation indicated by the directed line segment $\overrightarrow{AB}$. Mark these points X', Y' and Z' respectively.

    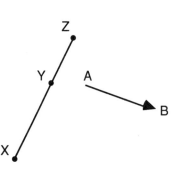

a. Draw the segment with endpoints X' and Z'. Is the point Y' on segment $\overline{X'Z'}$? (It should be!)

b. Translate $\overline{XZ}$ by using tracing paper. How does its image compare to $\overline{X'Z'}$?

c. Choose the *most complete* way of finishing the following statement:
The translation image of a segment is a
   A. segment.
   B. segment congruent and parallel to the original segment.
   C. segment congruent to the original segment.
   D. segment parallel to the original segment.

3. For the translation indicated by $\overrightarrow{AB}$, use tracing paper to find the images of the given ray, line, angle and triangle.

   Complete the following: The translation image
   of a ray is a _____ ,
   of a line is a _____ ,
   of an angle is an _____ ,
   and of a triangle is a _____ .

   How do the measures of the angle and its image compare?

   How do the size and shape of the triangle and its image compare?

   What is the relationship between the line and its image?

4. Finding images with tracing paper provides a good model of transformations. Imagine that the tracing paper is a copy of the plane. As you move the tracing paper, not only does P correspond to its image P', but each point of the plane corresponds to a unique point.

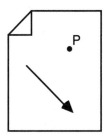

   a. Are there any points that correspond to themselves after a translation, that is, points that do not move?

   Summarize the properties of translations that you have found.

OBJECTIVE: **Investigate rotations and their properties**

You Will Need: Tracing paper

1. A **rotation** is a transformation associated with a turning motion through a specified **directed angle** around a fixed point, called the **center**. Follow the steps given next to rotate point P.

    a. The given angle and point C determine the rotation. Here the angle is drawn with its vertex at the center C.

    b. Lay a piece of tracing paper on top and trace the initial side of the angle and the point P.

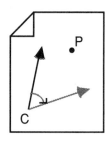

    c. Fix the center C with your pencil point and turn the tracing paper until the traced initial side of the angle coincides with the terminal side of the original angle.

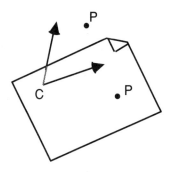

    d. With your pencil, press an indentation through the tracing paper at point P. On your original sheet of paper, mark the image point P'.

2. Using tracing paper, find the images of points X, Y and Z under the rotation indicated with center O and the given directed angle. Label these points X', Y' and Z'.

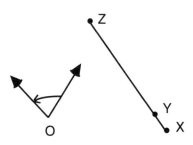

a. Draw the segment with endpoints X' and Z'. Is point Y' on this segment?

b. Rotate $\overline{XZ}$ by using tracing paper. How does its image compare to $\overline{X'Z'}$?

c. Describe the rotation image of a segment as completely as possible.

3. Using tracing paper, find the images of the given figures under the rotations indicated.

   a. Is the image of a line a line, the image of a ray a ray, and the image of an angle an angle?

      How do the measures of the angle and its image compare?

   b. Is the image of a triangle a triangle?

      How do the triangle and its image compare with regard to size and shape?

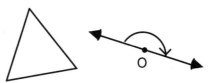

4. Tracing paper serves as a good model for finding images of the rotation transformation.

   a. Are there any points that remain fixed under a rotation?

   Summarize the properties of rotations that you have found.

OBJECTIVE: **Investigate reflections and their properties**

You Will Need: Tracing paper

1. A **reflection** is a transformation that gives a 'mirror' image across a line, called the **reflection line**. Follow the steps given next to find the reflection image of point P, which is not on the reflection line, and the point Q, which is on the reflection line.

   a. The given line determines a reflection. Mark a reference point, R, on the line.

   b. Lay a piece of tracing paper on top and trace the reflection line and the points P, Q and R.

   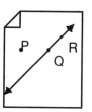

   c. Turn over the tracing paper so that it is face down. Be sure that the copy of the reflection line and the reference point each coincide with the original line and reference point.

   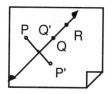

   d. Using your pencil, make an imprint through the tracing paper at points P and Q. Mark the image points P' and Q' on the original sheet of paper.

2. Using tracing paper, find the reflection images of P, Q and R across the line *l* . Label these points P', Q' and R'.

   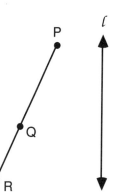

   a. Draw the segment with endpoints P' and R'. Does this segment contain Q'? (It should!)

   b. Reflect $\overline{PR}$ by using tracing paper. How does the image of $\overline{PR}$ compare with $\overline{P'R'}$?

   c. Describe the reflection image of a segment as completely as possible.

3. In each part use tracing paper to find the images of the given figures under the reflections in line *l*.

    a. 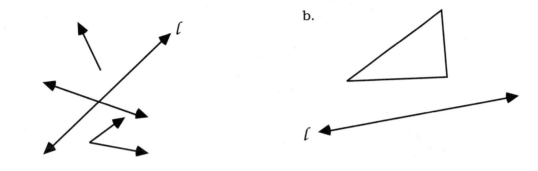   b.

    c. Is the image of a line a line, the image of a ray a ray, and the image of an angle an angle?

        How do the measures of an angle and its reflection image compare?

        How do a triangle and its reflection image compare?

4. Finding images with tracing paper also models the reflection transformation.

    a. Are there any points that correspond to themselves under a reflection; that is, are there any fixed points?

    Summarize the properties of reflections that you have found.

OBJECTIVE: **Investigate glide reflections and their properties**

You Will Need: Tracing paper

1. A **glide reflection** is a transformation that combines a translation and a reflection where the reflection line is parallel to the translation direction. Follow the steps given next to find the glide reflection image of a point P.

   a. The given line l and the directed line segment $\overrightarrow{AB}$ determine a glide reflection. Notice that $l \parallel \overrightarrow{AB}$. Mark a reference point on the reflection line and extend $\overrightarrow{AB}$ by drawing a dashed line $\overleftrightarrow{AB}$.

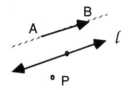

   b. Lay a piece of tracing paper on top. Trace the dashed line and points A and P.

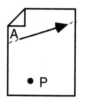

   c. Slide the tracing paper until point A is on top of point B. Be sure that the dashed line is still on top of itself.

   d. Trace the reflection line and the reference point.

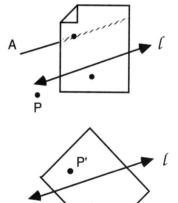

   e. Turn the tracing paper over so that it is face down. The reflection line and reference point should coincide with the original line and point.

   f. Mark the image point P'.

2. Repeat the glide reflection in part 1, except do the reflection first, followed by the translation. How do the images of parts 1 and 2 compare?

3. Perform the following glide reflections that are determined by the line l and the arrow $\overrightarrow{AB}$.

a.

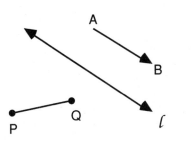

How does a segment compare to
its image in length?

b.

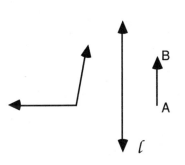

How does an angle compare
to its image in angle measure?

c. How does a triangle compare to its
image in size and shape?

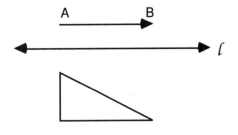

Summarize the properties of glide reflections that you have found.

OBJECTIVE: **Investigate magnifications and their properties**

You Will Need: Compass and straightedge

1. A **magnification** is a transformation that 'stretches' or 'shrinks' the plane away from or towards a specific point. Follow the steps given next to find the magnification image of point P.

    a. The **center** point O and a **scale factor** k determine a magnification. Here, let $k = 2$.

    b. Draw ray $\overrightarrow{OP}$.

    c. Measure $\overline{OP}$ and copy that segment such that P is one endpoint. Thus, OP'=2·OP.

    d. Mark the resulting image point P'.

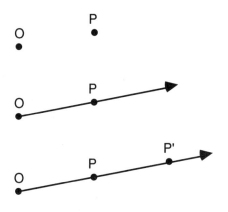

2. Using the technique from part 1, find the magnification images of points P, R and S where point O is the center and the scale factor k is 3. Label these image points P', R', and S' respectively.

    a. Does the segment $\overline{P'S'}$ contain R'?

    b. How do the lengths of $\overline{PS}$ and $\overline{P'S'}$ compare?

    c. How else are $\overline{PS}$ and $\overline{P'S'}$ related?

3. Using the technique described in part 2, magnify $\angle ABC$
    where O is the center and $k = 2$.

    a. Is the resulting figure also an angle? (It should be!)

    b. How do the measures of the two angles compare?

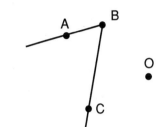

4. Draw the magnification image of $\triangle ABC$
    where O is the center and $k = 1/2$.

    a. Is the resulting figure also a triangle?
        (It should be!)

    b. How do the sizes and shapes of the two
        triangles compare?

Summarize the properties of magnifications that you have found.

The last activity looks at the relationship between translations,
rotations, and reflections.

OBJECTIVE: **Investigate combinations of reflections**

You Will Need: Tracing paper or Mira, straightedge, compass, and protractor

1. Lines *p* and *q* are parallel. Draw the reflection image of △ ABC across line *p*. Label the result △ A'B'C'.

   Draw the reflection image of △ A'B'C' across line *q*. Label the result △ A"B"C".

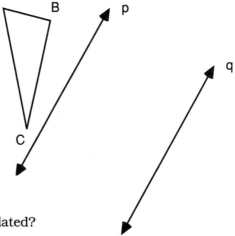

   a. Are the points A, A' and A" collinear? Test with a straightedge. Is the same true for the points B, B', and B", and the points C, C', and C" ?

   b. How are segments $\overline{AA"}$, $\overline{BB"}$, and $\overline{CC"}$ related?

   c. What single transformation will map △ ABC onto △ A"B"C"?

   d. Compare the lengths of segments $\overline{AA"}$, $\overline{BB"}$, $\overline{CC"}$ and the distance between lines *p* and *q*. What did you find?

   e. Describe the transformation you found in part (c) as completely as possible.

2. Lines *p* and *q* intersect at point M. Draw the reflection image of △ ABC across the line *p*. Label the result △ A'B'C'.

   Draw the reflection image of △ A'B'C' across the line *q*. Label the result △ A"B"C".

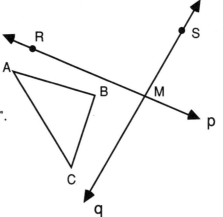

   a. Do the points A, A' and A" lie on a circle with center M? Is the same true for points B, B', B" and C, C', C"?

b. What single transformation will map Δ ABC onto Δ A"B"C"?

c. Compare the measures of ∠AMA", ∠BMB", and ∠CMC" and the measure of ∠RMS. What do you find?

d. Describe the transformation you found in part (b) as completely as possible.

MENTAL MATH

Given below are patterns that can be folded together to make a cube. Match each of the patterns on the left with its respective cube on the right.

A.

1. 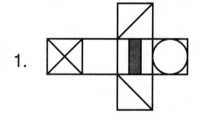   2.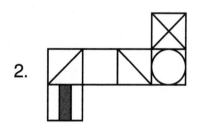

B.

3. 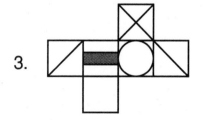   4.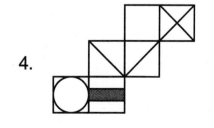

C.

D.

EXERCISES

FANCY "FREEZING"

The one-dimensional strip patterns given below are called **frieze patterns.** Imagine that they extend indefinitely to the left and right. Each one has translational symmetry; that is, sliding it to the right or left a certain distance maps it onto itself. Identify the other symmetries of these frieze patterns, if they exist. Note: No two of these patterns are equivalent, i.e. have the same list of symmetries.

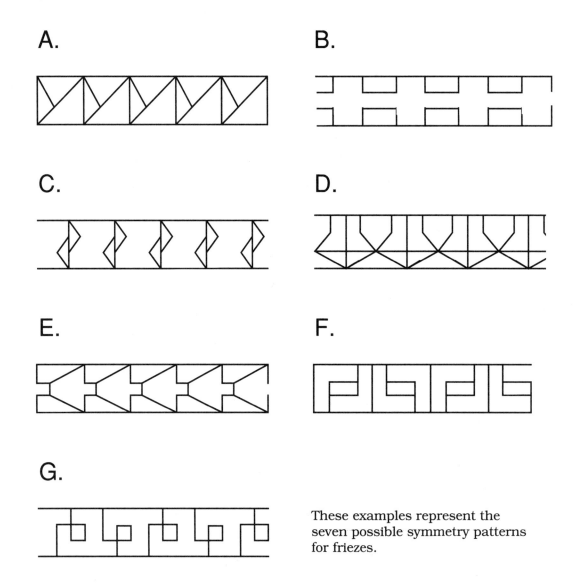

A.

B.

C.

D.

E.

F.

G.

These examples represent the seven possible symmetry patterns for friezes.

FOLDING PATTERNS

A sheet of paper is folded in half the long way, then in thirds as shown below.

While folded, a hole is punched through all thicknesses. The paper is then unfolded and spread out.

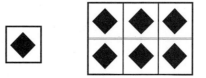

In each case below, the folded version is given on the left. Select the correct pattern for the spread-out paper on the right.

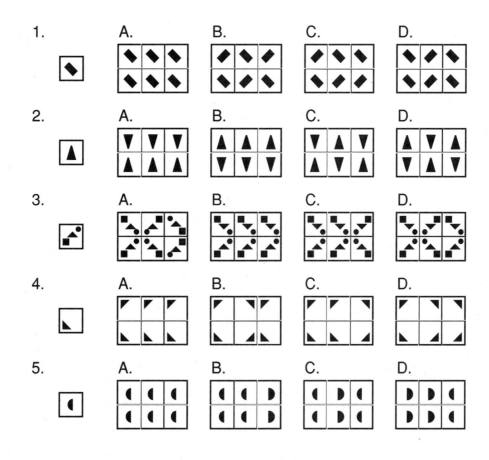

SELF-TEST

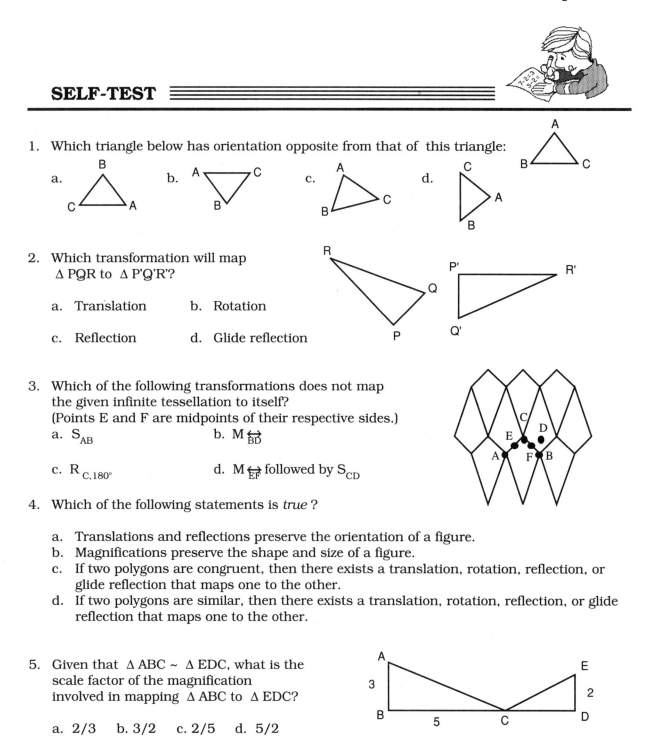

1. Which triangle below has orientation opposite from that of this triangle:

   a.   b.   c.   d.

2. Which transformation will map
   Δ PQR to Δ P'Q'R'?

   a. Translation   b. Rotation

   c. Reflection   d. Glide reflection

3. Which of the following transformations does not map
   the given infinite tessellation to itself?
   (Points E and F are midpoints of their respective sides.)
   a. S_{AB} b. $M_{\overleftrightarrow{BD}}$

   c. $R_{C,180°}$ d. $M_{\overleftrightarrow{EF}}$ followed by S_{CD}

4. Which of the following statements is *true* ?

   a. Translations and reflections preserve the orientation of a figure.
   b. Magnifications preserve the shape and size of a figure.
   c. If two polygons are congruent, then there exists a translation, rotation, reflection, or
      glide reflection that maps one to the other.
   d. If two polygons are similar, then there exists a translation, rotation, reflection, or glide
      reflection that maps one to the other.

5. Given that Δ ABC ~ Δ EDC, what is the
   scale factor of the magnification
   involved in mapping Δ ABC to Δ EDC?

   a. 2/3   b. 3/2   c. 2/5   d. 5/2

6. Each of the following is a property of an isometry *except* which one?

   a. An isometry maps a segment to a segment of the same length.
   b. An isometry maps an angle to an angle with the same measure.
   c. An isometry maps a line to a line parallel to the original line.
   d. An isometry maps parallel lines to parallel lines.

7. Triangle $\triangle$ ABC is congruent to $\triangle$ A'B'C' and $\overline{AB} \parallel \overline{A'B'}$. Point P is the midpoint of $\overline{AA'}$ and point Q (different from P) is the midpoint of $\overline{BB'}$ and $\overline{PQ} \perp \overline{AA'}$. Which of the following statements is necessarily true?

     a. A translation maps $\triangle$ ABC to $\triangle$ A'B'C'.
     b. A reflection maps $\triangle$ ABC to $\triangle$ A'B'C'.
     c. A glide reflection maps $\triangle$ ABC to $\triangle$ A'B'C'.
     d. Either a translation or a reflection maps $\triangle$ ABC to $\triangle$ A'B'C'.

8. Triangles $\triangle$ ABC and $\triangle$ A'B'C' are <u>congruent</u> and have the same orientation. The perpendicular bisectors of $\overline{AA'}$ and $\overline{BB'}$ intersect. Which transformation will map $\triangle$ ABC to $\triangle$ A'B'C'?

     a. Translation   b. Rotation   c. Reflection   d. Glide reflection

9. Which of the following does *not* map every line l to a line l' such that $l \parallel l'$.

     a. Reflection   b. Translation   c. Rotation of 180°   d. Magnification

10. Triangle $\triangle$ A'B'C' is the image of $\triangle$ ABC under $R_{P, 180°}$ followed by $R_{Q, 180°}$. Which single transformation maps $\triangle$ ABC to $\triangle$ A'B'C'?

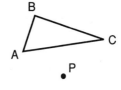

     a. Translation in the direction of $\overrightarrow{PQ}$ with distance PQ.
     b. Rotation of 180° about the midpoint of $\overline{PQ}$.
     c. Reflection in the perpendicular bisector of $\overline{PQ}$.
     d. Translation in the direction of $\overrightarrow{PQ}$ with distance 2·PQ.

SOLUTIONS

Warm-up
8:00, 4:30, 10:20

Hands-on Activities

Activity 1
2. b. They are the same segment.   c.   B
3. Ray, line, angle, triangle; They are equal. They are the same. They are parallel.
4. a. No
A translation maps a segment to a segment parallel and congruent to it, a line to a line parallel to it, an angle to a congruent angle, a ray to a ray, and a triangle to a congruent triangle.

Activity 2
2. a. Yes   b. The image of $\overline{XZ}$ is $\overline{X'Z'}$.   c. It is a segment with the same length.
3. a. Yes; They are equal.   b. Yes; They have the same size and shape.
4. a. Yes, the center point.
A rotation maps segments to congruent segments, angles to congruent angles, rays to rays, lines to lines, and triangles to congruent triangles.

Activity 3
2. b. The image of $\overline{PR}$ is $\overline{P'R'}$.   c. It is a segment with the same length.
3. c. Yes; They are equal. They have the same size and shape.
4. a. Yes, each point on the reflection line.
A reflection maps segments to congruent segments, lines to lines, angles to congruent angles, rays to rays, and triangles to congruent triangles.

Activity 4
2. They are the same point.
3. a. They have the same length.   b. They have the same measure.
c. They have the same size and shape.
A glide reflection maps segments to congruent segments, lines to lines, rays to rays, angles to congruent angles, and triangles to congruent triangles.

Activity 5
2. a. Yes   b. P'S' = 3PS   c. They are parallel.
3. b. They are the same.
4. b. They are the same shape, but the new sides are 1/2 as long.
A magnification with scale factor k maps a segment to a segment parallel to it and k times its length, an angle to a congruent angle, a line to a line parallel to it, a ray to a ray, and a triangle to a triangle with the same shape, but with sides k times the length of the original sides.

Activity 6
1. a. Yes; Yes   b. $\overline{AA''}$ || $\overline{BB''}$ || $\overline{CC''}$ and all are perpendicular to lines p and q.
c. A translation   d. $\overline{AA''}$ is twice as long as the distance between lines p and q.
e. It is a translation in the direction perpendicular to lines p and q with the distance equal to twice the distance between lines p and q.
2. a. Yes; Yes   b. A rotation
c. The measures of $\angle AMA''$, $\angle BMB''$, and $\angle CMC''$ are twice the measure of $\angle RMS$.
d. It is a rotation whose center is the intersection of the lines and whose angle has measure twice the measure of the angle from line p to line q.

Mental Math

1. D   **2.** C   **3.** A   **4.** B

Exercises

FANCY "FREEZING"
- **A.** Translation only   **B.** Rotation, horizontal and vertical reflections
- **C.** Rotation   **D.** Vertical reflection   **E.** Horizontal reflection
- **F.** Vertical reflection, glide reflection   **G.** Glide reflection

FOLDING PATTERNS
1. B   **2.** A   **3.** D   **4.** B   **5.** C

Self-Test

1. d   **2.** b   **3.** c   **4.** c   **5.** a   **6.** c   **7.** d   **8.** b   **9.** a   **10.** d

RESOURCE ARTICLES

Bidwell, James K. "Using Reflections to Find Symmetric and Asymmetric Patterns." *Arithmetic Teacher* 34 (March 1987): 10-15. *Activities exploring the idea of symmetry.*

Brieske, Tom. "Visual Thinking with Translations, Half-Turns, and Dilations." *Mathematics Teacher* 77 (September 1984): 466-469. *Helping students to think visually about algebraic operations and the associated mappings of the plane.*

DeTemple, Duane. "Reflection Borders for Patchwork Quilts." *Mathematics Teacher* 79 (February 1986): 138-143. *Geometric problem solving involving least common multiples and greatest common divisors.*

May, Beverly A. "Reflections on Miniature Golf." *Mathematics Teacher* 78 (May 1985): 351-353. *Application of reflections to miniature golf.*

Sawada, Daiyo. "Symmetry and Tessellations from Rotational Transformations on Transparencies." *Arithmetic Teacher* 33 (December 1985): 12-13. *Using transparencies to explore rotational transformations.*

Thompson, Patrick W. "A Piagetian Approach to Transformation Geometry via Microworlds." *Mathematics Teacher* 78 (September 1985): 465-471. *Developing the ability to apply a system of transformations.*

MATERIALS

CARDS

MATERIALS CARD 1.1

YOU WILL NEED: 3 paper clips and tape. Straighten one end of a paper clip and insert it through the base at point A. Repeat for points B and C. Bend curved portion of clip flat against the bottom of the base and tape in place.

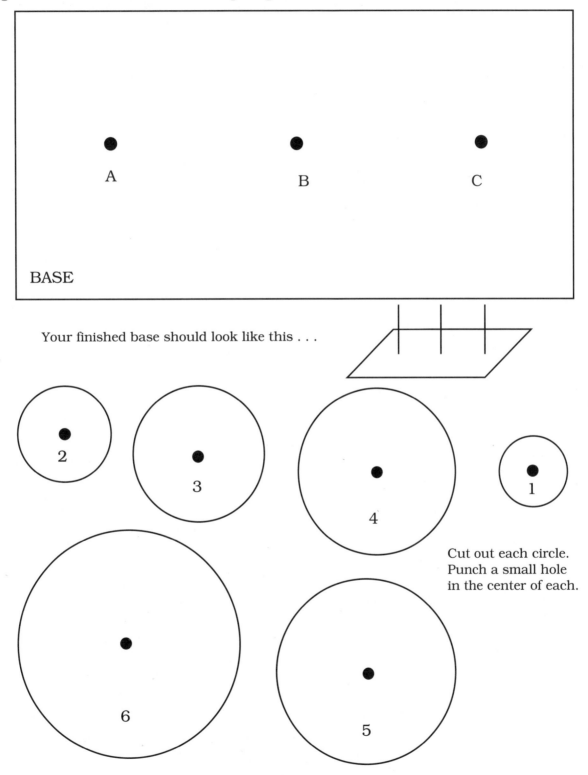

BASE

Your finished base should look like this . . .

Cut out each circle.
Punch a small hole
in the center of each.

MATERIALS CARD 1.3

Use the following as patterns. Cut several if needed.

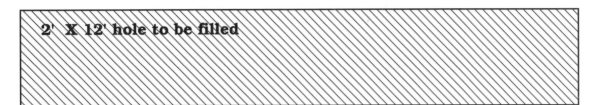

2' X 12' hole to be filled

3' X 8' piece of plywood

- -

MATERIALS CARD 1.5

Cut out each of these pieces.

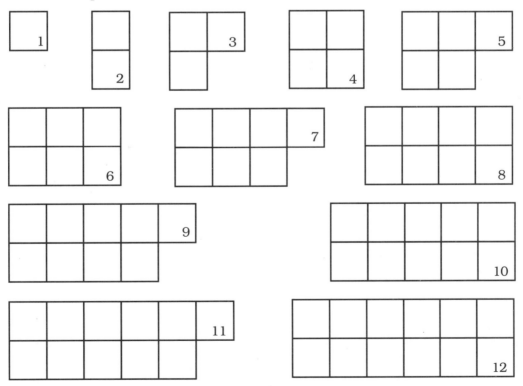

MATERIALS CARD 2.1

Cut out all of the following pieces.   Save these pieces for use later in the chapter.

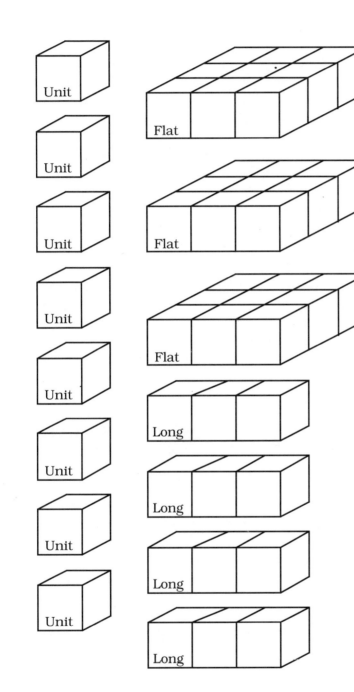

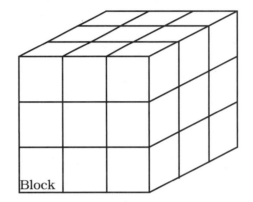

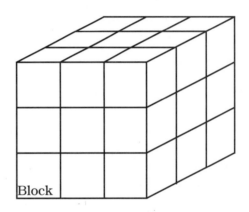

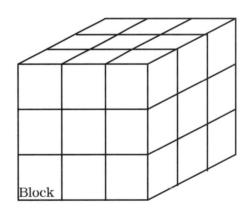

MATERIALS CARD 2.2

Cut out. Fold on all heavy
black lines. Put flap A on top
of flap B. Tuck flap C inside the
cube behind flap B. Tuck flap D
in. Tape if necessary.

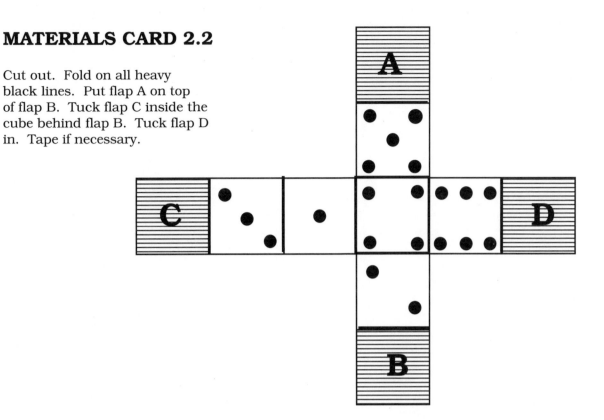

MATERIALS CARD 3.1   Cut out these strips and color them as labelled.

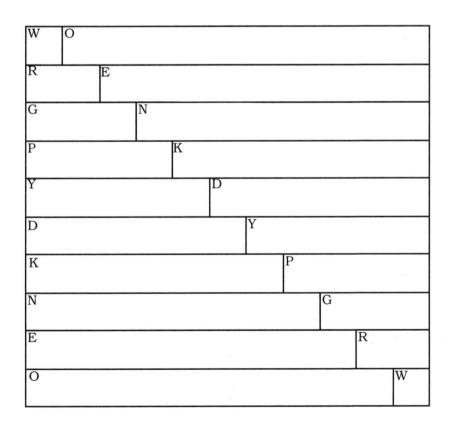

W = White
R = Red
G = Light Green
P = Purple
Y = Yellow
D = Dark Green
K = Black
N = Brown
E = Blue
O = Orange

Save these pieces
for use later in
the chapter.

MATERIALS CARD 3.7

Cut into squares to represent cubes.   Save these pieces for use later in the chapter.

MATERIALS CARD 4.1

Use coins or paper clips as chips. Save this for use later in the chapter.

3^3	3^2	3	1

MATERIALS CARD 4.5

Cut out the pieces on the next three pages.

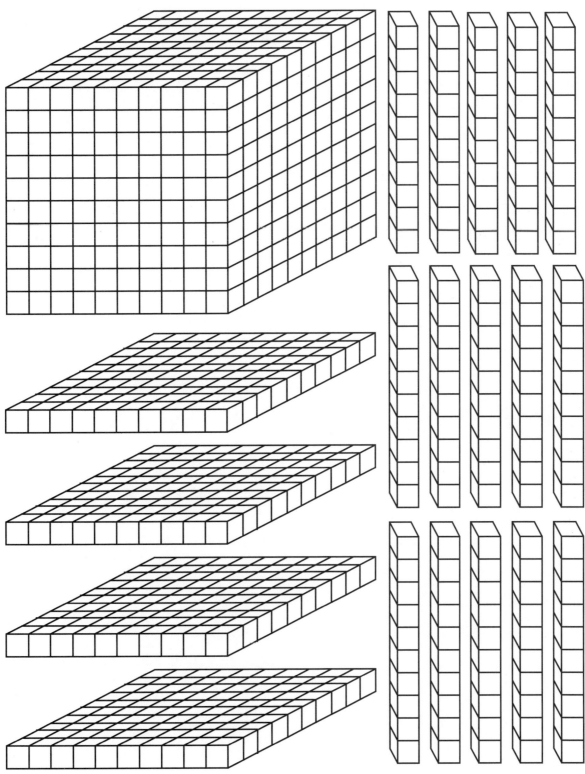

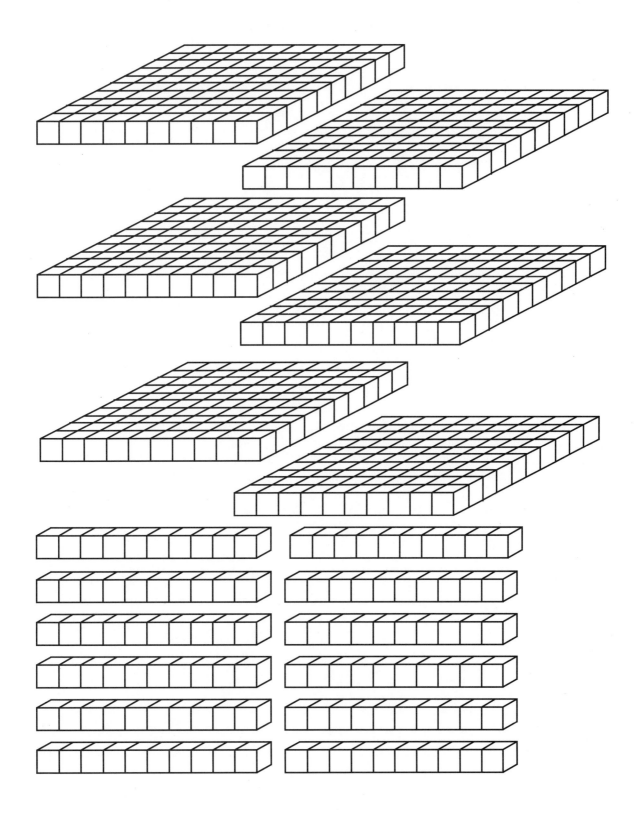

MATERIALS CARD 4.5, cont.

- -

MATERIALS CARD 5.1

Cut apart and use as cubes. Save these pieces for use later in the chapter.

MATERIALS CARD 6.1

Cut out these pieces. Color them as labelled. W = White.
Save these pieces for use later in the chapter.

					W	W	W	W	W	W
O=Orange										
E=Blue			P=Purple				W	W	W	
E			K=Black							
N=Brown		N								
R =Red	R	R	Y=Yellow		Y					
P	G=Green	G	D=Dark Green							
K		D			R	W				
R										

- -

MATERIALS CARD 6.2

Cut out the circles and then cut on all solid lines.
Save these pieces for use later in the chapter.

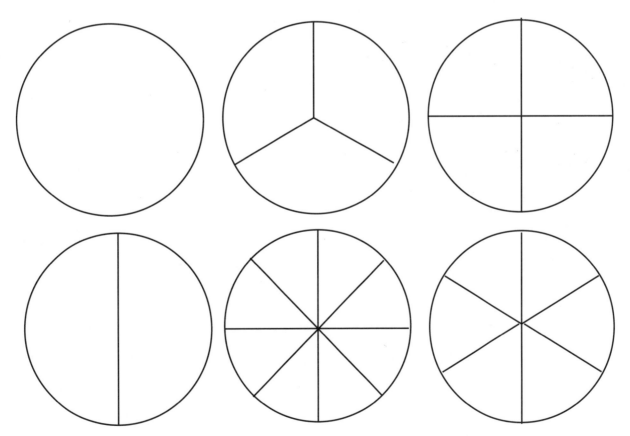

MATERIALS
CARD 6.3

Cut out the Tangram Puzzle
by cutting on all of the solid
lines. You will have 7 pieces.

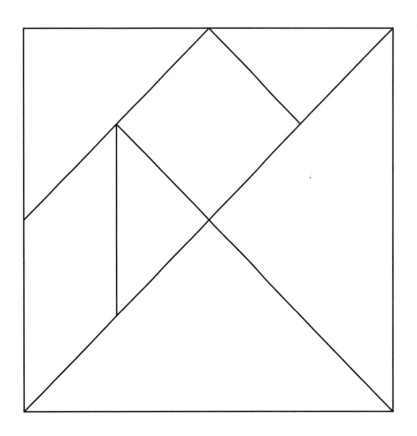

MATERIALS CARD 6.5

Cut out. Fold on all heavy black lines.
Put flap A on top of flap B. Tuck flap C
inside the cube behind flap B. Tuck
flap D in. Tape if necessary.

	A		
	1/2		
C 2/3	1/8	1/3	1/6 D
	1/4		
	B		

MATERIALS CARD 6.9   Cut out these squares.

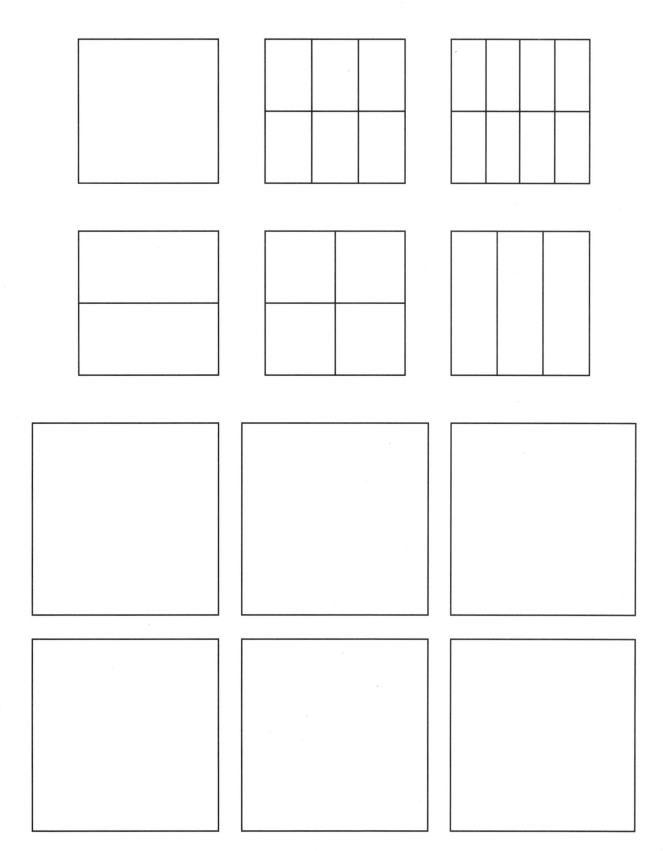

MATERIALS CARD 7.1

Cut out the circle to use as a decimal point marker.
Save these for use later in the chapter.

MATERIALS CARD 7.6

Cut into squares.

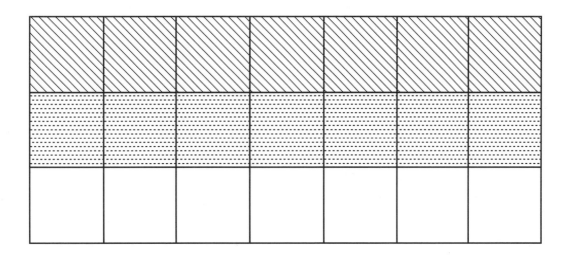

MATERIALS CARD 7.7

Cut into single triangles, rhombuses, trapezoids, and hexagons.

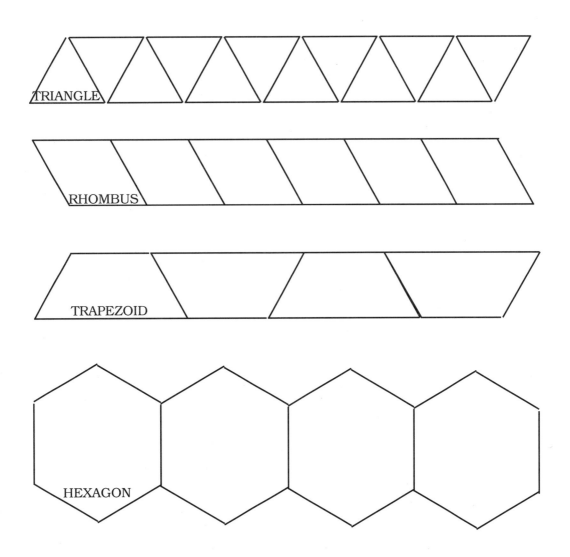

MATERIALS CARD 7.8

Cut into strips and tape the flap marked X under the next strip each time to construct a meter strip.

	1	2	3	4	5	6	7	8	9	1	
0	11	12	13	14	15	16	17	18	19	2	
0	21	22	23	24	25	26	27	28	29	3	
0	31	32	33	34	35	36	37	38	39	4	
0	41	42	43	44	45	46	47	48	49	5	
0	51	52	53	54	55	56	57	58	59	6	
0	61	62	63	64	65	66	67	68	69	7	
0	71	72	73	74	75	76	77	78	79	8	
0	81	82	83	84	85	86	87	88	89	9	
0	91	92	93	94	95	96	97	98	99	100	

MATERIALS CARD 8.1   Cut out these cubes. Save for use later in the chapter.

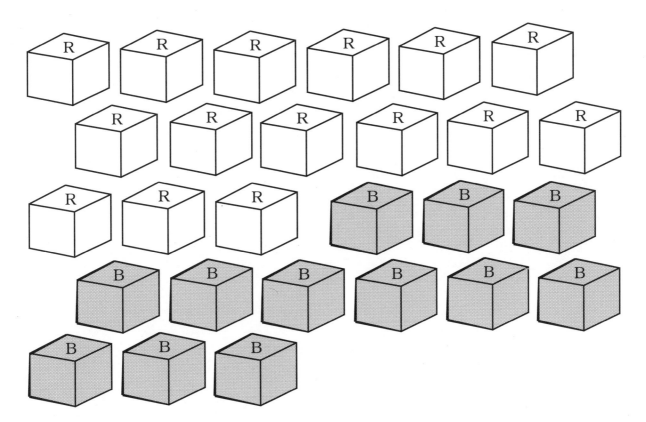

MATERIALS CARD 9.2

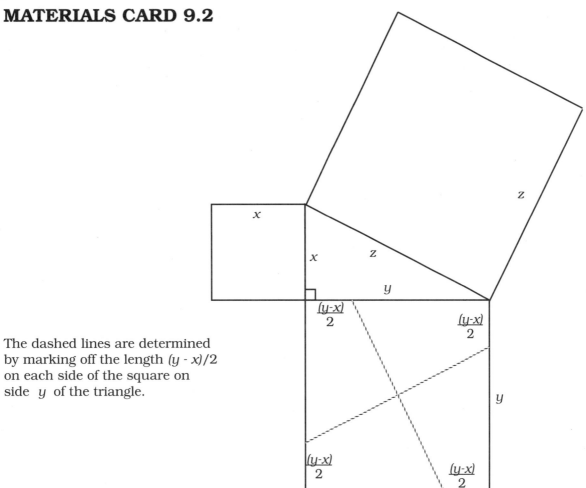

The dashed lines are determined by marking off the length $(y - x)/2$ on each side of the square on side y of the triangle.

x

x z

z

y

$\dfrac{(y-x)}{2}$ $\dfrac{(y-x)}{2}$

y

$\dfrac{(y-x)}{2}$ $\dfrac{(y-x)}{2}$

MATERIALS CARD 9.3

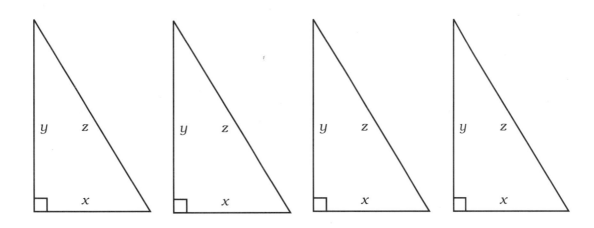

MATERIALS CARD 10.2

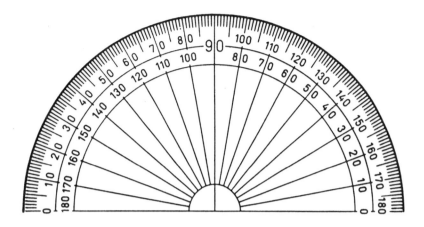

- -

MATERIALS CARD 11.1

Cut out these cubes.

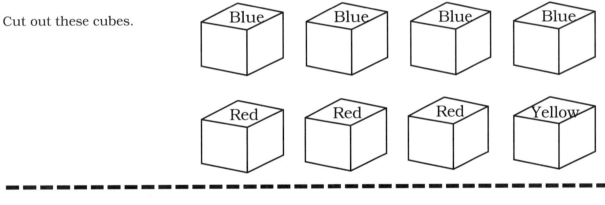

- -

MATERIALS CARD 11.2

Place the pencil point at the center of the disk through the end of a paper clip or safety pin as illustrated.

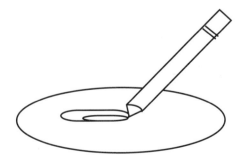

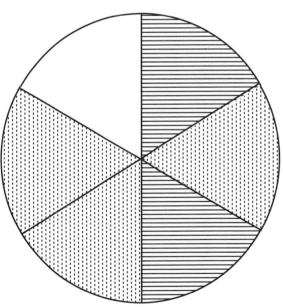

MATERIALS CARD 11.4

Cut out and fold for dice. Tuck
striped flaps inside. Tape in
place if necessary.

Save these for use
later in the chapter.

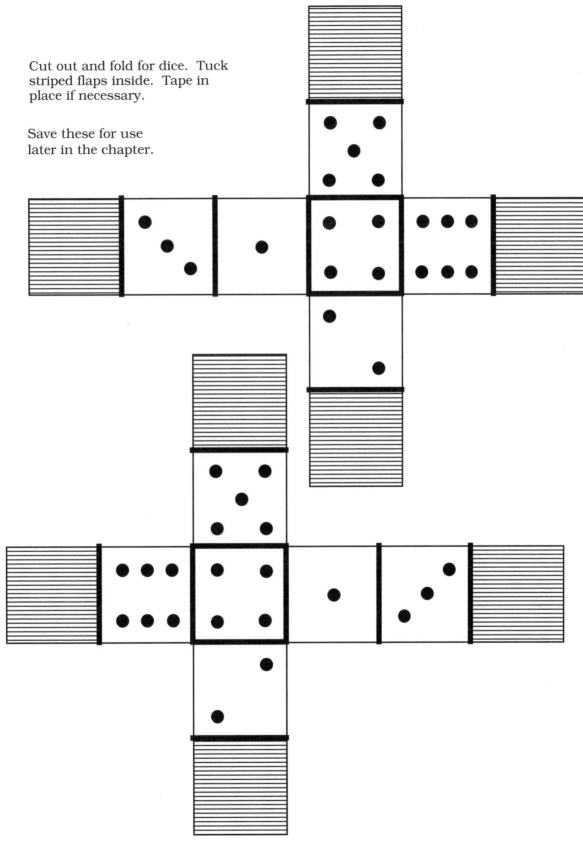

MATERIALS CARD 12.3

MATERIALS CARD 12.4

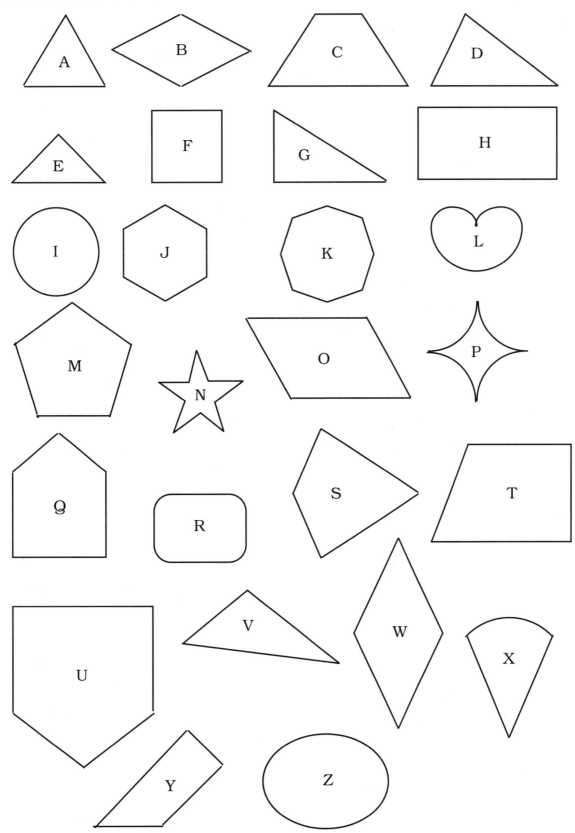

MATERIALS
CARD 12.5

Cut apart these pieces.

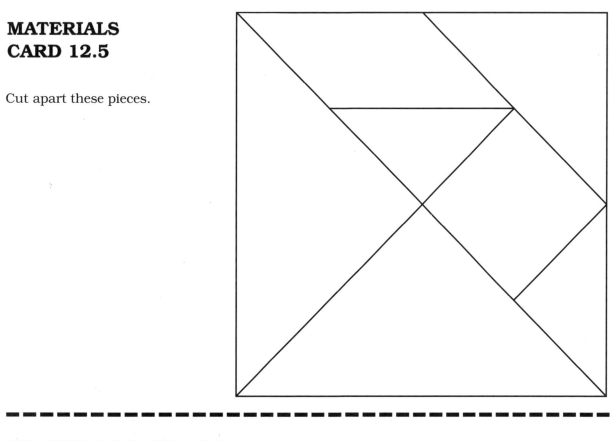

- -

MATERIALS CARD 12.6

Cut out another triangle.

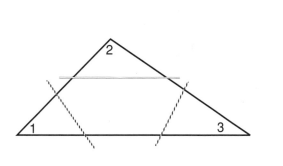

Cut out a quadrilateral.

MATERIALS CARD 12.7

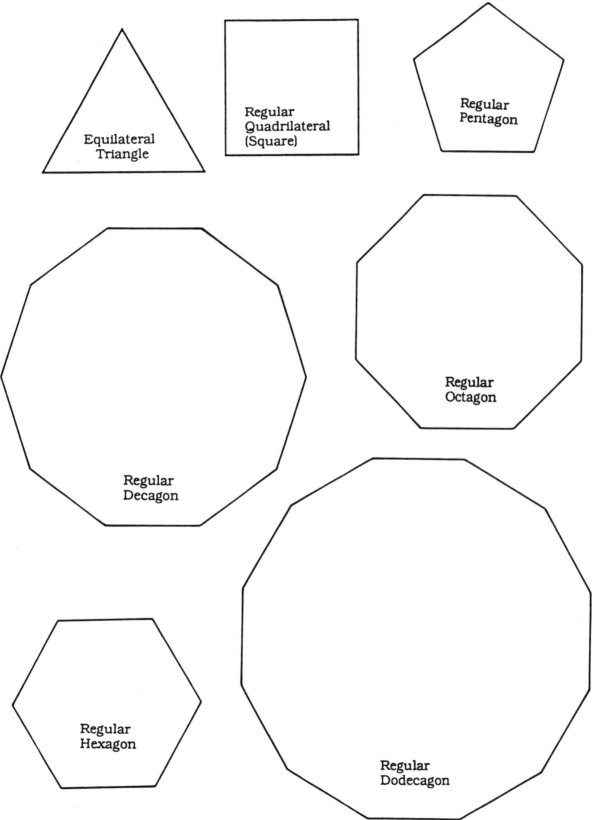

MATERIALS CARD 12.8

MATERIALS CARD 12.9

Cut out the circles to use as patterns.
Make the number of copies indicated.
Fold along dotted lines and put
together with paper clips or tape --
flaps on outside!

Make 20

Make 12

Make 12

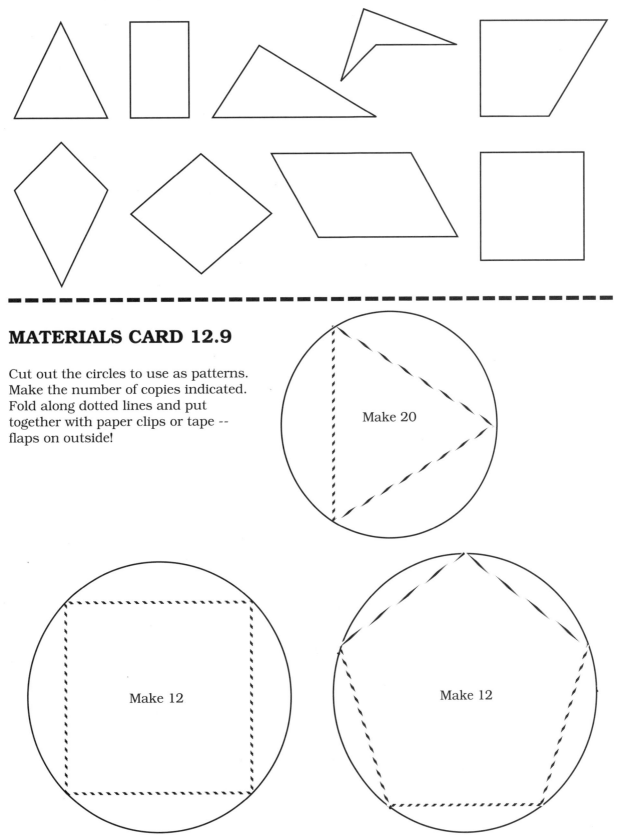

MATERIALS CARD 13.3

Cut the strips apart and tape or staple the tabs of each strip under the preceding strip.

	1	2	3	4	5	6	7	8	9	1	
0	11	12	13	14	15	16	17	18	19	2	
0	21	22	23	24	25	26	27	28	29	3	
0	31	32	33	34	35	36	37	38	39	4	
0	41	42	43	44	45	46	47	48	49	5	
0	51	52	53	54	55	56	57	58	59	6	
0	61	62	63	64	65	66	67	68	69	7	
0	71	72	73	74	75	76	77	78	79	8	
0	81	82	83	84	85	86	87	88	89	9	
0	91	92	93	94	95	96	97	98	99	100	

MATERIALS CARD 13.4

Cut out each figure; fold the cube
and tape in place. Roll the
rectangle into a long
cylinder and tape
in place.

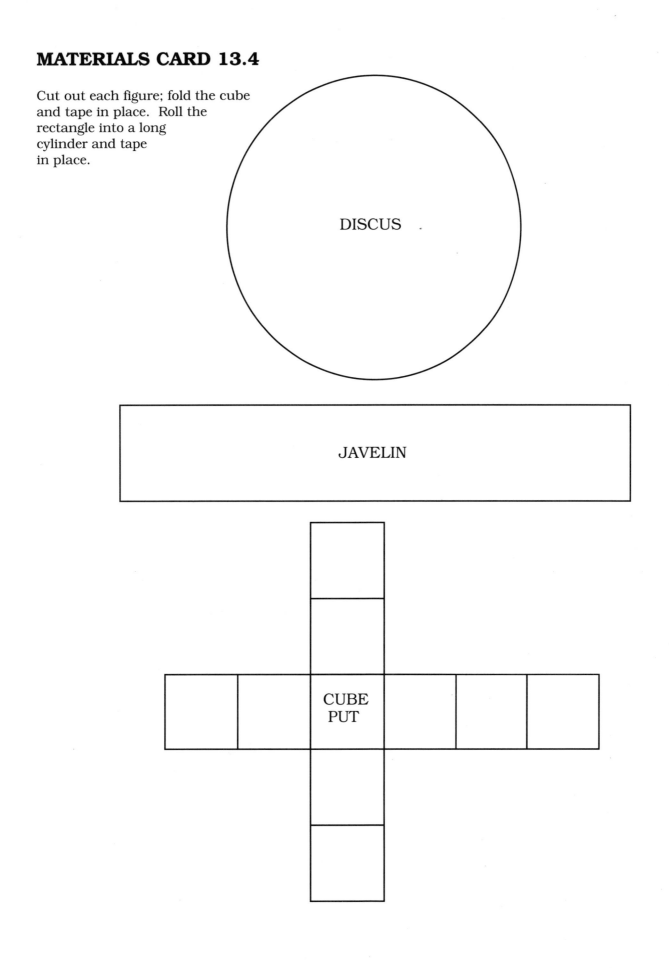

DISCUS

JAVELIN

CUBE
PUT

MATERIALS CARD 13.5

MATERIALS CARD 13.6

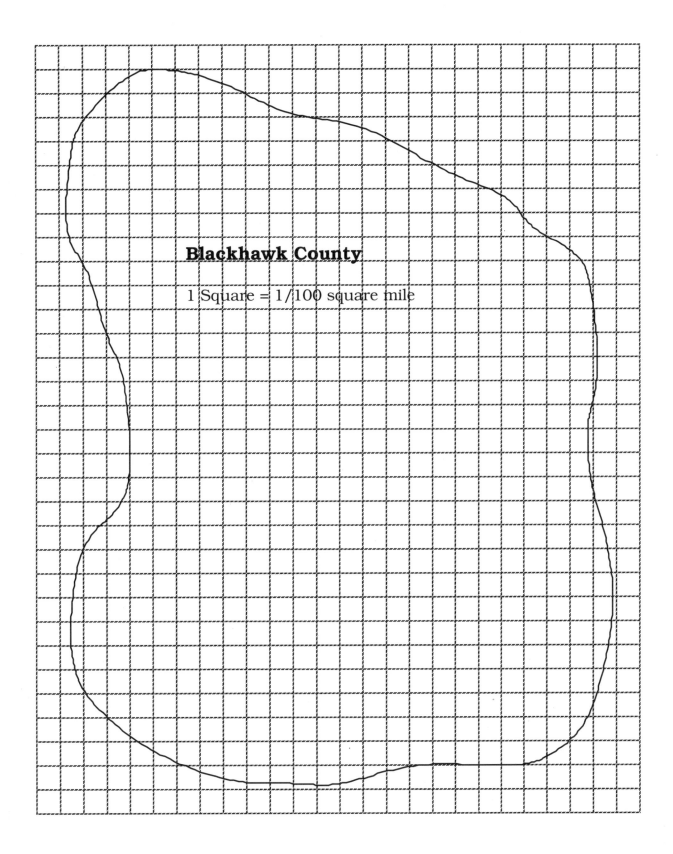

Blackhawk County

1 Square = 1/100 square mile

MATERIALS CARD 13.7

Cut out each figure and fold on the solid lines so that the
grid paper becomes the outside of the box. Tape in place.

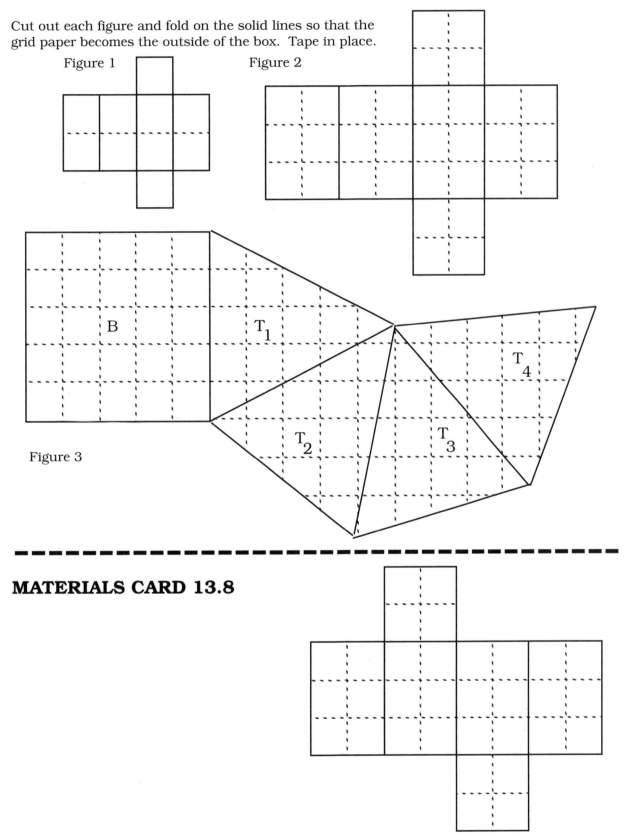

Figure 1

Figure 2

B

T_1

T_4

T_2

T_3

Figure 3

MATERIALS CARD 13.8

A

Overlap and tape securely.

B

C   Apex of cone

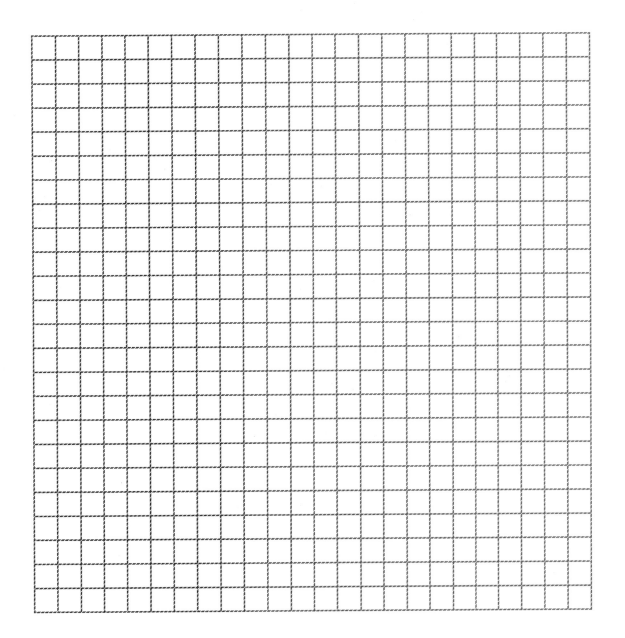